Culture and
Customs of
Taiwan

Culture and Customs of Taiwan

❦

Gary Marvin Davison
and
Barbara E. Reed

Culture and Customs of Asia
Hanchao Lu, Series Editor

GREENWOOD PRESS
Westport, Connecticut • London

Library of Congress Cataloging-in-Publication Data

Davison, Gary Marvin, 1951–
 Culture and customs of Taiwan / Gary Marvin Davison and Barbara E.
Reed.
  p. cm.—(Culture and customs of Asia, ISSN 1097–0738)
 Includes bibliographical references and index.
 ISBN 0–313–30298–7 (alk. paper)
 1. Taiwan—Civilization. 2. Taiwan—Social life and customs.
3. Taiwan—History. I. Reed, Barbara E. II. Title. III. Series.
DS799.4.D38 1998
951.24'9—DC21   97–43935

British Library Cataloging in Publication Data is available.

Library of Congress Catalog Card Number: 97–43935
ISBN: 0–313–30298–7
ISSN: 1097–0738

First published in 1998

Greenwood Press, 88 Post Road West, Westport, CT 06881
An imprint of Greenwood Publishing Group, Inc.

Printed in the United States of America

The paper used in this book complies with the
Permanent Paper Standard issued by the National
Information Standards Organization (Z39.48–1984).

10 9 8 7 6 5 4 3 2 1

Copyright Acknowledgments

The authors and publisher gratefully acknowledge permission for use of the following material:

Excerpts from the poems by Li Heng-tai: "Walls" (p. 64), "Dusk" (p. 65), "Landscape No. 1" (p. 66), "Landscape No. 2" (p. 66), "Dirty Faces" (p. 70), "One Party System" (p. 72), and "Taiwan" (p. 62), from John Balcom, "Modern Master, Native Son," *Free China Review*, December 1995. Reprinted by permission of *Free China Review*.

Excerpt from the poem "Nostalgia for My Hometown" by Yu Kuang-chung from Li P'eng (Coral Li), "The Rise of the Well-Versed Society: A Poetry Renaissance in Contemporary Taiwan," translated by Phil Newell, *Sinorama*, December 1995, p. 127. Reprinted by permission of *Sinorama*.

Excerpt from the poem "Coal" by Do She-sun from Li P'eng (Coral Li), "The Rise of the Well-Versed Society: A Poetry Renaissance in Contemporary Taiwan," translated by Phil Newell, *Sinorama*, December 1995, p. 127. Reprinted by permission of *Sinorama*.

Excerpt from the poem "A Sheet of Blotting Paper" by Chang Shiang-hua from Li P'eng (Coral Li), "The Rise of the Well-Versed Society: A Poetry Renaissance in Contemporary Taiwan," translated by Phil Newell, *Sinorama*, December 1995, p. 127. Reprinted by permission of *Sinorama*.

Excerpts from "Unexpected Encounter at Yuraku-cho" by Chen Fang-ming, *Free China Review*, July 1995, pp. 36–40. Reprinted by permission of *Free China Review*.

Every reasonable effort has been made to trace the owners of copyright materials in this book, but in some instances this has proven impossible. The authors and publisher will be glad to receive information leading to more complete acknowledgments in subsequent printings of the book and in the meantime extend their apologies for any omissions.

This book is dedicated to our beloved parents,
Myron and Frances Reed
Marvin and Betty Davison

And to our dear son who was born in Taiwan,
Ryan Davison-Reed

Contents

Illustrations

Series Foreword

GEOGRAPHICALLY, Asia encompasses the vast area from Suez, the Bosporus, and the Ural Mountains eastward to the Bering Sea and from this line southward to the Indonesian archipelago, an expanse that covers about 30 percent of our earth. Conventionally, and especially insofar as culture and customs are concerned, Asia refers primarily to the region east of Iran and south of Russia. This area can be divided in turn into subregions commonly known as South, Southeast, and East Asia, which are the main focus of this series.

The United States has vast interests in this region. In the twentieth century the United States fought three major wars in Asia (namely, the Pacific War of 1941–45, the Korean War of 1950–53, and the Vietnam War of 1965–75), and each had profound impact on life and politics in America. Today, America's major trading partners are in Asia, and in the foreseeable future the weight of Asia in American life will inevitably increase, for in Asia lie our great allies as well as our toughest competitors in virtually all arenas of global interest. Domestically, the role of Asian immigrants is more visible than at any other time in our history. In spite of these connections with Asia, however, our knowledge about this crucial region is far from adequate. For various reasons, Asia remains for most of us a relatively unfamiliar, if not stereotypical or even mysterious, "Oriental" land.

There are compelling reasons for Americans to obtain some level of concrete knowledge about Asia. It is one of the world's richest reservoirs of culture and an ever-evolving museum of human heritage. Rhoads Murphey, a prominent Asianist, once pointed out that in the part of Asia east of Afghanistan and south of Russia alone lies half the world, "half of its people and far more than half of its historical experience, for these are the oldest living civilized traditions." Prior to the modern era, with limited interaction and mutual influence between the East and the West, Asian civilizations developed largely independent from the West. In modern times, however, Asia and the West have come not only into close contact but also into frequent conflict: The result has been one of the most solemn and stirring dramas in world history. Today, integration and compromise are the trend in coping with cultural differences. The West—with some notable exceptions—has started to see Asian traditions, not as something to fear, but as something to be understood, appreciated, and even cherished. After all, Asian traditions are an indispensable part of the human legacy, a matter of global "common wealth" that few of us can afford to ignore.

As a result of Asia's enormous economic development since World War II, we can no longer neglect the study of this vibrant region. Japan's "economic miracle" of postwar development is no longer unique, but in various degrees has been matched by the booming economy of many other Asian countries and regions. The rise of the four "mini dragons" (South Korea, Taiwan, Hong Kong, and Singapore) suggests that there may be a common Asian pattern of development. At the same time, each economy in Asia has followed its own particular trajectory. Clearly, China is the next giant on the scene. Sweeping changes in China in the last two decades have already dramatically altered the world's economic map. Furthermore, growth has also been dramatic in much of Southeast Asia. Today war-devastated Vietnam shows great enthusiasm for joining the "club" of nations engaged in the world economy. And in South Asia, India, the world's largest democracy, is rediscovering its role as a champion of market capitalism. The economic development of Asia presents a challenge to Americans but also provides them with unprecedented opportunities. It is largely against this background that more and more people in the United States, in particular among the younger generation, have started to pursue careers dealing with Asia.

This series is designed to meet the need for knowledge of Asia among students and the general public. Each book is written in an accessible and lively style by an expert (or experts) in the field of Asian studies. Each book focuses on the culture and customs of a country or region. Each volume starts with an introduction to the land and people of a nation or region and includes a brief history and an overview of the economy. This is followed by chapters dealing with a variety of topics that piece together a cultural panorama, such as thought, religion, ethics, literature and art, architecture and housing, cuisine, traditional dress, gender, courtship and marriage, festivals and leisure activities, music and dance, and social customs and lifestyle. In this series, we have chosen not to elaborate on elite life, ideology, or detailed questions of political structure and struggle, but instead to explore the world of common people, their sorrow and joy, their pattern of thinking, and their way of life. It is the culture and customs of the majority of the people (rather than just the rich and powerful elite) that we seek to understand. Without such understanding, it will be difficult for all of us to live peacefully and fruitfully with each other in this increasingly interdependent world.

As the world shrinks, modern technologies have made all nations on earth "virtual" neighbors. The expression "global village" not only reveals the nature and the scope of the world in which we live but also, more importantly, highlights the serious need for mutual understanding of all peoples on our planet. If this series serves to help the reader obtain a better understanding of the "half of the world" that is Asia, the authors and I will be well rewarded.

Hanchao Lu
Georgia Institute of Technology

Acknowledgments

BREVITY MAY BE the soul of wit, but it is not my strong suit. Lest, however, I fill another book with the full story of my indebtedness to those whose humanity and scholarly inspiration have enabled me to co-write this book, I will attempt herein to cut across the grain of my personality and keep these acknowledgments succinct.

At each of the universities which I have attended en route to particular degrees, there are those who in their own zest for learning and encouragement of mine have inspired me to pursue further academic efforts, most notably professors Bradley Carter and Ronald Davis at Southern Methodist University; Stephen Vlastos at the University of Iowa; and Edward Farmer and Vernon Ruttan at the University of Minnesota. I wish to thank these latter three specially and respectively for support at a critical professional juncture; faith that my independence, eclecticism, and idiosyncratic ways would produce work of value; and countless, kind responses to requests for assistance.

In Taiwan, numerous people justified my faith that I could pursue a project based on people-to-people rather than formal institutional contacts: Huang Su-kuei, who lent me a chair in her hair salon; Ou-yang Ch'in, who offered a rental home and instructive comments on his experiences under the Japanese; Wu Ts'ung-hsien, Huang Chun-chieh, Hsiao Hsin-huang, and Hsieh Sen-chung (Samuel Hsieh), eminent scholars in Taipei; Tseng Li-hua, who facilitated the meeting with then Bank of China Governor Hsieh; and Yang San-ho, Lai Sen-hsiung, Yeh Li-tzu, and Mao Chih-ts'ung, agricultural researchers in Tainan County. Most of all, I wish to thank the farm family with whom I spent many days in the spring and summer of 1990 absorbing their wisdom relevant to Taiwanese agriculture and society: Huang K'un-shan, the family patriarch; Kao Chu-p'an (Mrs. Huang), the family matri-arch; their sons Huang Ts'ung-ming, Huang T'ien-te, and Huang Ming-kuei; and Lin Pu, Mr. Huang's mother.

Finally, on the most personal and important level, I wish to thank Barbara Reed, my partner in life; our precious son, Ryan; and all members of both our families whose love and interest energizes all my efforts.

Gary Marvin Davison

Taiwan began as a place of study for me, then a subject of study and finally a place that holds a part of my heart. I am grateful for those who nurtured my interests over the years. Yu Hsiao-jung, my friend and teacher while we were at the University of Iowa, taught me Chinese and told stories about her youth in Taiwan. Rotary International supported me generously for a year of study at Taiwan Normal University. Patrick and Lily Lee served as gracious hosts and lively storytellers about living between cultures. The faculty and staff at the Mandarin Training Center, the Foreign Students Office and the Chinese Literature Department at National Taiwan Normal University of-fered patient support to me as a confused graduate student during that first year encountering the ever-changing Taiwan. Later, the faculty and staff at the Stanford Center, formerly based at National Taiwan University, offered the same patience as well as support for a year of language study and research into Taiwanese religion to a still-confused professor. I also owe thanks to all the landlords, neighbors, store clerks, hospital staff, temple staff, and other acquaintances who generously guided me during my periods of residence in Taipei and Tainan.

St. Olaf College in Northfield, Minnesota, has turned out to be a good base from which to study East Asia. I thank the college for the generous support of sabbaticals and summer research grants which have allowed me to stay in touch with Taiwan. My colleagues in Asian Studies have offered a broader, more interdisciplinary perspective on East Asia from which to view Taiwan. Richard Bodman, in particular, is due thanks for suggesting that we undertake this project and providing the connections.

My special thanks to those who helped us most directly in preparing this book: Hanchao Lu as series editor and everyone at Greenwood Press, espe-cially Barbara Rader, Gillian Beebe, and Jennifer Wood. My deepest gratitude goes to Gary and Ryan who transform all undertakings into grand adventures.

Barbara Reed

Note on Romanization

WITH SOME EXCEPTIONS, the romanization system used in this book is *pinyin*. *Pinyin* literally means "spelled-out sounds." This descriptive name echoes the effort of all those who devise systems for achieving the difficult task of rendering Mandarin Chinese pronunciation into something approaching its "romanized" or English equivalent. After decades of favoring the Wade-Giles system with some use of early twentieth-century postal service renderings, publishers on Taiwan seem to be moving toward the pinyin system long used on the mainland People's Republic of China. The exceptions to our use of pinyin are place and personal names that have become conventional on Taiwan or which have been chosen by Taiwanese people themselves. Usually based on Wade-Giles or postal service renderings, these conventional spellings can be quite idiosyncratic. Given below are examples of these conventional spellings in comparison with the renderings in the Wade-Giles, pinyin, and Yale systems. The Yale system is included as a teaching tool probably most accessible to English-speaking students of the Chinese language in achieving reasonably close pronunciations.

Conventional	Wade-Giles	Pinyin	Yale
Lee Tenghui	Li Teng-hui	Li Denghui	Li Denghwei
Keelung	Chi-lung	Jilong	Jilung
Taipei	T'ai-pei	Taibei	Taibei

Conventional	Wade-Giles	Pinyin	Yale
Cheng Ch'eng-kung	Cheng Ch'eng-kung	Zheng Chenggong	Jeng Chenggung
Chiang Kai-shek	Chiang Chieh-shih	Jiang Jieshi	Jyang Jyeshr

Pinyin renderings are in general close to the Yale teaching system and thus fairly accessible to the English speaker. Some letters, though, have been chosen for the pinyin system to represent double consonant sounds or to dramatize the fact that the sound is not easily pronounced authentically by English speakers. Examples of the stranger-looking renderings are given below, with comparisons to other romanization systems. Again, the Yale system provides the best guide for relatively close pronunciation.

Pinyin	Wade-Giles	Yale
Qianlong	Ch'ien-lung	Chyanlung
Kangxi	K'ang-hsi	Kangsyi
cuo	ts'o	tswo

Chronology of the History of Taiwan

4,000 B.C.	First arrival of Neolithic Austronesian people (ancestors of aborigines) to Taiwan
202 B.C.–9 A.D.	(Former) Han dynasty in China
25–220	(Later) Han dynasty in China
239	Expeditionary force from mainland explores Taiwan
589–618	Sui dynasty in China
600s	First minimal migration from Chinese mainland
618–907	Tang dynasty in China
960–1127	(Northern) Song dynasty in China
1127–1279	(Southern) Song dynasty in China
late 1200s	Mongols take control of Penghu (Pescadores) Islands
1279–1368	Yuan (Mongol) dynasty in China
1368–1644	Ming dynasty in China

1517	Portuguese vessels pass Taiwan, calling it *Ilha Formosa* [beautiful island]
1624	Dutch establish themselves in Tainan area
1626	Spanish establish themselves in Tamsui area
1644–1912	Qing dynasty in China
1662	Cheng Ch'eng-kung's (Koxinga's) forces defeat the Dutch
1683	Qing dynasty ousts the family Cheng, incorporating Taiwan into mainland Chinese administration
1683–1895	Qing dynasty controls Taiwan as immigrants from Fujian and Guangdong come to greatly outnumber the aboriginal population
1842	Defeat of Qing forces by British in Opium Wars undermines Chinese power and makes peripheral areas vulnerable to European intrusion
1888–1892	Liu Mingquan lays foundation for modern infrastructure (railroads, electricity, telegraph)
1895–1945	Japanese greatly expand industrial and agricultural infrastructure on Taiwan
1945	Guomindang takes control of Taiwan following Japanese defeat in World War II
1947	February 28th Incident
1949	Communists defeat Guomindang in Chinese civil war; great mainlander immigration to Taiwan
1949–1958	Land reform and import substitution policy
1958–1968	Export orientation precipitates industrial takeoff
1969–1982	Taiwan acquires newly industrialized status
1975	President Chiang Kai-shek dies

1983–present	Transition to sophisticated technology and information-heavy exports
1987	Martial law lifted by President Chiang Ching-kuo
1988	President Chiang Ching-kuo dies
1988–1996	President Lee Teng-hui oversees political liberalization; Democratic Progressive Party becomes a factor
1996	Guomindang leader and President Lee Teng-hui wins first-ever popular presidential election
closing years of twentieth century	A thoroughly modernized Taiwanese society confronts crucial questions of political and social identity

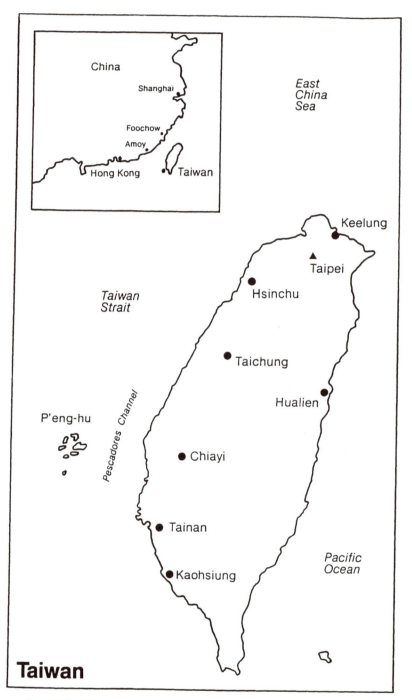

1.1 Map of Taiwan (Government Information Office, Taipei, ROC).

1

Land and History

ARRIVING ON TAIWAN in 1965 from the United States, a visitor might have felt that she or he had traveled back in time. Rickshaws were familiar parts of the urban landscape. Rural back roads and many urban streets and alleyways were unpaved and dusty throughways. A Westerner who set up residence in Taiwan found food prices ridiculously cheap, apartment rents payable in a pittance, and even a servant or two within a middle-class budget. These factors of Taiwanese life, especially the comparatively cheap prices, could be observed into the early 1980s, but by then Taiwan had become a very different place. Building on a historically solid economic foundation in an accelerating process that had become manifest just some thirty years before, the Taiwanese government and people had produced an economic miracle, and that economic miracle had itself engendered decided changes in the island's political economy. The traveler arriving in Taiwan in the late 1990s steps into a cultural environment full of sights, sounds, and smells very different from those of the United States but greets a society that in its level of economic development has pulled close to that of its onetime mentor.

What is the nature of Taiwanese society today? What special features can one detect in the Taiwanese people as they work and worship, establish communities and sustain families, cook their food and choose their attire, create literature and produce art, and build houses, commercial buildings, and the foundations for a civil society? What factors relevant to geography and history have made Taiwan and the Taiwanese people unique, influencing the main currents of the Taiwanese present, carrying these remarkable people toward the year 2000? This book seeks to provide readers of varying backgrounds and levels of knowledge, united in their interest in the place and the people of Taiwan, with information suggesting answers to those questions. This introductory chapter especially addresses itself to the latter question, to matters of geography and people in the context of Taiwanese history.

GEOGRAPHY, CLIMATE, AND NATURAL HISTORY

Once recovered from jet lag due to the effects of an approximately twelve-hour flight across the Pacific Ocean and the sixteen-hour time difference between Taiwan and the U.S. West Coast, the tourist coming to Taiwan has an island full of natural and human-made wonders to behold. It is an island about 245 miles long going northeast to southwest and 90 miles across at the widest point going northwest to southeast; it lies about 100 miles across the Taiwan Straits from China's Fujian Province. Taiwan's 13,900 square miles makes it a bit larger in land area than Massachusetts and Connecticut combined.[1] A trip across the width of Taiwan takes longer than the humble 90 miles might suggest, though. A mountainous spine runs the length of Taiwan, rising virtually from the sea on the east side of the island and extending to the western plains. Journeys across either of the two major east-west highways must traverse the mountains. With stops to admire breathtaking scenery such as that afforded by Taroko Gorge, and delays caused by occasionally falling boulders, highway construction, or traffic accidents, the spectacular trip can take up to six hours and, on a particularly eventful day, even more. The traveler to Taiwan should arrive with umbrella in tow. The island averages 100 inches of rainfall per year and in some years and places may get up to 200 inches; furthermore, the rainiest season in the north is winter, whereas in the south it is summer, so that the cross-island traveler may well be greeted by rain at some point in the trip. Temperatures and humidity levels will be familiar to those acquainted with the climate of places in the United States along the Gulf of Mexico. Summer weather lasts from April to November; a day in July will likely feature 90 degrees or above and high humidity. From December to March the temperatures drop and the traveler may even perceive the weather as turning cool at times; still, the mean temperature for these months is about 59 degrees.[2]

Almost all visitors to Taiwan arrive at Chiang Kai-shek International Airport, just outside Taipei at the northern end of the island, and proceed initially to some location within that city. Taipei is Taiwan's capital and largest city, housing the highest-level government offices on the island. Two

1.2 Rows of rice plants in rural Taiwan.

million of Taiwan's twenty-one million people live in Taipei. Another one million live in Kaohsiung at the southern end of the island; about 500,000 people live in each of the cities of Tainan, Taichung, and Keelung. In each of Taiwan's sixteen counties there are also sizable towns and small cities that serve the governmental and commercial needs of the surrounding rural population. A total of about 12.5 million people live in these towns and small cities, and another 3.0 million live in the countryside around them. Taiwan's population is well dispersed by comparison with other recently industrialized areas of the world, a condition that has contributed to an equitable distribution of wealth in the course of the island's rapid economic development. Although Taiwan has gone from a predominately agrarian society in the 1950s to a predominately industrial society at the close of the twentieth century, about 15 percent of the population still live in the countryside, and rural-urban differences are minimized by industrial zones and nearby towns that offer income-supplementing jobs and leisure activities to rural people.

Travelers to Taiwan are treated to a lush, mostly subtropical, partially tropical environment natural to its location between the twenty-first and twenty-sixth parallels, about the same latitude as Cuba. The island on which they find themselves has a prehistory fixing it firmly in a Southeast Asian ethnolinguistic cultural sphere and a history that has produced a highly unique society. A million years ago the island of Taiwan emerged from the sea according to geological processes similar to those that gave rise to the Japanese and Philippine archipelagos. Over the next several thousand years there evolved on Taiwan's rugged mountains and its fertile valleys a stunning landscape full of lush grasses on the western plains, 1,500 species of tropical and subtropical plants, and mixed forests of broad-leaved deciduous trees and conifers; the latter dominate the higher elevations, which rise frequently to 10,000 and as high as 13,114 feet above sea level.[3] Many millennia into its botanical evolution, a preceramic hunting, fishing, and gathering people were living on Taiwan, sharing its natural bounty with the Formosan black bear, foxes, flying foxes, wild boar, bats, squirrels, deer, many species of birds, and other animals that roamed the island.

ABORIGINAL POPULATION

If the traveler takes the advice of locals and ventures to the gorgeous, mountain-ringed body of water known as Sun Moon Lake, she or he can conveniently gain access to the new Nine Tribes Aboriginal Village, where experts have reconstructed the physical components of villages associated with all the enduring aboriginal groups. The ancestors of these people were neolithic Austronesian people who arrived on Taiwan in about 4000 B.C., following a pattern of migration that had taken a culturally and linguistically similar people from China, through Southeast Asia, and across Malaysia and the islands of Indonesia to New Zealand, Australia, and many islands of the Pacific Ocean. The Austronesian arrivals absorbed the previous human inhabitants and introduced an economy based on horticulture in addition to hunting, gathering, and fishing. These ancestors of the people known today as Taiwan's aborigines produced cord-marked pottery and sophisticated stone tools, including by 2500 B.C. stone knives associated with millet and rice agriculture.[4] They used those knives along with hoes and digging sticks as their primary tools for cultivating millet, rice, taro, yams, and sugarcane in the slash-and-burn style known as "swidden." The aborigines had no draft animals or plow agriculture. They raised dogs, pigs, and chickens; hunted deer and wild boar with bows and arrows, snares, and iron-tipped spears; and fished the rivers and coastal waters using basket traps, nets, and derris poison. The material culture of this aboriginal population would over the years demonstrate a range of styles suggesting interaction with cultures on the Southeast China mainland, Vietnam, and the Philippines. As the last centuries B.C. gave way to the first centuries A.D., these people were using iron forges with bellows of a type associated with the contemporary cultures of Indonesia. Wooden utensils carved with iron in time replaced the ancient pottery forms.

In producing distinctive woven goods, the aborigines employed the backstrap loom.[5]

Taiwanese aboriginal groups featured notable similarities. The aborigines organized themselves into villages independent of higher political authority, and the villages were generally egalitarian in social structure. Kinship served as an important but not exclusive organizing principle in aborigine villages; age grades, cult groups, and other nonkinship designations were also very important. Marriages were monogamous and families were nuclear or stem arrangements, so that households were discreet. The primary hunters of the village, however, occupied separate quarters at times during the year. Whereas males were the primary hunters and fishers, women were the main cultivators; they continued to gather naturally growing edibles even as horticulture took on greater importance. Taiwanese aboriginal society recognized rights to individual and household property; land was not traded or sold, though, and land demarcation was fluid. While traditional and contemporary patterns of village location were recognized, land immediately surrounding a village was understood to be the special hunting province of its members, and thus firm boundaries as such did not exist. Much land in Taiwan was taken as open territory for fishing, gathering, and especially hunting. Zones of security and primary usage were defended vigorously, however, and fighting was a prime male activity. Headhunting was common across ethnolinguistic groups and geographical areas, bringing high prestige to those who could return with evidence of a decapitated foe. The contemporary visitor to aboriginal village reconstructions may see model skeletons giving witness to the aboriginal propensity to hang these heads on poles or display them on outdoor shelves for the whole village to admire.[6]

Energizing drum beats and colorful music and dance performances at this site of the reconstructions give more uplifting representations of aboriginal culture and the cultural variety from group to group. Although sharing the common features cited, these aboriginal groups were distinguishable by numerous differences in housing, artistic motifs, personal ornamentation, village size, religion, and language. The aboriginal languages are all part of the Malayo-Polynesian family, but most are mutually incomprehensible. Cultural and linguistic differences among the Taiwanese aborigines gave rise to anthropological classification into six ethnolinguistic groups and, within those, twenty subgroups. Ten of those subgroups have survived as today's aboriginal "tribes"; the site of the reconstructions refers to nine villages because two of the groups have been included at one of the reconstructed villages. The aboriginal population could also be classified broadly into plains groups and mountain groups. The plains groups depended more on agricul-

1.3 Raised home with thatched roof reconstructed in the style of some aboriginal groups.

ture and coastal fishing than did the upland hunters, gatherers, and riverine fishers.[7]

Until the sixteenth century Chinese immigrants to Taiwan were peripheral to the main cultural life of the island, which was dominated by the aborigines. The first dependable citation of Chinese contact with the island comes to us from 239 A.D., when the emperor sent a large expeditionary force to explore, but not claim, Taiwan. Migrants from the Chinese mainland braved the turbulent Taiwan Straits as early as the seventh century A.D., but any resulting settlement was tiny. The Mongols took control of the Pescadores Islands during their thirteenth- and fourteenth-century rule, and during the same period pirates from China and Japan began to stake small claims along Taiwan's coast, but these claims were few and oriented toward the sea as much as to this particular island. Surprisingly, the Spanish and the Dutch contended for power on Taiwan before mainland Chinese dynastic power became a factor.

History

European Interest and the Brief Rule of the Dutch

Somewhere the visitor to Taiwan might have read of a European interest in the island during the days of seagoing exploration. She or he might seek to discover remaining physical evidence of the European presence on Taiwan. Evidence can be found at both ends of the island. Just north of Taipei is an area by the name of Tamsui, which during much of Taiwan's traditional history was an important port and city in its own right. Today the traveler to Taiwan finds in Tamsui a substantial suburban population with a thriving market and commercial life, a good university, stunning views of the East China Sea, and a fort where the government of Spain established headquarters from which it controlled the area for a time in the seventeenth century. At the other end of the island is a city named Tainan, the old capital heavily steeped in the culture of traditional Taiwan. Tainan features two forts, one located in the city, the other in the outlying area known as Anping. These endure as symbols of that time when the Dutch claimed the whole island after winning their competition with the Spaniards. The forts offer tangible representation of two enduring themes in Taiwanese history: the island's linkage to trade networks operating in the waters enveloping Southeast and East Asia; and Taiwan's strategic importance to those envisioning commercial or military contests in that part of the world.[8]

Taiwan's aborigines exchanged goods and ideas with people of other cultures through a Southeast Asian trade network that flourished for many centuries before outsiders began to press more aggressive claims on the island. By the sixteenth century, Chinese and Japanese pirates flourished in the waters of the South China and East China Seas. Chinese fishers from Guangdong and Fujian Provinces frequently anchored in the nearby Pescadores Islands and traded actively with the aborigines. Chinese traders also resided along the western coast, where they facilitated the exchange of dried venison and deerskins for salt, cloth, iron goods, porcelain wares, and jewelry. In 1517 Portuguese vessels en route to Japan passed by Taiwan and recorded their sighting as *Ilha Formosa* (beautiful island). A century later the Dutch found reason to do more than pass by: In 1622 they captured the Pescadores and used those islands as bases for controlling or otherwise harassing traders passing among Japan, China, and the Philippines. In 1624 the Dutch moved to Taiwan itself, abandoning the Pescadores by agreement with the Ming dynasty (1368–1644) government in exchange for limited trading rights along the southern China coast. In 1626 Spaniards seized the area around the modern city of Keelung as competition among European traders and their governments increased; two years later they established their key fort at Tamsui. The Dutch, though, won the European competition for Taiwan: In 1642 Dutch forces engaged and defeated the Spaniards in battle, quelled a Chinese rebellion with the help of aborigines, and established jurisdiction over the island.

Chinese migration to Taiwan increased greatly during Dutch tenure. The Dutch East India Company rented land, farm implements, and oxen to Chinese settlers with the understanding that they would grow sugarcane and several other cash crops. The Dutch authorities built forts, dug wells, conducted land surveys, and romanized aboriginal languages. Some aborigines in the Tainan area adapted to the Dutch and Chinese economic arrangement and began to practice agriculture in the Chinese style with Dutch-provided implements, helping to meet the demands of the colonial market. But Dutch control did not penetrate far beyond the southwest area centered on Tainan. The aboriginal population, over twice that of the 30,000 Chinese on Taiwan toward the end of the Dutch era, was largely left to follow traditional economic and cultural practices.[9]

Rule of the Family Cheng

At the outset of Dutch tenure a pirate named Cheng Chih-lung profited greatly by transporting across the Taiwan Straits Chinese seeking a better economic fate.[10] In the 1640s the faltering Ming dynasty commissioned Cheng to turn his attention from piracy to defense of the Chinese ruling house against Manchu challengers. Cheng gave a good account of himself and his naval forces, but by this time the Manchu conquest was inexorable. The Manchus secured Beijing in 1644, although in southern China they faced concerted opposition. Among those they faced was Cheng Ch'eng-kung, the half-Japanese son of Cheng Chih-lung, who inherited his father's forces, established a post with Dutch consent in northern Taiwan, and with 100,000 troops and 3,000 junks caused the Manchus major problems through 1658, at one point nearly capturing Nanjing.[11] During 1658–1661, though, Cheng Ch'eng-kung was relegated to limited forays along the southeastern China coast and in the latter year turned on the Dutch, aspiring to establish himself as the ruler of a post-Ming dynasty based on Taiwan. One of the two main Dutch forts fell quickly, but the other held out until early 1662. Cheng Ch'eng-kung died soon after taking Taiwan and establishing a Ming-style government, with a Chinese legal system, court, scholars, and advisers. Cheng Ch'eng-kung's son and brother fought each other for the vacated leadership position. The son, Cheng Ching, won. He not only consolidated his father's rule but also attempted to accomplish Cheng Ch'eng-kung's dream of restoring the Ming dynasty. After years of efforts, however, he retreated to Taiwan and in the family tradition died at an early age after exhausting efforts to fulfill his ambitions. Cheng Ching's death left the Cheng house in dissension and disarray. The Manchu government, which took the dynastic name of Qing, got wind of the weakened condition of the Cheng government, sent a naval expedition to the Pescadores (P'eng-hu), destroyed the Cheng fleet in battle there, and then landed on Taiwan and defeated the Cheng forces.[12]

While the traveler is in Tainan, she or he would do well to seek out historical reminders of the past that at this point in the story becomes considerably more complicated. The public university in Tainan, one of the island's finest, is named Ch'eng Kung University after the conqueror of the Dutch who then founded a family dynasty on Taiwan. Cheng Ch'eng-kung, also known as Koxinga, is a hero to many in Taiwan. A museum in Tainan honors him, housing archaeological artifacts and historical documents of his era and featuring paintings depicting his exploits. Yet when one ponders his story, the complexity of his and his family's activities and their legacies becomes evident. Cheng's father had a long career as a pirate, by definition a defier of the dynasty the Chengs then became famous for trying to save. Having failed to save the Ming dynasty, the Chengs opposed the Qing dynasty because it was not Ming and not ethnically Chinese. Yet the Chengs ultimately established their own minidynasty on Taiwan, defying the Manchus, who in embracing Chinese administrative techniques and high culture had begun to win over mainland residents.

So Cheng was half-Chinese, half-Japanese, a defender of a Chinese dynasty, the founder of a ruling house on Taiwan, and the stubborn opponent of a legitimate dynasty on mainland China, to which the family dynasty eventually lost Taiwan. Although there would be some malcontents, this Qing dynasty was then accepted by the Chinese population on Taiwan as the legitimate government. Still, for many Chinese, Cheng Ch'eng-kung remained a hero. Meanwhile the plains aborigines undoubtedly wished that all these outside contenders would just go away; the mountain aborigines at this point remained largely unaware of outside contenders.

Early Qing Dynasty Rule

When the Qing dynasty took control of Taiwan with the victory over the Cheng forces, it was the first time that any Chinese government aspired to establish a ruling apparatus on Taiwan. Taiwan was designated a prefecture of Fujian Province.[13] Below the prefectural government were three counties, one of them focused on Tainan, where the prefectural government was also ensconced, one at Feng-shan near present-day Kaohsiung, and one at Chu-lo at today's Chia-i.[14]

From 1683 to 1886 Taiwan was a rather wild and woolly frontier area on the Chinese periphery. The Qing rulers maintained their hold on Taiwan as an island of strategic value in an area of the world inundated with new European trade and missionary activity. The Manchus felt much ambivalence, though, as to how to use and govern the island. At the beginning, during the Kangxi imperial era (1662–1722), Chinese immigration into Taiwan was forbidden. The Manchus had much concern over potential conflict between the aborigines and the Chinese population as sedentary farmers moved northward along the western plains claiming lands where aborigines had practiced limited agriculture and hunted deer with abandon. Initially, and through most of the rest of the Qing period, the official response to potential Chinese-aborigine conflict was to stabilize the existing population and to minimize Chinese-aborigine contact by establishing clearly marked boundaries wherein the economic activities of each group were allowed.[15]

From the beginning, though, an alternative approach was voiced by activist officials who saw Taiwan as an outlet for economically depressed people from Fujian and other Southeast China provinces, as well as a fertile agricultural area capable of producing enough rice, sugar, and tea for profitable export. Activists further argued that an increased Chinese population would lay the agrarian foundations on which all Chinese civilization rested. On these foundations promoters of aggressive Chinese colonization of Taiwan hoped to build those institutions that sustained Chinese culture on the mainland. These foundations included strong, male-dominated families ideally housing several generations under one roof or at least in a common compound; a productive grain-growing agricultural economy; thriving commercial activity funded from surplus farm family funds, properly controlled, regulated, and exploited by the state; the development of a scholar-bureaucratic class that could in turn exemplify for the rest of society proper Confucian, humanitarian virtues in one's treatment of other people; and the Chinese religious complex mixing elements of Buddhism, Taoism, and propitiation of ancestors and a variety of gods in the practical service of supplicants.[16] This activist view enjoyed greatest prominence during the Yongzheng era (1723–1735), when the short but dynamic rule of Emperor Yongzheng foresaw full integration of Taiwan into the core of the Chinese Empire and the tapping of the island's value beyond matters of strategic concern. During the Qianlong era (1736–1795), however, the imperial government returned to a policy of population containment, guarantee of aboriginal territory for deer hunting and mixed economic activities, and stabilization rather than aggressive development of the Chinese frontier. Despite official policy, though, many people living on the more densely populated and overworked land of Guangdong and especially Fujian chose to defy the government and risk passage to Taiwan.[17]

For some fifty years after the Manchus overthrew the Ming and established the Qing dynasty, this illegal immigration was not a great problem as far as Chinese-aboriginal relations was concerned. Taiwan actually saw a drop in Chinese population through much of 1683–1722 as the stability provided by the new dynasty attracted more people back to the homeland in numbers greater than those who sought out the Taiwanese frontier. Through the middle years of the eighteenth century, Qing anti-immigration and aborigine-protection policies minimized conflict, having at least the effect of slowing Chinese penetration and providing some assurance to the aborigines of the government's concern for their welfare. But by the late eighteenth century Chinese immigration had become a steady flow. The Qing government recognized the reality of a steadily increasing population on Taiwan by establishing a new county with seat at today's Chang-hua and another roughly comparable, slightly higher level, administration at Tamsui.[18]

Thinking of the extraordinary poverty, daring, and energy of the Chinese immigrants who first ventured forth to Taiwan, the thoughtful traveler who becomes privy to this history might relate the information to contemporary images speaking to the temper of the Taiwanese people. One might do so, for example, when emerging visibly shaken from the effects of a grueling taxi ride during business hours back in Taipei, or when being swept along amidst densely crowded pedestrians moving swiftly on that city's sidewalks, thinking all the while that chaos rules this place. But then images of young people flooding into night schools to gain a leg up on passing high school or college entrance exams might take over. Or it might be the efficiency of travel by train or bus, or the wonders of Taiwanese technology that come to mind: excellent systems of roads and railroads, dams and other waterworks, the engineering feats required to blast tunnels and construct highways through sheer marble in the mountains towering above Taroko Gorge. The Taiwanese people are on the move, not at all chaotically, but with great sense of purpose, mustering colossal levels of energy, diligently applied above all to the pursuit of economic success. But a half-century ago Taiwan's people were by the standards of modern industrialized nations poor. They remember. Even most young people remember, vicariously. The ancestors of most of today's populace arrived in Taiwan poor. They also arrived under the influence of powerful cultural exhortations to seek opportunity, work hard, and do better. Another theme emerges and runs concurrently with the issue of Taiwanese identity: The Chinese who came to the island were the poorest of the poor, a practical, hardworking people who sought out a distant frontier as a place where they might improve their families' lots in life. The Taiwanese people today retain that legacy of extraordinary diligence applied to the tasks necessary for economic improvement.

Taiwan proved no easy place to live for an emigrant from Guangdong or Fujian. Death loomed as a definite possibility on the trip across the 100 miles of choppy waters of the straits. Land was available for the ambitious claimer but it required hard, backbreaking work to clear forests, prepare the soil, and initiate cultivation of virgin fields. Early pioneers from families of southeastern China were men who signed on in a tenancy relationship, cultivating land owned by someone else who had the economic wherewithal to procure the seeds, draft animals, and agricultural implements necessary to farm in the productive Chinese way. Once farmers were established on the land, security was their ever-present concern. Over the years many plains aborigines adapted to the Chinese presence, some switching to Chinese-style agriculture, others maintaining the traditional mixed economy on lands protected for that purpose by the Qing government. But as the Chinese tide proved ineluctable, the mood of many aborigines got angrier. It took a hardy, brave, imaginative Chinese soul to envision a better life on the tough Taiwanese frontier.[19]

Tainan provides rich indicators of the complexity of Taiwanese identity. With interest piqued by what she or he has found in the historic capital, still seeking a better understanding of the Taiwanese in the fullness of their identity, the traveler would do well to head up the west coast toward the old port city of Lukang, a rich repository of Taiwanese culture. Along the way the traveler might detour eastward just a bit to head for a small shrine honoring the historical character Wu Feng.[20] Here one finds oneself a few miles from Chia-i, a county seat in traditional and contemporary times. Nearby is Alishan, Taiwan's most scenic mountain, frequently enshrouded in a magical haze. Below one can view the expanses of the western plains and imagine the conflicts aroused by Chinese immigration, pressuring many plains aborigines to retreat into the uplands, where they in turn encroached upon the traditional territory of the mountain aborigines.

On a plaque at the site of the shrine one can read the story that made Wu Feng famous and speaks to these matters of cultural tension. Wu Feng was a Qing dynasty official who knew several aboriginal languages and served as liaison to Taiwan's indigenous people. Although sympathetic with the aborigines and dedicated to the improvement of their lives, he was reputedly deeply concerned about the ethics of certain aboriginal customs, especially the longtime practice of headhunting. For a time, the story goes, Wu Feng seemed to have convinced the aborigines to abandon the custom. After an extended drought, however, the aborigines told Wu Feng that they had to find a human sacrifice whose head could be offered to the rain god. Distraught at this reversal, Wu Feng told his indigenous friends that that evening a stranger wearing a red-hooded cape would come to them on horseback; if they insisted that they must decapitate someone for sacrifice, they should kill this man. That night the scene unfolded as Wu Feng predicted. When the aborigines pulled back the hood, they were aghast to see that the man they had killed was Wu Feng. They were so laden with guilt that from that moment they never practiced headhunting again.

Even today that story serves to illustrate the historical tension between the Chinese and the aborigines: Today's aborigines resent that story as a non-contextual misrepresentation of their culture and as a fabrication. Merely the stuff of legend, the story is not accurate even in its broad theme: Headhunting continued among some aboriginal groups into the early twentieth century. It does, though, serve to underscore two additional themes in the history of Taiwan: first, the island's social evolution as a pluralistic society where diverse groups had to find ways to live together and, second, the conflictual nature of the Taiwanese frontier.

Some aboriginal groups sustained the challenges to their traditional economy better than others, accommodating themselves to Chinese ways while maintaining a degree of cultural integrity. But in doing so they bucked an overall, gradual but inexorable trend whereby Chinese occupied the arable lowlands and either absorbed the plains aborigines or drove them into the mountains to join their ethnic cousins, who had always resisted Chinese penetration fiercely. Unassimilated lowlanders naturally became ever more intransigent as the Chinese took possession of their lands. Chinese heads literally rolled, in ample testimony of the fighting will of those who had inhabited Taiwan for nearly four millennia before the Spanish, Dutch, Cheng, and Qing intrusions.[21]

Late Qing Dynasty Rule

Society on Taiwan was conflictual, quite apart from the Chinese-aborigine tension. Another tension was that between the independent-minded Chinese settlers and the Qing government. The Qing ruled Taiwan with increasing vigor in the late eighteenth and early nineteenth centuries. Officials sought to bring more and more land onto the tax rolls while keeping the tax burden light.[22] Whereas Qing administration expanded and intensified as the eighteenth century wore on, Chinese rule traditionally penetrated only thinly below the county level, and on the frontier control over the populace, exercised by the county magistrate, was tenuous. In governing the territory for which he was responsible, the county magistrate depended on cooperation of the locally powerful. Sometimes this meant looking the other way when local strongmen evaded tax responsibility or encroached on land occupied by the less powerful. Local self-defense groups were common, and the line between defense and aggression was thin. In general Chinese farmers were secure in their productive labor, but in many areas their security came at the price of "protection fees" paid to local strongmen.[23] Qing officials had to maintain enough order to enable agriculture to thrive and to collect enough taxes so the island could repay at least a significant percentage of the expenditure required to govern it. The worst armed conflicts, and certainly direct challenges to the dynasty, had to be countered with effective force, and indeed Qing forces met bald challenges with overwhelming reply. But given its premodern political economy, the government could not afford to attend to every local disturbance.

Living amidst these local and central contenders for power, acutely aware of the dangers posed by their encroachment on aboriginal territories, farmers on the Taiwanese frontier formed a society oriented toward survival and to the pursuit of economic prosperity under tough conditions. The frontier produced a hardworking, independent, pragmatic populace supremely dedicated to the socioreligious imperative to increase family fortunes and highly impressed with the necessity for flexible adjustment to prevailing circumstances. Such ability to adjust flexibly to the demand of the moment ensured survival and maximized chances to make prosperous the family, including not only the living family but ancestors and future generations. Pragmatism in the service of ancestors, to sustain them in the realms of the world beyond this one, and in behalf of descendants, who could thrive and build upon solid economic foundations deep into the future, became a value of the highest order on the Taiwanese frontier.[24] Taiwanese pragmatism emerges as a thematic stream flowing into the confluence of themes riding the currents of a unique history.

Beyond Chinese-aborigine tensions and those between government and society lay the tensions produced by subethnic rivalries. The Hakka, a small but significant portion of the population, had until the first centuries A.D. lived in Hubei Province but under persecution found their way to Guang-

1.4 Fishing boats off the coast of Taiwan.

dong and western Fujian Provinces. They were ethnically Chinese but featured certain distinct cultural practices. Although outwardly reticent in demeanor, their women worked actively in agricultural cultivation and abhorred the practice of footbinding. Their work hats with veils to protect them from the sun were distinctive, as were other Hakka fashions. The Hakka were the first Chinese to arrive on Taiwan, coming in small numbers since the time of the Tang dynasty; a notable Hakka migration to Taiwan occurred in the sixteenth century, and there would be significant arrivals in the late seventeenth and eighteenth centuries as well.[25]

But during these centuries Taiwan was occupied predominately by people arriving from Fujian Province, principally from two densely populated prefectures, Quanzhou and Zhangzhou. The language of the Fujianese, Minnan, gave rise to the closely related form often referred to as "Taiwanese." The Hakka, in addition to maintaining distinct cultural features, speak a language mutually incomprehensible with Minnan. Fujianese and Hakka people fought each other with considerable frequency on the Taiwanese frontier. Within the Fujianese group, news of conflicts between those tracing their roots to Quanzhou and those hailing from Zhangzhou never shocked anybody.[26]

People on Taiwan grew accustomed to the rivalries of contentious aboriginal, Hakka, and Fujianese populations. Each of these possessed interests potentially disharmonious with that of the government. Government officials in Taiwan operated far away from the center of Qing administration in

Beijing, and they operated at an unusual distance from the provincial administration across the straits in Fujian. They frequently struck independent stances in immediate response to the tasks of governance. These officials therefore constituted yet another discreet group on the pluralistic, notoriously turbulent, frontier.[27]

Moving back to the main highway from the Wu Feng shrine and Chia-i, thence to the west coast and the old city of Lukang, the traveler comes to a place where it is still possible to get a real sense of old Taiwan. The city features numerous old temples; chief among them are a temple in honor of Mazu, the patron goddess of sailors, and Lung Shan Temple, a chief pilgrimage site for adherents of popular Buddhism. Traditional urban architecture graces Lukang's streets, where shops emit sweet-smelling fragrances from religious statuary and caskets carved from native woods by highly skilled local artisans. After a leisurely morning observing the temple scene and strolling the streets, taking lunch perhaps at one of the excellent seafood restaurants, the visitor would delight in spending a sizable chunk of time at the Lukang Museum, the island's best repository of Taiwanese material culture. Here one finds among other things clothes demonstrating Chinese fashion at different stages of Taiwanese history; items worn by officials and degree holders of various levels; furniture typifying the homes of successful scholars, merchants, and members of the local gentry; traditional dress of the ten surviving aboriginal groups in Taiwan; and various coins, documents, and other items giving evidence of Taiwanese interaction with foreign governments, missionaries, and traders.

Emerging from this museum after a day spent in Lukang, the visitor has a richer understanding of the island's complex culture and identity. Various aboriginal groups, Chinese immigrants of different ethnicities and social classes, officials and scholars, local traders and entrepreneurs, and foreign commercial interests have all found representation in the museum. Taiwan's long history of foreign commercial contacts and interaction with outside powers is well reemphasized as the history of Taiwan in the nineteenth and twentieth century is considered. During the nineteenth century the island's economic life reached new heights of commercialization as surplus family labor opened enterprises in urban areas to produce goods for sale on the international market as well as on the domestic market.[28] These products of Chinese crafts and entrepreneurial diversification joined rice, sugar, tea, camphor, deerskins, venison, and many other items as sought-after goods for trade in China, Japan, the Philippines, and Southeast Asia. European traders handled a hefty chunk of this trade, even though forbidden to do so under the Qing dynasty's Canton system of the late eighteenth and early nineteenth centuries. European commercial involvement with Taiwan increased as defeats in the Opium Wars (1839–1842) and the Anglo-French War (1858–1860) forced the opening of twenty-one Chinese-governed ports, including Taiwan's Tamsui and Keelung. By the late nineteenth century Taiwanese farmers and urban entrepreneurs had considerable experience producing for a multisectoral, cross-island, trans-China, and international economy.[29] These facts highlight another important theme in Taiwanese history: the Taiwanese openness to entrepreneurial endeavors targeted at domestic and foreign markets.

Economic flexibility as demonstrated by nineteenth-century Taiwanese entrepreneurs connects easily with another theme that developed as the Qing dynasty gave ever more attention to Taiwan's strategic utility: Taiwan as the focus of ambitious goals of economic development by outside powers. As European pressure on China increased in the nineteenth century, the Qing court developed an elevated awareness of the economic and especially the strategic importance of Taiwan. Made a province in 1886, Taiwan was de-tached from Fujian and given parity with it. The provincial governor from 1888 to 1892 was Liu Mingquan, a farsighted official in sympathy with the Chinese self-strengthening movement on the mainland. Liu brought in-creased road and railroad mileage, electrification, the telephone, the tele-graph, shipbuilding, and industry to Taiwan. By 1895 Taiwan was among the most highly developed areas of China and far more connected to the international economy than most. Its people retained the hardworking, prag-matic, success-oriented attitudes that Chinese culture in the context of a frontier society had instilled in them. But the society had become ever more sophisticated. Here and there members of the local elite, often with roots to a strongman past, succeeded in the civil service examinations and attained rank among the scholar-bureaucrats. Unique forms of puppetry, folk theater, and religion brought cultural flash and dash to this outpost of Chinese society. Above all, new levels of achievement were reached in agriculture, commerce, and trade, all abetted by the elements of modern economic in-frastructure that Liu Mingquan brought to the island.[30]

The Japanese Period

Throughout a trip around Taiwan the traveler can hear and observe many indicators of a former Japanese presence. While in the course of the last four decades Mandarin has been the language of official and common commu-nication, many people in the countryside remain vastly more comfortable with the Minnan ("Taiwanese") or Hakka dialects. People over fifty years of age often comprehend little and speak less of Mandarin. Those Taiwanese over sixty would be more likely to understand Japanese, and some in this age group are fluent in that language. The visitor might well have heard some older people speaking to each other in Japanese. Someone might have pointed out the Japanese-style houses that can be seen in cities throughout Taiwan. One might have learned along the way that Taipei and Keelung to the north, Kaohsiung and Tainan to the south, and Taichung in the middle along the western coast feature populations in excess of one million. The locations of these large cities indicate these are of Taiwan's dispersed pattern of population, traceable to policies inaugurated under Japanese authority. The farmers' association buildings and many agricultural research stations were built by the Japanese, as were many government buildings in Taiwan, including most notably the huge edifice housing the central government of Taiwan today, even as it did during the Japanese era. That era began in 1895 when island rule passed from Sino-Manchu to Japanese hands by the terms of the Treaty of Shimonoseki, following Japan's defeat of Qing forces in a war fueled by competition over Korea and the Manchu ancestral lands of China's Northeast.

Vaguely resembling the Manchus in their early debates over exactly what to do with Taiwan, the Japanese at first evidenced considerable indecisiveness about the shape their colonial rule would take. That indecisiveness ended with the arrival of Governor-General Kodama Gentaro and his civil administrator Goto Shimpei in 1898.[31] These two activist Japanese administrators initiated surveys to discover pertinent facts about Taiwanese topography, people, and economic potential. A multitiered system of land ownership and tenancy that had evolved on Taiwan ended as great amounts of land that had hitherto escaped taxation were brought onto government tax rolls. When surveys revealed Taiwan had humble endowments of minerals, precious metals, and fossil fuels, the self-aggrandizing Japanese focused on intensive cultivation of Taiwanese fields for production of the traditionally important crops of sugar and rice. For these crops new higher-yielding, pest-resistant strains were introduced and eventually exceeded in production those varieties traditionally cultivated on Taiwan. The Japanese also introduced sophisticated new sugar-refining factories and food-processing industries.

During the 1930s and 1940s the Japanese added metallurgical and machine industries as their nation geared up for war in the Asian-Pacific region. The Taiwanese east coast remained relatively underdeveloped, but the Japanese administration otherwise built systems of power generation, dams, irrigation works, roads, and railroads from north to south across the island. Freezing the social structure, the Japanese overlords recognized the prerogatives of the rural gentry, whom they co-opted and used to maintain social order. Japanese administration reached down into the villages of Taiwan; Taiwanese were severely restricted in pursuit of higher education on Taiwan, and the most important positions in government went to the Japanese. The Japanese did, however, introduce universal education; as the Japanese era unfolded, a majority of the people on Taiwan gained at least a primary school level, rudimentary formal Japanese education in the Japanese language. Also, ambitious members of favored gentry families could attain higher education in Japan, where they evaded the discrimination they faced in Taiwan. These privileged students gained further understanding of modernity through such study. For all the harshness of Japanese rule, the whole Taiwanese society had been exposed to significant elements of advanced industrial society by the time World War II and Japanese rule on Taiwan ended in 1945.

Chiang Kai-shek and the Guomindang: New Rulers from the Mainland

Just east of that huge central administration building in Taipei, on Chung-shan South Road, the visitor cannot miss the main gates to a memorial of similarly impressive size. To the left and to the right of the main gates are theaters established for the performance of serious concerts and dramatic works. These are appealing structures mixing Western and Chinese styles of architecture, but they are afterthoughts, built in the 1980s. Across an immense square with well-attended gardens lies the main building built a decade and a half earlier than these other structures. Inside is a museum documenting the history of the Guomindang regime of Chiang Kai-shek. On the top floor is a statue of similar size and pose to that of Lincoln at the memorial in Washington, D.C. Unlike the memorial to Lincoln, though, the Chiang Kai-shek Memorial was established by its namesake, in his own honor, to glorify his rule and to amplify the prestige of the Guomindang, the party that he led. The Chiang Kai-shek Memorial constitutes a massive statement of the power of a ruler and the party he led.

The Potsdam Declaration of July 1945 gave control of Taiwan to the Guomindang government. This government, led by Chiang Kai-shek, traced its heritage to Sun Yat-sen and his efforts to overthrow China's last traditional dynasty, the Qing (1644–1912). A tireless revolutionary, Sun Yat-sen made many failed attempts to topple the Qing, finally inspiring a successful revolutionary effort that began on October 10, 1911, and lasted until the Qing leaders officially stepped down in February 1912. The Guomindang ("Party of the Nation's People," often referred to as the "Nationalists") was formed by Sun, those who had followed him in the years before the Revolution of

1911, and those who wanted a constitutional democracy for China. The Guomindang was the leading party in the national legislature of the "Republic of China," which succeeded dynastic rule. But Sun Yat-sen conceded the presidency to the strongest military figure, Yuan Shikai. Yuan was at heart no proponent of Republican democracy, though; he quickly acted to end any effective power held by the national legislature and even made a failed attempt to become emperor of a new dynasty shortly before his death in 1916. Yuan's death brought on a period during which China was partitioned by "warlords" who competed for control of territory throughout China. The Republic of China continued to exist, but the power of the national government in Beijing was limited. Before his death in 1925 Sun Yat-sen laid the groundwork for a joint effort by his Guomindang and the Chinese Communist Party (established in 1921) to rid China of warlordism. Chiang Kai-shek emerged as the new leader of the Guomindang in the wake of Sun's death, and during 1926–1928 led the military initiative known as the "Northern Expedition," beginning in the southern province of Guangdong and proceeding through central China toward Beijing. On the expedition, Chiang turned on his communist allies, killing many of them. From that time until 1949, the Chinese Communist Party and army, under Mao Zedong's guidance from the mid-1930s, continually challenged Guomindang power. The Guomindang and the Chinese Communist Party formally joined forces again to oppose the Japanese invasion and occupation of China during 1937–1945. But in practice, the two Chinese parties opposed each other as much as they did the Japanese. After the August 1945 Japanese concession of defeat in World War II and withdrawal from China, the armies of the Guomindang and Chinese Communist Party soon clashed openly, beginning the Chinese Civil War of 1946–1949.

During Chiang Kai-shek's leadership on the Chinese mainland, his Guomindang government based itself in the central China city of Nanjing from 1928 until 1938, when Japanese pressure forced it to move westward to Chongqing (also known as Chungking) in Sichuan Province. Chiang's administration made notable advances in bringing modern finance, transport, and communication to China. But Chiang had an authoritarian administrative style that countered the democratic spirit that Sun Yat-sen had articulated; Chiang purged those within the Guomindang who sought to keep that spirit alive, and despite success as a modernizer he ran a government whose methods in squelching dissent were reminiscent of Nazi Germany and Fascist Italy. Despite considerable frustration with Chiang, the U.S. government supported him because of his anticommunist stance, giving his Guomindang generous material assistance in its struggle against the communists in the

Chinese Civil War. The Chinese Communists were much less well endowed in weaponry than the Guomindang, but they used their well-cultivated links to the peasant population in pursuing a brilliant guerrilla warfare strategy.

By 1948 the Chinese Communists were routing the Guomindang in conventional battle as well and by October 1, 1949, were in a position to claim themselves the leaders of a new People's Republic of China. Guomindang government officials, soldiers, and supporters retreated to Taiwan, already occupied by members of the Guomindang party and army since 1945, with the intention of eventually mounting an attack on the Communists and returning to rule the mainland.[32]

Between 1945 and 1949 the Guomindang gave every indication that they could produce a disaster on Taiwan equal to that which they had wrought on mainland China. The war years had been tough on the Taiwanese people, on whose island the Allies had dropped significant enough tonnage to destroy about one-half of Taiwan's transportation networks, communications facilities, power generating plants, and factories. They had eaten poorly while witnessing Japanese authoritarianism at its height. For younger members of the populace, especially, this served to blur Japan's record of momentous achievements on Taiwan: the modern infrastructure; education, health, and sanitation improvements; and economic productivity. Most Taiwanese people welcomed their Chinese ethnic kin, expecting them to rule with a lighter, more benevolent hand. Instead, the hand came down even harder. Guomindang troops looted industrial and agricultural goods for their own aggrandizement and in general acted in a haughty, cruel manner toward the Taiwanese people.

On February 27, 1947, Guomindang troops initiated their most infamous actions of this early period of their rule. On this date Guomindang troops began harassing a woman selling black market cigarettes in front of the Taipei railroad station and then shot and killed a man who came to her defense. The next day crowds of angry citizens unleashed their pent-up anger at the Guomindang in violent demonstrations that came to be known collectively as the February 28th Incident.[33] As news spread across Taiwan, over the next several days people in other cities staged their own protests. Over the next several months the Guomindang ruthlessly quelled the resistance, and during the next few years the Chinese succeeded in tracking down and subjecting to life imprisonment or to death not only those suspected of fomenting or abetting the February 28th Incident but also the best and brightest among the elite who might be capable of providing the Taiwanese people with an independent voice against the brutal Guomindang regime.

Beginning in 1949 the Guomindang government began to dig itself out of the hole it had dug for itself on Taiwanese soil. With substantial U.S. assistance and heavy pressure, the Guomindang superintended a showcase land reform that launched the Taiwanese countryside toward an owner-cultivator society.[34] Currency reform, price controls, and an infusion of U.S. foodstuffs and monetary aid ended astronomic inflation. A policy of import substitution secured the home market for domestic producers of agricultural commodities, processed foods, textiles, and other labor-intensive light industrial items. With the saturation of the home market, in 1958 the government switched gears, revising multiple exchange rates in favor of a more unified structure, lowering tariffs, offering five-year tax holidays to selected transnational corporations, and designating specific industries for favorable tax treatment and raw material supply; the latter included the textile, electric and electronic products assembly, plastics, and petrochemical industries willing to produce for the international market. In 1965 an export-processing zone was established at Kaohsiung for foreign and domestic entrepreneurs and industries producing exclusively for the export market; in return for productive efforts that proved to be a collective boost for the Taiwanese economy, such export-oriented industries escaped taxation on all but the value-added portion of their products. They also got cheap energy, convenient communications and transportation, and hardworking, literate, highly competent labor at bargain basement prices. The export-processing zone concept worked so well that within a few years two additional zones were established, another one close to Kaohsiung and one near Taichung. Between 1960 and 1973 the export-driven Taiwanese economy grew at about 11 percent annually, industrial production increased 17 percent annually, and industry superseded agriculture as chief export sector and economic engine.[35]

To its credit, the Guomindang had made a startling comeback, cutting what to this point has been an enduring deal with the Taiwanese people, the benefactors of the world's hottest economy and an income distribution that is an international marvel for its equity. In return for their majority owner share in the newly industrialized economy, the Taiwanese people remained for a long time politically quiescent. The latent contentiousness in their character was overruled by the historical quest of the Taiwanese for a better economic life for their families. But the 1970s saw more attention given to political matters.[36] Farmers were restive as they packed their young men and women off to factory jobs that boosted family incomes but saw their enormous gains in agricultural productivity siphoned off through various fiscal mechanisms to fuel the industrial economy. Better- and better-educated Taiwanese youth joined other intellectuals in questioning policies that had given short shrift to environmental concerns, cultural development, and democratic aspirations of a growing middle class. The Guomindang weathered these criticisms through use of both soft gloves and a stinging whip: The government reversed the policy of agricultural resource extraction, turning to subsidization instead. Ethnic Taiwanese membership in national political organs increased, although mainlander domination continued. But political dissidents were arrested and treated ruthlessly, and Guomindang propaganda continued to promote the view that Taiwan was a temporary base from which the Chiang government would recapture the mainland.[37]

That propagandistic message, though, had lost force; no one, not even Chiang and his government, believed it any longer. President Richard Nixon's secretary of state, Henry Kissinger, traveled to the People's Republic of China in July 1971, paving the way for Nixon's historic trip the following January that culminated in the Shanghai Communique, a vaguely worded document that nevertheless left little doubt that the United States now recognized the communist regime of Mao Zedong as the legitimate governing authority on the mainland. At about the same time the United States dropped its opposition to the entrance of the People's Republic of China into the United Nations; the government of the Republic of China on Taiwan accordingly lost its U.N. seat and a major international forum for its claim to be the legitimate government of all China. President Jimmy Carter announced in December 1978 that beginning on January 1, 1979, official diplomatic relations would be established with the People's Republic; accordingly, the official diplomatic offices on Taiwan were converted to unofficial sections doing many of the same things but signaling an alteration in the United States–Taiwan relationship.[38]

Political and Economic Trends at the Close of the Twentieth Century

Chiang Kai-shek died in April 1975; power passed to his son, Chiang Ching-kuo. Especially after a nasty government clash with dissidents in Kaohsiung in 1978, Chiang Ching-kuo began to cultivate a populist image and ever so slowly to loosen the Guomindang's grip on society. In July 1987 the younger Chiang lifted martial law and let it be known that he was grooming as his successor an ethnic Taiwanese, former provincial governor Lee Teng-hui. Lee did inherit the government and party leadership when Chiang Ching-kuo died in 1988. Between 1988 and 1996 he oversaw a liberalization process by which his party's leadership could be more fairly challenged. A significant new player, the Democratic Progressive Party, was allowed to organize and compete in local, provincial, and national elections. A first-ever popular election of the president was held in spring 1996; Lee won in what outsiders judged an adequately fair and open process.[39] The Guomindang seems on the verge of another miracle. The Guomindang first managed a miracle of survival, made possible by the miracle of economic transformation. Now the party and the government seem on the verge of producing the political miracle of democratization, transforming the nature of the formerly rightest dictatorship and the society over which it ruled.

Continued success for the Guomindang hinges on continued economic progress, which will call for the flexible adjustments that the government made in achieving the economic miracle. From the late 1970s through 1996 the government showed the necessary flexibility. Government policymakers nudged the economy in productive new directions even as it divested itself of much of the direct ownership that it maintained in key industrial, communications, and transportation systems. Through advice and targeting of resources the government skillfully facilitated a move of industry away from labor-intensive operations in the late 1970s and early 1980s toward more capital-intensive industry using machines to do many of the tasks formerly done by human labor alone.[40] Then as the 1980s came to a close, with accelerated pace in the early 1990s, Taiwanese businesses were induced to move into highly sophisticated, knowledge-intensive, low-energy-use industries that seemed destined to give Taiwan rough parity with the United States, Germany, and Japan, as a postindustrial economy able to take its place among world leaders as to per capita gross national product and household income by the year 2000.[41]

Although economic success is the key to the future of the Guomindang, there are social and cultural adjustments to be made, as well. The mainlanders brought with them a variety of Chinese dialects different from the Chinese dialects of the Fujianese Minnan-speakers and the Hakka. Before they ever lost to the Communists, the Guomindang had already begun to push the northern dialect of Mandarin as the language of common communication on the mainland. The party would continue to promote Mandarin in Taiwan, where it became the medium of communication in the government, schools, and media. The Communists would do the same on the mainland. Many Chinese across the world have since recognized Mandarin as the language of common communication. The Taiwanese on the whole seem to have no great problem with this role for Mandarin, but there is now a push to allot a greater role for Minnan, used more widely at the close of the twentieth century on television, radio, and public gatherings than politically possible even during the 1980s. There is in general a growing interest in those things specifically Taiwanese in culture. Defining "Taiwanese" culture and society, synthesizing Fujianese, Hakka, mainlander (those whose families came to Taiwan only after the Guomindang defeat in the Chinese Civil War), and aboriginal elements is a truly exciting but challenging task for Taiwanese society and the Guomindang government that still seeks to govern it.

Achieving an enduring international identity is also a major concern. Military muscle is periodically displayed by the mainland People's Republic of China government in its naval and aerial exercises conducted in the South China Sea. The mainland government has made clear that the return of Hong Kong to its control is a precedent for the eventual inclusion of Taiwan in its territories of governance. Especially since the Tiananmen incident of June 1989, in which mainland leaders brutally put down student protesters, Taiwan's people have shown decided distaste for any such political reunion. Commercial and postal contacts between the mainland and Taiwan have developed rapidly since the mid-1980s, and the Taiwanese people remain enthusiastic about maintaining economic and cultural links to the land of their ancestry. Any forcible attempt to bring Taiwan under People's Republic of China control, however, would almost certainly meet with vigorous and effective military opposition mandated by Taiwan's government and supported by Taiwan's people. Furthermore, although Taiwan's international political status is extremely murky, the island is a powerhouse in matters of international trade; the world's major economic powers, including the United States, have a deep interest in the island's security.

Thoughtful travelers to Taiwan will remember certain compelling themes from Taiwanese history as they board their planes for the return home. These themes loom large in considering the present shape of Taiwanese society. Taiwan had early links to the trade networks of Southeast and East Asia, and European powers recognized the island's value as a base for realizing their international trade objectives. Recent Taiwanese society has thrived economically by its willingness to seize the opportunities of the international marketplace and to turn to its own advantage the strategic interests that others have in the island's polity and economy. Having developed an abiding spirit of pragmatism, hard work, and entrepreneurial will as the result of harsh historical realities, the Taiwanese people were positioned to seize the opportunities presented by recent history. Prepared by a past in which outsiders exploited the island's economic potential, the Taiwanese people have of late enthusiastically embraced modern economic development to realize their historical goal to increase the prosperity of their families. Born of a history that saw the conflicting interests of competing groups played out on a rough and ready frontier, the Taiwanese have ultimately endured harsh colonial rule and the politically oppressive reign of the pre-1990s Guomindang. Beyond enduring, they have thrived. In enduring their tumultuous past and thriving in their promising present, the Taiwanese have evolved a rich and fascinating culture, revealed in its fullness in the remaining chapters of this book.

NOTES

1. John F. Copper, *Taiwan: Nation-State or Province?* (Boulder, CO: Westview Press, 1990), p. 5. See pp. 4–6 for general geographic information on Taiwan.

2. *Taiwan Agricultural Yearbook* (Taichung, Taiwan: Department of Agriculture and Forestry, Taiwan Provincial Government, 1990), pp. 336–37.

3. Copper, p. 2.

4. John Robert Shepherd, *Statecraft and Political Economy on the Taiwan Frontier* (Stanford, CA: Stanford University Press, 1993), pp. 28–29.

5. Ibid., p. 29.

6. Ibid., pp. 30–32; Chen Kang Chai, *Taiwan Aborigines: A Genetic Study of Tribal Variations* (Cambridge, MA: Harvard University Press, 1967), pp. 38–48.

7. Shepherd, pp. 30–32.

8. Copper, pp. 18–19.

9. Ibid., p. 19; Shepherd discusses at length the aborigines' fate under the Dutch, pp. 47–90. For even more information on Dutch rule on Taiwan, see William Campbell, *Formosa under the Dutch* (Taipei: Ch'eng-wen Publishing Company, 1967).

10. Copper, p. 19. For a lengthier discussion see Gary M. Davison, *Agricultural Development and the Fate of Farmers in Taiwan, 1945–1990* (Ph.D. dissertation, University of Minnesota Department of History, 1993), pp. 17–18.

11. Copper, p. 19.

12. Ibid., pp. 19–20; Shepherd, pp. 91–104.

13. Shepherd, pp. 106–7.

14. See Shepherd's discussion of the early Qing rule on Taiwan, pp. 104–34.

15. Ibid., p. 139.

16. This capsule summary of the essential elements of Chinese culture is our own. For a discussion of the Qing dynasty debates on what do with Taiwan, see Shepherd, pp. 137–42.

17. See both table and text in Shepherd, p. 161.

18. See Shepherd's maps on pp. 196–97, 200–201, and 202–3. For a complete discussion of ongoing administration and debates during the Qing dynasty, see pp. 178–214.

19. See Shepherd, pp. 239–307, for a full exposition of aborigine land rights under the Qing.

20. This is a familiar story to those acquainted with Taiwanese history and culture. There is a colorful summary of the story, with accompanying picture of the

shrine, in Joseph Nerbonne, *Formosa at Your Fingertips: Guide to Taipei and All Taiwan, Republic of China,* 8th ed. (Taipei: Caves Books, 1985), p. 107.

21. Refer to Shepherd's discussion, pp. 239–307, for further details on the aborigines' reaction to expanded Chinese migration northward along the west coast.

22. See Shepherd's discussion of Qing fiscal administration on Taiwan, pp. 215–36. This, and other information in this paragraph, is consistent with information coming to us through our wide reading of Chinese language source material on the subject.

23. For an excellent discussion of the role of the strongman in Taiwanese frontier society, see Johanna Meskill, *A Chinese Pioneer Family: The Lins of Wu-feng, Taiwan* (Princeton, NJ: Princeton University Press, 1979), pp. 86–102.

24. This is our own characterization of the Taiwanese family, based on readings over the years and field experiences in Taiwan during 1980–1981 and 1988–1990. It is consistent with Hugh D. R. Baker, *Chinese Family and Kinship* (New York: Columbia University Press, 1979). For other information on the Taiwanese family, see Arthur Wolf, "Domestic Organization," and Lung-sheng Sung, "Property and Family Division," pp. 361–78, both in Emily Martin Ahern and Hill Gates, eds., *The Anthropology of Taiwanese Society* (Stanford, CA: Stanford University Press, 1981).

25. Copper, p. 37.

26. See Harry Lamley, "Subethnic Rivalry in the Ch'ing Period," in Emily Martin Ahern and Hill Gates, eds., *The Anthropology of Taiwanese Society* (Stanford, CA: Stanford University Press, 1981), pp. 282–318, for additional information on subethnic tensions on the Taiwanese frontier.

27. Shepherd, pp. 198–208. Johanna Meskill's book also gives an excellent feel for the challenges Taiwan's location presented to the Qing government.

28. See Myron L. Cohen, *House United, House Divided: A Chinese Family in Taiwan* (New York: Columbia University Press, 1976), for a highly insightful analysis of the Taiwanese family's rational use of surplus labor.

29. Much of this information on Taiwan's connections to international trade networks by the nineteenth century comes from our reading of Chinese language source material. Discussions of this subject can also be found in Thomas B. Gold, *State and Society in the Taiwan Miracle* (Armonk, NY: M. E. Sharpe, 1986), pp. 25–30; and Copper, p. 21.

30. For information on the Liu Mingquan era, see, for example, Gold, pp. 29–30.

31. See Copper, pp. 22–25, for a summary of Taiwanese society and economy during Japanese tenure. See also Gold, pp. 32–46. For a longer treatment see Chang Han-yu and Ramon H. Myers, "Japanese Colonial Development Policy in Taiwan, 1895–1906: A Case of Bureaucratic Entrepreneurship," *Journal of Asian Studies,* vol. 22, no. 4 (August 1963); and for a monograph on Goto Shimpei see Yukio Hayase, *The Career of Goto Shimpei: Japan's Statesman of Research, 1857–1929* (Ph.D. dissertation, Florida State University Department of History, March 1974).

32. For treatments of the Guomindang period in Taiwanese history, see Copper, pp. 25–32; and Gold, pp. 47–133.

33. For years discussion of the February 28th Incident was taboo in Taiwan; scholars had difficulty getting accurate details. Now the government itself has released a credible, if probably understated, study of the incident, and a major park in Taipei has dedicated a memorial to those who suffered its consequences. Short summaries of the incident may be found in Copper, p. 27; and Gold, pp. 50–51. Numerous lengthier works are also now available in Chinese and English.

34. For material on land reform in Taiwan, see Copper, p. 77; and Gold, pp. 65–66. Davison deals with this topic in considerable detail on pp. 48–71. Martin Yang, *Socio-Economic Results of Land Reform in Taiwan* (Honolulu: East-West Center Press, 1970), deals with this important subject in book-length detail.

35. See Davison, pp. 77–114, for a detailed summary of industrial development on Taiwan during the Guomindang era, based on Chinese source material. See also Gustav Ranis, "Industrial Development," in Walter Galenson, ed., *Economic Growth and Structural Change in Taiwan: The Postwar Experience of the Republic of China* (Ithaca, NY: Cornell University Press, 1979). Gold, pp. 74–96, also has a helpful summary; and John C. H. Fei, Gustav Ranis, and Shirley Kuo, *Growth with Equity: The Taiwan Case* (Oxford: Oxford University Press, 1979), is a classic statement written for the World Bank and expressive of liberal Western economists' view of Taiwan's growth experience under the Guomindang. Shirley Kuo has been finance minister in Lee Teng-hui's administration.

36. See Gold, pp. 97–121, for a summary of Taiwan's rather startling recent experience in democratization. Much of our discussion here is based on personal fieldwork in Taiwan and reading in Chinese source materials.

37. See Gold, pp. 111–21, on the matter of political dissidents in Taiwan.

38. These events are by now famous and covered in many sources. See, for example, Copper, pp. 31–32; Gold, p. 93; and John King Fairbank, *The United States and China*, 4th ed. (Cambridge, MA: Harvard University Press, 1983), pp. 458–60.

39. This election was covered frequently in U.S. newsmagazines and newspapers and in issues of the Hong Kong–based English language *Far Eastern Economic Review* in spring 1996.

40. See Davison, pp. 117–23; and Gold, pp. 97–111.

41. Copper, p. 119.

SUGGESTED READINGS

Ahern, Emily Martin and Hill Gates, eds. *The Anthropology of Taiwanese Society.* Stanford, CA: Stanford University Press, 1981.

Copper, John F. *Taiwan: Nation-State or Province?* Boulder, CO: Westview Press, 1990.

Gold, Thomas B. *State and Society in the Taiwan Miracle.* Armonk, NY: M. E. Sharpe, 1986.

Meskill, Johanna. *A Chinese Pioneer Family: The Lins of Wu-feng, Taiwan.* Princeton, NJ: Princeton University Press, 1979.

Rubinstein, Murray A., ed. *The Other Taiwan: 1945 to the Present.* Armonk, NY: M. E. Sharpe, 1994.

Shepherd, John Robert. *Statecraft and Political Economy on the Taiwan Frontier.* Stanford, CA: Stanford University Press, 1993.

2

Thought and Religion

TAIWAN IN THE 1990s has experienced a flourishing of modern democratic and scientific thought at the same time traditional Taiwanese folk traditions are being renewed and adapted to a modern industrialized society. The economic gains of recent decades have brought a boom in renovating and building Buddhist and Taoist temples. New religious groups have arisen that meld traditional Chinese religious ideas with modern concerns.

Taiwain's religious culture reflects a unique status as a culture brought by immigrants from Fujian and Guangdong, influenced by Japanese and Western presence, and then regulated by the Guomindang Party since 1947. The dominant religious activities are ancestral rituals and community temple festivals. According to 1994 ROC statistics, 11.2 million out of the 21 million people in Taiwan identify themselves as religious. Of these religious Taiwanese, 43 percent are Buddhist, 34 percent Taoists, 8 percent Yiguandao, 6 percent Christians, and 9 percent followers of other religions.[1] These figures do not adequately portray the rich diversity of religious rituals, sects, temples, and deities that are part of Taiwanese life. Moreover, the ongoing vitality of Taiwanese folk religion and ancestor reverence makes the distinction between Buddhists and Taoists more a matter of preferred designation than actual practice.

2.1   Relaxation at the temple.

CONCEPTS OF NATURE, TIME, AND SPACE

Traditional Chinese concepts of humanity, nature, time, and space continue to be meaningful to the Taiwanese despite the dominance of the modern scientific worldview. The traditional worldview envisions humans living in harmony with the natural order, usually referred to as Tian, or Heaven. Human beings should live in harmony with the natural order by understanding and adjusting their lives to the natural order as seen in the changes of the seasons and the landscape of the earth. The transformation within this natural order is known as Dao, or the Way. Dao is not only the way of nature; it is the way humans should follow to live in harmony with self, others, and the natural world. All religious and philosophical approaches teach the Way, but with different emphases and interpretations.

According to the Chinese view of a harmonious natural order, all things of heaven and earth are connected by the life force, *qi*. *Qi* is the breath of the universe, and in humans, the breath of life. The flow of *qi* and the patterns of change are understood in terms of two polar opposites: *yin* and *yang*. *Yin* and *yang* are polar opposites seen in the transformations and relationships of all things. Cold and hot, male and female, dry and wet, moon and sun, night and day, all are examples of *yin-yang* dichotomy. Another Chinese concept that interprets relationships and change is that of the five agents: wood, fire, earth, metal, and water. These traditional concepts—*qi*, the five agents, and the *yin-yang* polarity—are used to conceptualize and order all aspects of nature and society. Seasons can be understood in terms of the ebb and flow of *yin* and *yang* and the alternating dominance of the five agents. Historical change can be seen as the movement of the five agents overcoming each other. Most significantly, the human being is a microcosm of the natural universe. Like the rest of the universe, human life is governed by *qi*, the five agents, and the *yin-yang* polarity. The major organs of the body are dominated by the five agents; the forces of *yin* and *yang* are balanced in a healthy body.

In Taiwan two different calendars mark the passing of time: the Western calendar for business, school and government, and the lunar calendar for religious observances and personal guidance. The Western (Gregorian) solar calendar is the official calendar and the basis for government-designated national holidays: Founding Day of the Republic of China, Women's Day, Youth Day, Children's Day, Armed Forces Day, Teachers' Day (celebrated as Confucius's birthday), Double Ten (National Day), Taiwan's Retrocession Day, and Constitution Day: These days celebrate ROC nationalism and social progress. The official government calendar begins with the founding of the Republic of China in 1911, so the date of "retrocession" of Taiwan to China would be given as the year 34. Some government holidays conveniently coincide with Western and Christian holidays: Founding Day is January 1, and Constitution Day is December 25, Christmas Day.[2]

Chinese festivals follow the traditional lunar calendar. This calendar is based on twelve lunar months and twenty-four solar divisions and is eleven days shorter than the Western solar calendar. The biggest festival for families in Taiwan is the lunar New Year's Day, also known as Spring Festival. On New Year Taiwanese families try to share a meal of abundance with the entire family as they face a year of new beginnings with new clothes, newly clean homes, new finances, and renewed hope for good fortune. (See Chapter 3 for more information on festivals.) The Chinese almanac gives information about the lunar festivals and information about auspicious and inauspicious activities for each day. For example, the Taiwanese may consult the almanac or a specialist to find out the most auspicious days for opening a new business, getting married, or moving.

To live in harmony with nature, the Taiwanese have used the tradition of *fengshui*. In the natural landscape there is the interaction of *yin* and *yang* and the flow of *qi*. Humans must live in accordance with those natural forces and not disrupt them when they build new structures. In building temples, homes, or gravesites, the Taiwanese continue to acknowledge the need for humanity and nature to live in harmony. Thus the natural-urban landscape is conceptualized through traditional concepts such as *yin-yang* and *qi*. The Chinese science of *fengshui* (wind and water) is a tradition in which experts attempt to analyze the landscape in order to see the flow of *qi* and the relationships of *yin* and *yang*.[3] *Fengshui* experts are consulted to position a building or a grave in a way harmonious with its surroundings and therefore auspicious for its inhabitants (or their descendants). A well-positioned home or temple brings good fortune, wealth, and good crops to the family or community. Poor positioning brings various kinds of ill fortune. The tools of the trade include ancient manuals and a special compass (*luoban*) that incorporate the eight trigrams (*bagua*), the nine primary stars and twenty-eight constellations, the five elements, and the twelve-year and sixty-year cycles. (For more information, see Chapter 6, "Architecture.") Although fully trained traditional experts are few, a generalized knowledge of *fengshui* principles is widespread. Popularizers of *fengshui* are numerous, and the field has become quite lucrative for those consulted in the construction of large building projects. Now interior design and furniture placement have become areas for the application of popularized *fengshui* principles.

MORAL AND POLITICAL THOUGHT

Moral philosophy and political philosophy play central roles in Taiwanese history, just as they have in China since the time of Confucius (born ca. 551 B.C.). The Confucian tradition emphasizes moral cultivation of the individual and harmonious ordering of society. The *Analects*, written by Confucius's students to represent his teachings, places great value on the moral virtues of benevolence (*ren*) and propriety or ritual (*li*). The more specific virtue of filial piety (*xiao*) is also extolled in the *Analects* and countless philosophical and popular texts seeking to inculcate this respect and obedience to parents and ancestors. Much of Confucian philosophy resonates with folk tradition and organized religion in Taiwan. The Confucian ideal of filial piety, for example, is ritually expressed in Taiwanese funerals, ancestral shrines, and religious festivals. The Confucian tradition is also strongly hierarchical because it emphasizes the obligations in a hierarchically ordered society centered around the bonds of father and son, elder brother and younger brother, husband and wife, elders and juniors, and rulers and subjects. The authoritarian and patriarchal tendencies of these relationships are increasingly being questioned by the more egalitarian, democratically minded Taiwanese.

The official ideology of the Guomindang Party and the Republic of China came from the father of the ROC, Sun Yat-sen, and his "Three Principles of the People" (*sanmin zhuyi*). Sun Yat-sen was a product of the meeting of East and West. With his Western training, lack of classical Chinese training, and life in Western-influenced ports such as Macau and Hong Kong and abroad, he advocated a form of Chinese revolution that was highly Westernized. His three principles were nationalism, democracy, and the people's livelihood—basically concepts from the modern West sufficiently vague to be embraced by a large portion of the Chinese. Chiang Kai-shek, successor to Sun Yat-sen and leader of the Guomindang government in Taiwan for thirty years, had a less-Westernized background and was more interested in traditional Confucian morality. His New Life Movement advocated four Confucian virtues as a means of strengthening the party and the nation. He defined the classical moral virtues of propriety (*li*), righteousness (*yi*), integrity (*lian*), and a sense of shame (*chi*) in modern terms of regulated attitude, right conduct, clear discrimination, and real self-consciousness. He envisioned a highly disciplined, rational, and frugal lifestyle. The New Life Movement was a failure in China, but its ideas took new forms in ROC educational and social policies.

There has always been a strong Confucian emphasis in the ideal culture supported by the Guomindang government. Chiang Kai-shek's political and moral program reflected the Confucian commitment to virtues as the foundation of leadership and government. The Guomindang Party's early commitment to Confucian culture is seen most visibly in Taipei with its streets renamed for Confucian virtues and its temple celebration for Confucius's birthday on September 28. Textbooks used to teach language, literature, and social studies contain moral tales illustrating the Confucian values of filial obedience, loyalty, and frugality. The Confucian orientation of education in Taiwan goes back to the examination system by which Chinese men were trained and tested in classical texts in order to become government officials. The official examination system entered Taiwan in 1687 and lasted until 1895. Under Japanese rule until 1945, the educational system in Taiwan was carried out in Japanese language to further Japanese colonial rule. When the Guomindang Party came into power in 1949, education became a means of inculcating an ideal of reunified Chinese culture. Teaching was conducted in the Mandarin Chinese dialect, a dialect unknown to most Taiwanese. Inculcation of loyalty to the Republic of China and its party leaders was

accomplished in the schools through civics and history classes and through
the rituals of Chinese patriotism with the ever-present ROC flag and portraits
of Dr. Sun Yat-sen, President Chiang Kai-shek, and later Presidents Chiang
Ching-kuo and Lee Teng-hui. President Lee Teng-hui, the first native Taiwanese president and the first to be directly elected by the people of Taiwan,
officially upholds the ideal of reunification with China but also seeks greater
democratization and a larger international role for Taiwan.

Although the "Three Principles of the People" and the reunification of
Taiwan with China are official ideology of the Republic of China, they are
now being challenged openly and with vigor. With growing awareness of
Taiwanese identity, many Taiwanese express resentment at an educational
system that has taught them about the history and geography of an idealized
China and nothing about Taiwan and its local culture. Education and the
philosophy of education is in the midst of Taiwanization. Advocates of education reform seek to change the examination system to make it more com-
patible with a modern, pluralistic society. This would include the elimination
of testing on the "Three Principles of the People," which critics say should
not be singled out as the only political thought appropriate to modern Taiwan. With the lifting of martial law in 1987 and growing freedom for dissent,
advocates of Taiwanese culture and Taiwanese independence have become
more vocal and more numerous. The Taiwanese have been embracing their
own history and culture, often suppressed by the Guomindang Party to foster
a sense of identity with China. Instead of being viewed as inferior, Taiwanese
language and customs are now extolled as the culture of a free Taiwan.
Especially since the first direct presidential elections in 1996, the Taiwanese
have great pride in their embodiment of democratic ideals. Democracy, freedom, and political autonomy are the new ideals for many Taiwanese.

Philosophical interests mirror Taiwanese social changes. In the 1960s during rapid social change and industrialization, intellectuals and students were
drawn to translations of existentialists: Sartre, Camus, Kafka, and Heidegger.
Some philosophers in Taiwan are engaged in the centuries-old effort to
synthesize Chinese philosophy, particularly Confucianism, with Western
philosophy. For example, the "contemporary Neo-Confucian synthesis"
represented by T'ang Chün-Yi and Mou Tsung-san incorporates the idealistic
school of Neo-Confucianism (emphasizing texts by Mencius and Wang
Yangming) and the German philosophers Kant and Hegel. New intellectual
trends have mirrored new social concerns. Recently philosophers have begun
work on the philosophy of science and technology to understand the place
of humanity in the highly technological society in which the Taiwanese now
find themselves. Groups silent in the past have found their voices in the more

open political and social environment. Environmentalists write essays, songs, and poetry in support of a renewed appreciation and concern for the ecological well-being of the island in the face of nuclear energy and naphtha cracker plants. Feminists such as Lyu Xiulian (Annette Lu) have offered critiques of Confucianism as they involve themselves in Taiwanese politics. The single voice of the "Three Principles of the People" has been replaced with a multitude of voices struggling to define moral and political principles for a modern Taiwan.

POPULAR RELIGION

The renewal of interest and pride in a distinctively Taiwanese culture shows itself clearly in Taiwanese folk religion. Taiwanese folk religion is the oldest of all religions in Taiwan, with the exception of aboriginal religions.[4] Folk religion is overwhelmingly the most prevalent of all religious activity. The early settlers from Fujian and Guangdong brought with them the devotion, rituals, and images of their villages and countryside. Early immigrant life was rough and difficult. Religious and intellectual elites were not among the immigrant groups that developed early religious life and folk traditions. The immigrants' safe arrival in Taiwan was often marked by the building of simple shrines for their protector deities as a means of repaying them for their safe arrival on the island. Towns formed by immigrants from the same counties created temple traditions that gave them a sense of community in spite of the loss of their older clan traditions. Some of these temples later became the enormous temple complexes in modern Taiwan.

Many deities worshipped in Taiwan have their roots in traditions found throughout China, such as Guanyin Bodhisattva and Lord Guandi. The Chinese Buddhist Guanyin Bodhisattva is worshipped not only by Taiwanese Buddhists but also by Taiwanese who see her as a goddess of mercy in the folk tradition. She is worshipped for saving people from sea wrecks, fires, and illnesses and also for bringing children to women who pray for them. The god Guandi, originally a general of the Three Kingdoms period, has been known in China as a loyal, brave hero and later as a god. In Taiwan his status and perceived power have grown; today he is worshipped as a healing god and a patron of businesspeople. These two figures, Guanyin and Lord Guandi, are the deities most often pictured on the family ancestral shrines.

Most deities of Taiwan are portrayed in religious art and literature with images of bureaucratic power. Gods and goddesses are emperors, empresses, or appointed bureaucratic or military officials who have received imperial

2.2   Offerings to the city god of Taipei: spirit money, liquor, and food.

designations of their status. Gods of folk tradition look like Qing dynasty officials sitting on thrones in their palatial temples. The Stove God, Zaojun, is one of the lower members of this supernatural hierarchy. His image is found in homes, especially during the New Year's Festival. Another popular god, Lord Tudi, sits in small shrines to bring good fortune to the farms, towns, businesses, and surrounding area. The Jade Emperor is at the top of the hierarchy, but he is not all powerful or by any means the most important of Taiwanese gods: He reigns on high, but other deities are emotionally and practically more significant to the Taiwanese.

Other Taiwanese deities are more local spirits or divinized heroes and saints. They are valued for their healing powers and for the protection they afford from plagues and natural disasters. Offerings and promises made to the deities ensure their continued protection. In Taiwanese folk religion, deities are worshipped primarily because of community membership, but individuals may also choose to worship a specific deity because of his or her reputation for providing protection, good fortune, or healing.[5]

One of the most popular deities of Taiwanese folk religion is the goddess

2.3 Small shrine to the earth god commonly found in businesses.

Mazu. In fact, she is often considered the patron goddess of the island. According to Taiwanese traditions, Mazu grew up in the tenth century as a pious child on the island of Meizhou in Fujian Province. When she was just sixteen she miraculously saved her father and brother from a shipwreck. Miraculous stories of her saving interventions multiplied, and after her death a temple was built in Meizhou. Worship of Mazu eventually spread throughout the southern coastal fishing and farming villages and onward to the Taiwanese frontier. She is affectionately called Mazu-*po*, or "Granny," by the Taiwanese, but she has numerous exalted titles given to her by Chinese emperors. In 1409 she was given the title Tian Fei, or Imperial Concubine of Heaven. Then in 1683 she was further elevated to Tian Hou, or Consort of Heaven.

Mazu temples and festivals are the grandest in Taiwan. One of the Mazu temples in Peikang traces its history back to 1694, when a statue of Mazu from Meizhou was enshrined in gratitude for her protection. Peikang's annual festival for Mazu attracts more pilgrims than any other religious festival in Taiwan. Busloads of pilgrims from Taiwanese communities travel to Peikang to bring their Mazu statues home to the mother temple and to participate in feasting, processions, and rituals. Taiwanese celebrated the 1,000th anniversary of her ascent to heaven in 1987 with an elaborate procession and special rituals. Since the opening of travel to the mainland, some pilgrims have made religious journeys to the island of Meizhou to worship Mazu at the original mother temple. Bringing back images and incense from older temples in Fujian has been one way in which Taiwanese temples have increased their stature in relation to competing Taiwanese Mazu temples. The ties between Fujian and Taiwanese temples is a complex issue in the current discussion of Taiwanese identity. The connections to Fujianese religions and culture reinforce specifically regional—that is, Taiwanese—culture at the same time that they acknowledge the close cultural ties to China.

Numerous temples in Taiwan are devoted to the Wangye, or Royal Lords—deities who drive away evil spirits and protect against plagues. There are over 700 registered temples to Royal Lords on the island, but the identities of the "lords" and the rituals honoring them vary locally. Some folk traditions tell of a lord who died while trying to stop plague spirits from harming people. The status of Royal Lords in the supernatural hierarchy is low; they are simply ghosts who have been elevated to the status of gods. Their powers have expanded in Taiwanese traditions to include not only preventing plague (no longer of grave concern) but also bestowing general healing and prosperity. The Royal Lords festivals involve the destruction of plague spirits by the burning of wooden or paper boats on which the evil spirits have been placed.[6]

In addition to the gods and goddesses, Taiwanese popular religion also recognizes other spirit-beings, particularly ancestor spirits and ghosts. Gods, ghosts, and ancestor spirits are all closely related to the human realm. Ancestor spirits are simply the deceased and honored ancestors who contributed to a family's patrilineal line. The honoring of ancestors is an important part of most family rituals and religious festivals. One of the highest moral values in Taiwanese society, filial respect (*xiao*), is ritually expressed through offerings to the ancestors and the maintenance of a family shrine for the ancestors' tablets.

Ghosts are the spirits of dead strangers, particularly the dead who died a violent death or have no descendants to make offerings to them. Offerings are given to them to prevent them from causing accidents or illnesses. The seventh lunar month is a period of heightened awareness of the dangers of ghosts because they are allowed out of the underworld to roam freely. Ghosts are an active part of the popular Taiwanese imagination: They appear in fearsome and humorous forms in folk tales, modern horror movies, and popular television series. Ancestor spirits and ghosts are similar to the gods of folk religion because the gods are often ancestors or ghosts who eventually became respected and worshipped for their power in a larger community.

The temples and festivals of Taiwanese folk religion are the foundation of Taiwanese folk arts, puppet and opera theaters, and community identity. Temples are the center of more than just community religious life. They are a place to socialize over tea, to play chess, or to watch Taiwanese opera during festivals. The elaborate festivals for the community temple bring the Taiwanese together in ways that celebrate folk traditions and solidify community leadership, hierarchy, and relationships. Communities strengthen mutual ties by sending representatives to one another's religious processions; representatives include temple leaders, musical bands, statues of the temple's gods, and groups of young men to perform the lion dance. Grand feasting at Taiwanese festivals celebrates and expresses hope for continued good fortune in the community. The temple deities are given offerings of pigs, roosters, wine, tea, fruits, and sweets. (Buddhist-related deities and the celibate goddess Mazu are generally not offered meat or wine.) An abundance of food is offered to the gods and then eaten with family or a larger group. This extravagant feasting at festival time or for weddings or other special social events contrasts to the relatively frugal meals of daily life.

Taiwanese folk religion has changed over the past decades. Temples and festivals have modernized along with society. Religious processions include elaborate lighted floats with modern nightclub entertainers. Moreover, the Guomindang government has worked to simplify and regulate Taiwanese folk religion to reduce waste and expense.[7] In some temples, such as the popular Xing Tian Gong in northern Taipei, the government's influence has been successful in eliminating elaborate offerings of livestock or spirit money. Also banned are spirit mediums who become possessed by gods and spirits at other temples. At Xing Tian Gong and other "reformed" temples worshippers seek the healing power of the enshrined god through the burning of incense and the making of petitions. Blue-robed volunteers assist and advise visitors needing help with the ritual or interpretation of the written fortunes.

HEALING TRADITIONS

The traditional healing arts of China are based on concepts such as *yin-yang*, the five agents, and *qi*. Traditional Chinese medicine is also based on several millennia of experimentation. *Yin* and *yang* are polar opposites that exist in all of nature; in the human body these two polar opposites must be in harmony for one to be healthy. The five elements of wood, fire, metal, earth, and water are symbolic means of ordering the universe and the human body. The human body is a microcosm of the universe, containing the movement of *yin* and *yang* and the five major internal organs associated with the five elements. In the human body it is *qi*, the life force, that circulates and animates the body; it is the breath as it moves through the respiratory and circulatory system.

Chinese medicine brings order and harmony to a body out of balance and maintains balance for the healthy. The practice of Chinese medicine goes back to traditions recorded in texts beginning in the third century B.C.: the *Nei jing* (ca. 221–207 B.C.). And it is heavily dependent on the influential *Ben cao gang mu* by Li Shizhen of the Ming dynasty (A.D. 1368–1644). Based on this ongoing tradition, herbalists in Taiwan prescribe medicine to treat imbalances in their patients, usually by combining plant and animal products into a mixture made into a tea and ingested.

Two other means of bringing harmony back to an unhealthy body are acupuncture and moxibustion. Acupuncturists insert slender needles in order to stimulate *qi* within the body and harmonize the *yin* and *yang* energies. Today the acupuncturists often use mild electrical current at the acupuncture points instead of puncturing the skin in order to achieve the same effect. Moxibustion is based on similar principles; it is the technique of burning Chinese mugroot at certain points along the channels through which the *qi* flows.

Modern Western medicine is widely available in Taiwan. Some Taiwanese continue to value traditional medicine for its ability to maintain health and its gentle means of restoring balance. At the same time many Taiwanese view modern medicine as a necessary means of dealing with major health problems requiring surgery, though often too harsh for less serious and chronic conditions.

The Taiwanese concern for good health is also evident in the resurgence of interest in the practice of *qigong* and the martial arts. In *qigong* practitioners direct the movement of their *qi* in order to heal themselves and increase their energy. Someone who has very strong *qi* is able to use it to heal others as well. *Qigong* is taught through self-help books, in classes, and even on television.

Chinese martial arts make use of the understanding of *yin-yang* and *qi* to strengthen and discipline the body and mind, as well as to prepare for the defense of the person. There are some 100 different kinds of martial arts (*guo-gong*). The gentle art of *taijiquan*, popular with both the young and the old in Taiwan, is now taught at Chinese Culture University and is part of the Asian Games. One often sees its practitioners in the early morning in parks or on temple grounds exercising for good health and emotional calm.

Traditional medicine, *taijiquan*, and *qigong* are health practices derived from traditional religious and philosophical concepts. They can, though, be practiced independently of one's religious worldview; indeed, these traditions are increasingly used in the West as alternative medical treatments that are gaining increased attention from the Western medical community.

Although truly religious means of healing have declined in popularity with the increased accessibility of modern medicine, they continue to be popular for chronic or incurable conditions. Offerings are made to gods and goddesses known for their healing power along with petitions for help. When healing does occur, the worshipper returns to the temple or shrine with more offerings in order to *bao en*, or repay the deity for its help. Those who worship the Buddhist Guanyin Bodhisattva typically seek her healing power by chanting her name a specified number of times. To repay her for her help, a follower may continue chanting or perhaps become a vegetarian for a period of time.

RELIGION AS FOLK PSYCHOLOGY

Taiwanese gods and goddesses are known for more than just physical healing. Individuals seek divine power to protect their children from harm, to become pregnant, to do well on the college entrance examinations, and to prosper financially. Religion provides much in the way of folk psychology. In Taiwan, religion continues as a popular means of self-help and therapy despite rapid Westernization in most other areas. Western therapeutic models that require revealing personal and family problems to a stranger are quite at odds with Taiwanese family ideals. Religious books on self-cultivation through the Book of Changes, through various forms of meditation, and by traditional divination techniques remain popular. Fortune telling thrives in various traditional forms. Fortune telling is not primarily about predicting the future but, rather, about understanding the factors that influence a person's life and must be understood if one is to make decisions in harmony with the conditions of one's life. Some experts base their conclusions and personal advice on facial physiognomy. Others rely on Chinese astrology to interpret the influence of a person's exact time of birth on his or her present circumstances. In temples, visitors throw crescent-shaped, red divination blocks in order to receive from the gods answers to their questions.[8] Then a numbered stick may be chosen to determine which numbered fortune should be applied to their problems. The printed text of these "fortunes" is ambiguous, classical Chinese that can be freely applied to questions of marriage, illness, relocation, or a troubled child. Temples have professional interpreters or volunteers who assist in the reading and application of the printed text.

For those inclined to high-tech advice, modernized divination appears in the form of computer software of the Book of Changes or astrological texts.

ORGANIZED RELIGIOUS GROUPS

Whereas participation in the festivals and rituals of folk religion generally comes from membership in a community, participation in an organized religious group is a matter of individual decision. There are Taoist, Buddhist, Christian, and syncretic religious sects registered with the government as religious groups.

Taoism as a religion is difficult to define. According to 1994 government figures, 34 percent of Taiwan's population who identify themselves as religious consider themselves Taoist. Often, though, this term is used to describe the vibrant folk religion of Taiwan that draws on ideas, images, and figures from Taoist, Buddhist, Confucian, and regional folk traditions whose temples usually rely on Taoist priests for cyclical rituals. This Taoist-identified folk religion was brought in various forms to Taiwan with Fujian and Guangdong immigrants who worshipped their ancestors and a variety of gods, goddesses, and other spirits. During the Japanese occupation, Taoism was suppressed because it was viewed as supporting Chinese patriotism. Some community temples switched to a Buddhist identity until after the Japanese left. These changes of identity between Taoist and Buddhist temples aided the syncretism of Taoist and Buddhist traditions in the Taiwanese temples. In many Taiwanese temples, Taoist goddesses are worshipped in Buddhist temples while a Buddhist Bodhisattva is worshipped in a Taoist temple. Organized Taoism as a separate religious sect was brought to Taiwan by Zhang Enpu and other Taoist priests of the Zheng Yi sect after 1945. In 1994 there were two Taoist seminaries and 31,950 Taoist priests.

Chinese Buddhism in Taiwan has undergone a renaissance in recent years. About 22 percent of the population identifies itself as Buddhist, but the visibility of Buddhism seems greater than that number would indicate. Books on popular Buddhist masters are on bestseller lists. The numbers of monks, nuns, and temples have risen sharply in the 1980s and early 1990s. Large lay organizations have founded new schools and hospitals. College student groups have become more visible and active on campuses. The growing importance and influence of Buddhist leaders based on the island extends beyond Taiwan to the large number of Taiwanese living in North America and elsewhere. Their followers, however, are not limited to people from Taiwan or even to Asians.

Buddhism in Taiwan has in the course of the twentieth century experi-

2.4 White-robed Guanyin Bodhisattva.

enced radical changes that have eventually led to this renaissance. Before this century, Taiwanese Buddhism was a folk tradition of the frontier. Fully ordained monks were few, and nuns nonexistent. Many of the monks were simply temple caretakers with little Buddhist education. With the Japanese rule of Taiwan came the sudden presence and oversight of Japanese Buddhist schools, which led to new organizations for Taiwanese Buddhist temples and lay Buddhist groups. Then the end of Japanese rule and the end of the Chinese Civil War between the Guomindang and the Communists brought large numbers of prominent Chinese monks to Taiwan with the Guomindang army and government.

Monks and nuns in Taiwan follow Chinese ordination traditions requiring celibacy, the shaving of the head, and numerous other practices in addition to the five precepts recommended for lay Buddhists. With the lay precepts,

Buddhists vow to abstain from killing living beings, stealing, engaging in sexual misconduct, lying, and partaking of alcohol or addictive drugs. The Mahayana form of Buddhism in Taiwan has as its religious ideal the Bodhisattva, who embodies Buddhist wisdom and compassion. Buddhists who take the Bodhisattva vows seek full enlightenment through the cultivation of wisdom and moral perfection and at the same time endeavor to lead all other living beings out of ignorance into enlightenment. The Bodhisattva is both a high moral ideal and an object of devotion to those less advanced on the Buddhist path.

Most Taiwanese Buddhism emphasizes the teachings of two Chinese Buddhist traditions: the Chan (meditation) and the Pure Land traditions. Pure Land teachings focus on the compassion of Amitabha Buddha, whose compassionate power will cause his followers to be reborn in his pure buddhaland after death and to be assured of enlightenment. People chant Amitabha's name as individuals or in groups to call on his compassion and as a form of meditation to calm and concentrate the mind.

The practice of the Chan tradition is primarily sitting meditation (*zuo chan*), more popularly known in the West by the Japanese terms of Zen and *zazen*. The Chan schools teach that all living beings contain the potential to become buddhas; one merely needs to see into one's own true buddha-nature. Although serious practitioners of Chan are few, the general influence of Chan on Chinese painting, poetry, and other arts is generally appreciated by the Taiwanese.

Buddhist monks and nuns have become popular and influential figures in Taiwan since the early 1980s. Although some Taiwanese believe Buddhist monks are primarily ritual specialists for funerals and death anniversaries, the presence of highly educated and socially engaged monks and nuns has changed that image in the minds of many Taiwanese. This can be seen from the great popularity of the published teachings, biographies, and tapes of leading Buddhist figures.

The most influential Buddhist teachers are still those monks who came to Taiwan with the Guomindang after the Chinese Civil War. Master Hsin Yun is one of the most influential of monks both within Taiwan and internationally. Born in Jiangsu, he came to Taiwan after the communists' victory over the Guomindang in China. He founded the Fo-kuang shan temple and educational institution in order to spread knowledge of Buddhist teachings. Another internationally known monk, Master Sheng Yen, was born near Shanghai and became a monk at the young age of thirteen. Educated in Buddhism first in China, he received a doctorate in Buddhist literature from Rissho University, a Buddhist university in Tokyo. He heads a Chan meditation center in New York and monasteries in Taiwan. His organizations have encouraged the study of meditation and the engagement with social issues such as environmental protection.[9]

Master Cheng Yen is the best known of Buddhist nuns in Taiwan and one of the most charismatic leaders of Buddhist social action.[10] Unlike most of the leading monks, she was born in Taiwan—in 1937 near Taichung. She is founder and leader of the Compassionate Relief Society, whose members work in social welfare, healthcare for the poor, assistance for the aged, and disaster relief. This organization's efforts in soliciting bone marrow and blood donations have been very effective. Recently her teachings and the organization's efforts have expanded to include environmental issues. The Compassionate Relief Society is based in Taiwan but has groups in the United States, Canada, Europe, and elsewhere.

Tantric Buddhism has become popular in Taiwan only recently. Exiled Tibetan monks have come to Taiwan and attracted attention. In spring 1997 the leader of Tibetan Buddhists, the Dalai Lama, visited Taiwan and met with government leaders as well as with members of the Buddhist community. Taiwanese Buddhism has become greatly internationalized. Not only does it have organizations throughout the world; it is also influenced by Buddhists from other traditions.

Among organized religions, the third most popular is the new religion of Yiguandao, with a membership of about 4–5 percent of the total population. This religion teaches a universal truth encompassing the plurality of religious expression. Related to the White Lotus Sect that sought the overthrow of the Yuan dynasty (1271–1368), Yiguandao worships a Universal God who encompasses all the gods and buddhas of Buddhism, Taoism, Christianity, Islam, Judaism, and Hinduism. Although Yiguandao emphasizes the unity behind all religions, the language and rituals it uses are distinctively Chinese.[11] It promotes personal moral development and places importance on family relationships. Ancestor worship is emphasized and carried out at family shrines. Yiguandao followers are vegetarians and run 90 percent of Taiwan's vegetarian restaurants.

There are other, smaller organized sects in Taiwan. Many of them share with Yiguandao a concern for bringing together pluralistic religious images under one umbrella. Zhaijiao, brought to Taiwan in the seventeenth century, is a syncretic school that focuses on the worship of the Buddha and Guanyin Bodhisattva, but also includes aspects of Taoism, Confucianism, and folk traditions. Li-ism, founded by Yang Lairu in the seventeenth century and brought to Taiwan by mainlander priests, is another syncretic religion that focuses on worship of Guanyin.

Xiajiao, brought to Taiwan during the Japanese period, focuses on the worship of Confucius, Laozi, the Buddha, and the sixteenth-century founder of Xiajiao, Lin Zhaoen. Tiandejiao, founded by Xiao Zhangming in China in 1923, was introduced to Taiwan in 1953 but recognized by the government only in 1989. Tiandejiao masters guide followers in meditation and healing in a tradition that brings together elements of Confucianism, Taoism, Buddhism, Christianity, and Islam.

Although Christianity's influence is obvious in the syncretic sects of Taiwanese religion, only a small number of Taiwanese are Christian. Approximately 6 percent of Taiwanese are Christian, but their influence is significant both religiously and politically. Politically, the influence of Christianity is felt within the ruling Guomindang Party and within the political opposition. The last three presidents and a disproportionate percentage of government officials have been Christian. Yet the Presbyterian Church is seen as having significant political force within opposition politics, especially the Taiwanese independence movement.[12]

Protestant and Roman Catholic Christianity first arrived in Taiwan in the early seventeenth century. When the Dutch arrived, around 1624, missionaries from the Reformed Church began to evangelize among the indigenous people in southern Taiwan. Dominican missionaries arrived in northern Taiwan with the Spaniards in 1626 and converted aborigines as well. The Dutch drove the Spanish out of Taiwan; then the Dutch themselves were driven out by Cheng Ch'eng-kung (Koxinga). When Jesuits arrived in Taiwan in 1714, they found few of these Dutch and Spanish converts remaining. In 1860 British missionaries arrived in the Taipei area, and in 1864 the Presbyterian Dr. James L. Maxwell began preaching in southern Taiwan. Then in 1872 the influential Canadian Presbyterian George L. Mackay arrived in northern Taiwan to continue the most successful missionary work—that of the Presbyterians.[13]

During the Japanese occupation Roman Catholicism grew slowly, Protestantism somewhat more rapidly. With the influx of mainlanders with the Guomindang government in 1949, the number of Christian denominations grew from three to about forty in 1955. Today there are fifty-seven Protestant denominations, with the Presbyterian Church by far the largest. An advocate of opposition politics, the Presbyterian Church has been an important participant in Taiwanese independence movements.

In addition to the presence of Christian denominations in Taiwan is the presence of secularized Western Christian rituals and imagery. Like much of East Asia, Taiwan celebrates Christmas with department store sales, Christmas parties, and holiday decorations. Large hotels have joined the retail industry in encouraging the celebration of Christmas with parties and decorations. Christmas in Taiwan has become part of the winter celebrations embracing the winter solstice, New Year's, and the Lantern festival, in all a great boon to commerce.

Other religious groups in Taiwan are somewhat apart from both Taiwanese folk religiosity and Christianity. The Muslim population, around 52,000 in 1994, supports five mosques, two in Taipei and one each in Kaohsiung, Taichung, and Lungkang. The first Muslims in Taiwan were soldiers who arrived with Koxinga, whose descendants became assimilated by non-Muslim Chinese. In 1949 about 20,000 Muslim soldiers and government workers accompanied the Guomindang government to Taiwan. The small Jewish population in Taiwan consists mainly of expatriate families from the United States, Europe, and Israel. Government statistics identify the presence of other religions from foreign countries: Baha'i, first brought to Taiwan in 1954 by an Iranian couple, has about 15,000 members; Mormonism, whose missionaries arrived in Taiwan in 1954 and now have about 22,000 followers; Tenrikyo, introduced to Taiwan during the Japanese occupation, has about 29,000 believers.

Organized religion, community-based popular religion, individualistic self-help traditions, all are going strong in Taiwan. This widespread interest in and support of religion may surprise those who know Taiwan primarily though its high-tech industries and capitalist successes. But the technological and economic successes have in common with much of Taiwanese religion a certain pragmatism and this-worldly orientation. The religious practices in fact celebrate and express hope for the physical and financial well-being of families and communities.

NOTES

1. Statistical information about religious membership and registered religious groups is from the government publication *Republic of China Yearbook, 1997* (Taipei: Kwang Hwa Publishing, 1997).

2. Information on government commemorative days and lunar festivals is found in the *Republic of China Yearbook, 1997.*

3. For a discussion of *fengshui* see Ronald G. Knapp, *China's Traditional Rural Architecture: A Cultural Geography of the Common House* (Honolulu: University of Hawaii Press, 1986), pp. 108–21. On page 97 he notes the ways in which the practice of *fengshui* in Taiwan differs from the canonical tradition formalized in northern China.

4. Information about the culture of Taiwan's indigenous peoples is included in Chapter 4, "Music and Dance."

5. For a good introduction to Chinese gods and spirits, see Arthur P. Wolf,

"Gods, Ghosts, and Ancestors," in Arthur P. Wolf, ed., *Religion and Ritual in Chinese Society* (Stanford, CA: Stanford University Press, 1974). This volume includes other articles concerning Taiwanese folk religion.

6. Paul Katz has studied the *wangye* cults of Taiwan and Zhejiang. His most accessible study of the cult in Taiwan is "Demons or Deities?—The *Wangye* of Taiwan," in *Asian Folklore Studies*, vol. 46, no. 2 (1987), pp. 197–215.

7. An excellent study of government control of temples in Taiwan is found in Stephan Feuchtwang, "City Temples in Taipei under Three Regimes," in Mark Elvin and G. William Skinner, eds. *The Chinese City between Two Worlds* (Stanford, CA: Stanford University Press, 1974), pp. 263–301.

8. For an interesting study of divination by these crescent-shaped blocks, see David K. Jordan, "Taiwanese *Poe* Divination: Statistical Awareness and Religious Belief," in *Journal for the Scientific Study of Religion*, vol. 21, no. 2 (1982), pp. 114–18.

9. Because he has an organization in the United States, Master Sheng Yen's teachings are more available in English than those of many Buddhist teachers. A good introduction to Chan Buddhism is Sheng Yen, *Dharma Drum: The Life and Heart of Ch'an Practice* (Elmhurst, NY: Dharma Drum Publications, 1996).

10. A biography of Master Cheng Yen has been published: See Yu-ing Ching, *Master of Love and Mercy: Cheng Yen* (Nevada City, CA: Blue Dolphin Publishing, 1995).

11. For a study of Yiguandao, see David K. Jordan, "The Recent History of the Celestial Way: A Chinese Pietistic Association," *Modern China*, vol. 8, no. 4 (1982), pp. 45–62. See also Joseph Bosco, "Yiguan Dao: 'Heterodoxy' and Popular Religion in Taiwan," in Murray A. Rubinstein, ed., *The Other Taiwan: 1945 to the Present* (Armonk, NY: M. E. Sharpe, 1994).

12. See James Tyson, "Christians and the Taiwanese Independence Movement: A Commentary," *Asian Affairs*, vol. 14, no. 3 (1987), pp. 163–70.

13. For a thorough but somewhat outdated study of Christianity, see Hollington K. Tong, *Christianity in Taiwan: A History* (Taipei: China Post, 1961). For a more recent study focusing on Protestant churches, see Murray A. Rubinstein, *The Protestant Community of Modern Taiwan: Mission, Seminary, and Church* (Armonk, NY: M. E. Sharpe, 1991).

SUGGESTED READINGS

Dean, Kenneth. *Taoist Ritual and Popular Cults of Southeast China.* Princeton, NJ: Princeton University Press, 1993.

Jordan, David K. *Gods, Ghosts, and Ancestors: The Folk Religion of a Taiwanese Village.* Berkeley, CA: University of California Press, 1972.

Jordan, David K. and Daniel L. Overmyer. *The Flying Phoenix: Aspects of Chinese Sectarianism in Taiwan.* Princeton, NJ: Princeton University Press, 1986.

Wolf, Arthur P. *Religion and Ritual in Chinese Society.* Stanford, CA: Stanford University Press, 1974.

3

Festivals and Entertainment

HOLIDAYS AND COMMUNITY festivals have long provided a celebratory break in the busy lives of the hardworking Taiwanese. On such occasions the traditionally frugal Taiwanese feast and party while reinforcing family structures and community ties. Calendrical and temple festivals have also supported many of Taiwan's folk arts, namely, Taiwanese opera and puppet theater, specialty foods, and crafts. In recent years the popularity of movies and television has threatened the survival of Taiwan's performing traditions, but operas and puppet theaters have learned that if you can't fight television, you can be on television.

The Taiwanese celebrate three kinds of festivals. First are the official government commemorative holidays based on the modern solar calendar. These mainly honor important events and leaders of the Republic of China. Second are the major lunar festivals known and celebrated by most Taiwanese. Third are the community-based or temple-based celebrations of the birth of regional goddesses or gods, the ascension of temple deities, or other regional or ethnic religious events.

COMMEMORATIVE DAYS

The Republic of China's commemorative days are honored by closing of schools and government offices and by often extravagant government parades and decorations.[1] These days honor the founding fathers and historical events

3.1 Monument built to honor those Taiwanese who died in the February 28, 1947, uprising.

of the Guomindang and the Republic of China. In the past these days were an occasion to demonstrate the prestige of the Guomindang Party and the power of the Republic of China's military. Since the late 1980s, however, the military significance has lessened. Moreover, new political pluralism and Taiwanization movements have raised questions about the propriety and significance of these commemorative days. One might even see the February 28th Incident ceremonies, commemorating the 1947 uprising against the Guomindang in Taiwan, as a new unofficial commemorative day honoring a long-repressed tradition of political dissent.

The first commemorative day of the year is January 1, **Founding Day** of the Republic of China. The day marks the anniversary of the inauguration of Sun Yat-sen as the provisional president of the Republic on the first day of 1912. Flags, banners, and portraits of Sun Yat-sen and Chiang Kai-shek are displayed throughout the island, but particularly in the area around the Presidential Office building in downtown Taipei. Bands play the national anthem, which extols the "Three Principles of the People" formulated by Sun Yat-sen.

Double Ten National Day marks the Republic of China's birth at the uprising in Wuchang on October 10, 1911. The day is marked by political and cultural celebrations. The central events in the capital city of Taipei are ceremonies, parades, and the presidential address at the Presidential Office building. Parades and evening ceremonies present traditional Chinese and ethnic dancers, school bands, folk artist performers, and other entertainment. The day no longer conveys the strong militaristic image of earlier decades, however. Instead it celebrates in fireworks, music, and dance a successful capitalist island. The birth of the Republic of China in Taiwan is marked by Taiwan's **Retrocession Day**, officially extolled on October 25 to commemorate the end of Japanese rule in Taiwan in 1945.

Armed Forces Day is celebrated on September 3 to honor all armed forces, whose divisions had their own separate days of honor until they were combined in 1955. The day is meant to honor the Chinese who fought against the Japanese in World War II. **Youth Day**, March 29, began as Revolutionary Martyrs Day. Like Armed Forces Day, it commemorates soldiers, in this case especially the seventy-two soldiers led by Huang Xing who died in the 1910 Canton Uprising against the Qing government. On this day the president of the Republic of China officiates at a service for all soldiers at the Martyrs of the Revolution Shrine in Taipei. As the war recedes in memory, the day has become more a celebration of youth.

December 25 is an official government holiday in Taiwan. The official reason is to celebrate not Christmas but **Constitution Day**, designated as such in 1963 to honor the completion of the constitution by the Constitutional Convention after the war. That a government holiday conveniently falls on Christmas reflects the Christianity of many prominent Guomindang leaders. In practice, for most Taiwanese December 25 is just part of the New Year's period. Thus Christmas decorations in hotels and department stores add to the New Year's festive atmosphere.

Two of the government commemorative days, **Women's Day** on March 8 and **Children's Day** on April 4, were inspired by international efforts to improve the well-being of women and children. Women's Day follows the international designation by the International Women's Conference in Denmark in 1910 to raise women's issues through an international day for women. Children's Day was inspired by the 1925 conference on children in Switzerland, which urged countries to designate a day for children. In Taiwan, the April 4 holiday promotes children's activities and honors model students.

The government honors Confucius and all teachers on the September 28 commemoration of Confucius's birthday, **Teachers' Day**. The day obviously

3.2   Ceremonial dance of traditionally costumed boys at Confucius's birthday.

emphasizes the important Confucian value of education and respect for teachers. It also serves to symbolize the government's commitment to represent true Chinese culture, especially in its elaborate ritual celebration at dawn in the Confucius Temple. The elaborate ritual includes traditionally clothed dancers, ancient ceremonial music, and the traditional sacrificial offering of an ox, a pig, and a goat.

LUNAR FESTIVALS

The colorful religious festivals in Taiwan follow the Chinese lunar calendar.[2] By far the most important are those festivals centering on the Chinese New Year. **New Year's Festival** or **Spring Festival** is a celebration of family past and present and an expression of hope for family prosperity and good fortune. Unlike some East Asian nations, Taiwan has clung to the traditional lunar celebration of the New Year, rather than transfer the festival into a more "Western" or "modern" event based on the Western solar calendar. The festivities embody values too close to the Taiwanese heart—family, prosperity, and tradition—to be switched to the solar calendar.

Prior to New Year's festival itself, the **Ascension of the Kitchen God** on the twenty-fourth day of the twelfth lunar month begins the traditions associated with the coming of the new year. Taiwanese traditions say that on this day the Kitchen God of every home reports to the Jade Emperor about the activities of the family. To ensure a positive report on the family, members offer meat, sweet rice balls, and spirit money to the god before he ascends to heaven.

Preparations for New Year's festivities are hectic. People send out New Year's cards to friends and business associates. Families do a thorough spring cleaning to prepare for the new year. On the doorways of homes and businesses, vertical red banners express auspicious sentiments for the New Year. Shoppers stock up on the traditional cakes and snacks for New Year. Taiwanese eat peanuts, which symbolize long life; melon seeds, which symbolize many descendants; and perhaps red dates, which express a woman's desire to give birth to a healthy child. Shopping must be done ahead of time because many shops close for several days or even weeks during the New Year's period. Preparations also include paying off current debts so that the family may begin the year with a rosy financial picture.

In Taiwan New Year's Eve is a time for family. In the afternoon many Taiwanese worship their ancestors by offering them wine and special New Year's cake. Family members place on their family altars offerings of cooked food, fresh fruits, flowers, pastries, spirit money, and incense. Worship of ancestors, gods, and Buddhas is followed by the noisy sendoff of firecrackers. If possible, all Taiwanese try to return home to share the last evening meal of the year. If someone cannot return because he or she is working or studying far away, then a place is left empty at the table in remembrance. This ritual meal consists of favorite foods full of symbolic meaning. A platter of fish (*yu*), for example, represents the hoped-for abundance (*yu*) of the coming year because the two words sound alike. To ensure the abundance, no one will eat the last of the fish. After dinner older members of the family distribute red envelopes (*hongbao*) filled with money to the excited junior members of the family. This ritual giving of wealth to the younger generation not only is great fun for children but is also said to ensure the family's future prosperity. Some even say that the giving of red envelopes encourages reciprocity and filial piety in the younger generation, who will be expected to show respect for their elders and give them financial support.

New Year's is great fun. Taiwanese families spend New Year's Eve playing mahjong or other games, snacking on nuts and seeds, watching television specials, and exploding firecrackers. Loud explosions are meant to drive away evil spirits, but many boys love lighting the long strands of red and gold firecrackers for sheer joy. The Taiwanese may stay awake until dawn of New Year's Day as part of a New Year's vigil traditionally meant to ensure the longevity of one's parents.

New Year's Day itself is full of more festivities: lighting firecrackers, making offerings to ancestor spirits and gods, playing games, and watching endless television specials. The Taiwanese give each other greetings for a prosperous New Year. They take great care to avoid inauspicious words or actions that might start the year off with bad luck. Death should never be mentioned, nor should articles associated with death be present.

The spirit of New Year continues until the **Lantern Festival** on the fifteenth day of the first lunar month. Taiwanese families enjoy making rice-flour dumplings as offerings to their ancestors and as delicious treats for themselves. The evening glows with brightly decorated lanterns and fireworks. The temples of Taiwan have long hung lanterns on this evening. Lanterns have traditionally been made of paper and bamboo, but the newer electric versions use a variety of materials. Colorful lanterns combine traditional folkcrafts and designs with modern creativity. Often, decorative themes come from Chinese legends like the story of the White Snake or historical stories such as the *Romance of the Three Kingdoms*. The most popular animal depicted is usually the zodiac sign for the new year. The largest lantern competition is now held at the spacious plaza at Chiang Kai-shek Memorial Hall, but in southern Taiwan the Tainan Yanshui Fireworks Display attracts the largest crowds.

The **First Head Feast** (second month, second day) and the **Final Head Feast** (twelfth month, sixteenth day) both honor the hugely popular Tudi Gong, the local earth god present everywhere in Taiwan. The First Head Feast is often seen as a birthday celebration for Tudi Gong. He is offered meat and spirit money to ensure his blessings and protection. On this day of their patron deity, business owners may provide a banquet for their workers. At the Final Head Feast banquets of the past, business owners fired an employee by pointing the head of a rooster in his or her direction. In general, the end of the year is the time for settling business accounts and making arrangements for the obligatory, and often quite generous, New Year's bonuses.

The **Tomb-Sweeping Festival** marks the day when the Taiwanese pay respects to their dead ancestors at their gravesites. Traditionally Tomb-Sweeping Day has been marked as the 105th day after the winter solstice. But this day is one festival that has been modernized and clearly politicized. This festival is now celebrated on April 5, which is the date of Chiang Kai-shek's death in 1975. There have always been subethnic variations in the timing of this ancestral ritual. The Taiwanese from Zhangzhou, Fujian, have traditionally swept their ancestors' tombs on Tomb-Sweeping Day itself, whereas Quanzhou descendants have traditionally swept just before the festival. The Hakka people allow a long period during which to sweep their ancestors' graves, because their long migration on mainland China required them to be flexible if they were ever to return north to their ancestors' tombs. The "sweeping" of the tomb means removing weeds and repairing the grave. Family members burn incense offerings to Tudi Gong, who protects the grave, as well as to their ancestors. Pieces of gold or multicolored paper are weighted down on the gravesite to offer ancestors spirit money and to show the community that the family's ancestors are well cared for.

The **Dragon Boat Festival** (fifth lunar month, fifth day) is unusual because it commemorates a historical person, Chu Yuan, the poet and minister of the ancient state of Chu. According to tradition, Chu Yuan threw himself into a river out of despair about the state of political affairs. Friends and subordinates threw offerings of food wrapped in bamboo leaves into the river to appease his disturbed spirit. Today the Taiwanese honor his memory by eating rice and meat dumplings wrapped in bamboo leaves (*zongzi*) and competing in dragon boat races.

The **Birthday of the Seventh Goddess** is celebrated on the seventh day of the seventh month. This goddess protects children under age sixteen. In a sense this day marks transition to adulthood as children leave the goddess's protection on this day. Some families may burn paper pavilions for the Seventh Goddess to thank her for protecting their children who turned sixteen in the previous year. The day is also celebrated as a "Chinese Valentine's Day" because it celebrates as well the romantic legend of the Cowherder and the Weaving Girl, now constellations, reunited once a year on this day when birds form a bridge to reunite the couple. There exist countless versions of this folk tale. In one, the Weaving Girl was the beautiful daughter of the Emperor of Heaven, who married her to the handsome Cowherd. They fell so deeply in love that the Weaving Girl failed to make garments for the deities of the heavens and the Cowherd failed to milk the cows of heaven. When the gods complained, the Emperor of Heaven responded by separating the loving couple except for this one day of the year.

The seventh month is the **Ghost Month**, a great danger to those who believe in the wandering ghosts who venture forth during this period. The seventh month is a time to avoid starting a new home, a new business, or especially a new marriage to someone who might turn out to be a ghost. Even the most educated of Taiwanese expressed surprise and disbelief when we packed up our belongings to move from Taipei to Tainan during this

month. On the first of the month the gates of the netherworld are opened
to release the spirits for a month of wandering. Taiwanese families and temples make offerings to the wandering spirits to encourage them to keep moving rather than to stop and bother them. The fifteenth of the month is the
day to make offering to the spirits of one's own ancestors and to release
floating lanterns. On the last day of the month, many Taiwanese set out
offerings of food, beer, and cigarettes for the spirits as they return to the
netherworld. Not surprisingly, all these offerings are gone by the next morning.

The **Mid-Autumn Festival** (eighth lunar month, fifteenth day) is simply
a beautiful, contemplative festival. On mainland China the day used to be a
celebration of the end of the harvest, but in Taiwan today the agricultural
season extends almost throughout the year. Now the modern Taiwanese
primarily admire the beauty of the full moon on this night. Families honor
their ancestors and gods with offerings, but the focus is on the enjoyment of
viewing the moon and eating varieties of the treat specific to this festival—
moon cakes. The love of the moon is expressed in several legends retold by
the Taiwanese. One story tells of the beautiful Chang O and her husband
Yi, the famous archer who saved the world by shooting down nine of the
ten suns that appeared in the sky one day. The Queen Mother of Heaven
rewarded Archer Yi by giving him an elixir that would confer immortality.
The beautiful but greedy Chang O stole the elixir and swallowed it. She
attained immortality, but she also found herself ascending to the moon,
where she has lived forever after. Chang O lives in a beautiful jade palace
full of dancing fairies—a lovely but rather bittersweet image to see while
contemplating the full moon.

Numerous other lunar festivals are celebrated. The **Double Nine Festival**
(ninth month, ninth day) is a day for hiking and ancestor worship; it is also
traditionally a time for flying kites. A traditional holiday figured according
to the solar calendar, the **Winter Solstice** is celebrated with red and white
rice balls offered to the ancestors and to the gods (and then, of course, eaten).

RELIGIOUS FESTIVALS

In addition to traditional lunar festivals celebrated, or at least acknowl-
edged, by most Taiwanese are numerous festivals celebrated by communities
in honor of their deities. These festivals, known as *baibai*, are the liveliest,
loudest celebrations held by Taiwanese towns, villages, and even urban communities. One of the biggest community festivals is truly an islandwide celebration of Taiwan's patron goddess Mazu. The *baibai* celebrates the birthday

3.3 Mazu statues brought "home" to her Luermen Temple for a festival.

of this saving goddess on the twenty-third day of the third lunar month. This is the most important Taiwanese festival honoring a particular god or goddess. Festivals and processions are held throughout the island, but the destination of the most devout Mazu followers is the gigantic festival in Peikang. Representatives of hundreds of temples carry their goddess statues in palanquins to Peikang's central Mazu temple. One might consider this festival with its ritual offerings, folk operas, noisy processions, and spirit mediums as the height of authentic Taiwanese religious consciousness.

Growing numbers of Taiwanese Buddhists honor their tradition on special Buddhist festival days. Their most important festivals celebrate the birthdays of Sakyamuni Buddha and Guanyin Bodhisattva. The birthday of Sakyamuni Buddha, the historical Buddha, is honored on the eighth day of the fourth lunar month. At the Longshan Temple in Taipei, a golden statue of the Buddha is brought out and washed in dew water on this day. Buddhists celebrate the birthday of the Bodhisattva of compassion, Guanyin, on the nineteenth day of the second lunar month and repeat the celebrations on the nineteenth day of the sixth and ninth months. Celebrations are held at the Longshan Temple and in Guanyin temples all over the island. Moreover, every local temple has a special festival.

Subethnic groups celebrate their own special days and hold festivals unique to their own communities. The Hakka, the largest minority group in Taiwan, celebrate festivals for the *yimin*, or "righteous citizens," on various days to commemorate Hakka heroes who died in battles for which they were frequently recruited by Qing troops. Twenty-one *yi-min* temples in Taiwan honor the remains of Hakka fighters involved in the Zhu Yigui Rebellion (1721), the Lin Shuangwen Rebellion (1786), and the Dai Zhaozun Rebellion (1862). The *yimin* festival in Hsinchu features elaborate processions, Hakka music, and the honoring of "King Swine," the winner in the competition to raise the largest pig as an offering to the *yimin*.[3]

CHINESE OPERA

As a modern, industrialized people, the Taiwanese enjoy entertainment and leisure activities that are highly technological. Temple-centered entertainment such as Taiwanese opera or puppet theater has yielded to television, movies, and electronically produced music. Taiwanese opera and puppet theater receive the support of fans who seek a renaissance in the folk arts, but it is doubtful Taiwanese children love Taiwanese opera as much as they love cartoons made in Taiwan, Japan, or the United States.

Taiwanese opera (*gezaixi*) has adapted to modern technology by using high-tech staging techniques and televising their productions. Because Taiwanese opera is a local folk art that most expressively conveys distinctively Taiwanese culture and language, it has benefited from recent interest in reviving Taiwanese culture and identity. Taiwanese opera reached its peak in the 1960s as a form of music theater with elaborate costumes and symbolic makeup. Through the 1970s it was performed throughout the island at temple festivals, birthdays, weddings, and other festive occasions.

Truly a product of the experiences of the Taiwanese, Taiwanese opera developed from the *beiguan* and *nanguan* operatic forms brought to Taiwan by immigrants from Fujian and Guangdong. Its musical style derives from the folk songs of Ilan County, which were in turn influenced by aboriginal songs. Opera music is performed by a group consisting of the four-stringed *pipa*, the flutelike *dongxiao*, the three-stringed *sanxian*, the double-reeded *suona* horn, and of course a smattering of drums and gongs. Ilan County remains a fertile source for the development of Taiwanese opera. In 1992 the county government planned the first county-sponsored Taiwanese opera troupe, the Lan-Yang Opera Troupe. There are several hundred Taiwanese opera troupes, including high-quality troupes that have moved from outdoor stages to impressive new indoor stages like the beautiful National Theater in Taipei.

Opera in Taiwan is in a constant state of adaptation. It has absorbed diverse cultural influences and adapted to modern technology. Televised performances of operas began in the 1960s, intensifying modernization of opera form with recorded music and elaborate lighting techniques. One of the oldest and most popular troupes, the Ming Hwa Yuan Troupe, established in 1929, tours internationally with a style that combines the best of Taiwanese tradition with high-tech staging. The most popular performers today tend to be women playing men's roles, such as the actresses Ye Jing and Yang Lihua. Ironically, traditionally Taiwanese opera, like Beijing opera, was performed only by men.

Other theater traditions live on in Taiwan. The Henan operatic style, sung in a natural voice, is represented by the Flying Horse Henan Opera Troupe led by actress Wang Hailing. Cantonese and Hakka opera troupes have also performed in Taiwan. Older *beiguan* operatic forms are performed by several troupes on the island, and the subtle music of *nanguan* opera is being promoted by the Nanguan Opera Performance Program of the National Institute of Arts.

Until recently, the Guomindang government strongly supported the production of Beijing opera over all other theater forms. Beijing opera developed in the Chinese capital city from several regional opera forms during the Qing dynasty. In Taiwan during the early period of Japanese administration, troupes crossed the Taiwan Straits to entertain Taiwanese audiences. But since 1949, Beijing opera has been dominated in Taiwan by the military. Beginning in 1951 military opera troupes were organized into three troupes in the army, airforce, and navy—each with its own opera schools until 1986. Until disbanded in 1994, the troupes performed regularly for the military troops and at the National Armed Forces Center. These military troupes were replaced by the Kuo-kuang Opera Company, sponsored by the Ministry of Education, with the expectation that Beijing opera could adapt to the new pluralistic Taiwanese culture.[4]

With Taiwanization of the island, Beijing opera has declined in political importance and popularity. Nonetheless, the Kuo-kuang Opera Company and the National Fu-hsing Dramatic Arts Academy, both government sponsored, have responded to change by reaching out to younger and nonmainlander audiences. Even though the Beijing form of opera has declined in popularity in Taiwan, the influence of Beijing opera on Taiwanese opera, puppet theater, and film is undeniable.

Traditional Beijing opera is performed on an almost bare stage that serves as a background for the colorful costumes, bright facial makeup, and stylized movements of the actors. "No sound except singing, no motion except dancing." Every sound and movement is carefully orchestrated to convey the emotion and narrative elements of the play. Singing, often in a high falsetto voice, is accompanied by stringed instruments. Action is often marked by gongs and drums.

Many stories, acting roles, and symbolic elements of Chinese opera are similar in Taiwanese opera, Beijing opera, and puppet performances in Taiwan.[5] Character roles in opera and puppet theater are highly defined. The many female roles, traditionally played by men, are all called *dan*. The *laodan* is an older, dignified woman, the *huadan* a flirtatious younger woman. The *qingyi* is a virtuous woman who traditionally wears a blue robe. The *daoma dan* is the acrobatic and fierce "saber-horse" *dan*, who is usually a warrior or a military sprite. There is also the female clown, the *choudan*. Male roles cover three general categories: the *sheng*, the *jing*, and the *chou*. The *sheng* can be either older (*lao sheng*) or younger (*xiao sheng*) or a child (*wawa sheng*). One popular *sheng* character is the attractive, moral young scholar who embodies all Confucian virtues. The *jing* is the painted-face character by which the Chinese opera is most known in the West. The *jing* are colorful characters, both figuratively and literally. One legend tells the origin of the painted face in the Qin dynasty. A handsome and rather delicate-looking king wished to appear fierce and fearsome to his opponents. His solution was to paint a fierce-looking mask on his face. His army won, and his face painting supposedly evolved into the intricately painted mask designs of Chinese opera makeup. The painted designs on the actors' faces convey a wealth of information about these strong characters whose ranks include military heroes, gods, and monsters. Red faces convey courage and honesty; white faces represent deceitfulness. Silver and gold are used only on gods or other supernatural spirits. The fourth general category is the male clown, the *chou*, who often wears a small patch of white centered on his face.

Since Beijing opera stages usually have only a table and chairs as stage props, elaborate stylized gestures convey information about props and changes of location. Although Taiwanese operas use more elaborate backdrops, they too use the same stylized gestures and movements. Actors wear Ming dynasty costumes with long sleeves. About fifty different stylized sleeve movements are used to communicate with the audience. The "aside sleeve," the raising of the right hand so that the sleeve hangs down from the fingers, means that the actor's statement, perhaps a secret plan or a warning, cannot be heard by the other actors on stage. Holding the sleeve to cover the face conveys embarrassment or hiding from others. Hand gestures similarly convey a wealth of narrative information: the helpless hands, the hindering hand, the fighting fist, the swimming hand, and the variety of pointing gestures.

Foot movements are stylized into stage walking, stage running, the staggering steps of a drunk, the slipping step of someone on wet ground, and the upstairs and downstairs steps (done on level stage). Special movements represent mounting or dismounting a horse, boarding a boat, or climbing a wall or hill.

PUPPET THEATER

Taiwanese puppet theater shares many conventions and stories with Taiwanese and Beijing opera, but the puppets are free to fly or transform into other beings. Until the intrusion of television in the 1960s, puppet theater was immensely popular. To survive, puppet theater has adapted with the times. Now puppet theater is seen on television enhanced with popular music, fantastic lighting, and special effects.

Three forms of puppetry popular in Taiwan were imported by immigrants in the early nineteenth century: glove puppets, shadow puppets, and marionettes.[6] Glove puppets, *budai xi*, are the most popular puppets today; about a foot high, they wear elaborately embroidered costumes similar to those seen in Taiwanese or Beijing opera. These puppets perform on an intricately carved, multilevel stage painted gold. Master puppeteers manipulate the puppets and provide the voices for a variety of characters. Accompanying the puppets is a group of five musicians playing *beiguan* music behind the stage. Traditionally, temples have sponsored performances for their major festivals. The puppet stage may face the temple to give the temple gods a good view. The first story performed at the temple is a religious tale dedicated to the god or goddess of the temple. Later in the evening the most popular, high-action plays are presented to the large crowds that have gathered.

Shadow puppets, *piying xi*, are hinged puppets carved of leather and painted. These shadows appear on a white screen behind which the puppeteer manipulates the puppets. Shadow puppet theater, which spread throughout China during the Ming and Qing dynasties, arrived in Taiwan in the early nineteenth century with the Fujian and Guangdong immigrants. This art form has been most popular in the south around Kaohsiung and Tainan. The tunes of Taiwanese shadow theater are called "Chao-tunes," reflecting their probable origin in Chaozhou, Guangdong.

Marionette theater, *guilei xi*, is a bit scary. Carved of wood, these beautifully costumed puppets are about two feet high and have interchangeable heads. They are scary because they have been used primarily to exorcise evil spirits. Communities or families sponsor a *guilei xi* performance to drive out the evil from a destructive fire or terrifying accident. The first performance is by Zhong Kui to drive away evil; after his performance some viewers have felt safe enough to watch the subsequent plays. In this highly demanding art form, the puppeteer must command all the vocal skills of an opera performer plus the skill to manipulate nine to twenty strings of a single marionette. Despite the high level of artistry demanded, the fears and taboos surrounding this theater have long limited its general appeal. Fans of the folk arts have become alarmed at the possible demise of this art form as the great puppet masters die off. Groups committed to reviving this puppet version of Chinese opera have now sprung up in Taiwan.

Popular stories appear and reappear in all the theater forms: glove puppets, marionettes, shadow puppets, Taiwanese opera, Beijing opera. One popular legend told and retold is the *Tale of the White Snake.* In this tale, a white snake and her servant, a green snake, transform themselves into women. The white snake falls deeply in love with the typical Chinese hero, a young scholar, who does not know she is a snake. This is one of the most passionate and popular of Chinese romances, yet it involves a man and a snake. (The female passions were more acceptable in a snake than in a human woman in the Confucian society in which this tale developed.) Other popular tales involve the heroic military figures of the *Romance of the Three Kingdoms* and the Monkey King and his assorted supernatural and human companions from the *Journey to the West.* Militaristic plays include impressive acrobatic feats by human and spirit warriors to enthrall audiences of all kinds. Glove puppet theater has advanced the military genre into modern *gongfu* dramas that easily draw younger audiences.

DRAMATIC THEATER

Musical theater, whether with human actors or puppets, has a long tradition in China and Taiwan, whereas spoken drama is relatively new. The only precedent for spoken drama is the Qing dynasty *xiangsheng* dialogues of comic social criticism. This vaudevillian presentation has reappeared in Taiwan because it allows flexible use of vernacular and contemporary social references. The "revival" can be traced to the Stan Lai's Performance Workshop production of "The Night We Became Xiangsheng Comedians."[7] Other forms of spoken drama first appeared on the mainland in the early twentieth century, developed by students returning from study abroad.

In Taiwan, nonmusical theater became popular in the 1970s, beginning with independent production of Yao Yiwei's "Red Nose." Innovation in the 1970s continued with the presentation of a Chinese opera in modern language by the Lan-ling Drama Workshop. Its production of Ho Zhu's "New

Match," an adaptation from Beijing opera, led the way to even more creative drama. Another innovative organization, the New Aspect Art Center, founded in 1978, produced famous Western plays and Taiwan's first made-in-Taiwan musical, "The Chess King." Slapstick comedy has flourished with the presence of troupes like the Pin-Fong Acting Troupe directed by Lie Kuo-hsiu, sometimes referred to as the "Chinese Woody Allen." Although Taiwanization affects all dramatic arts, it is the special focus of the U Theater led by Liu Ching-min. Performers work in traditional Taiwanese art forms to develop theater with a contemporary Taiwanese identity. Drama troupes are now found in southern Taiwan, far from the dynamic arts center of Taipei. The Nan Feng Theater Troupe in Kaohsiung, for example, has worked to train performing artists and promote the arts.

MOVIES

Chinese movies are facing strange times in Taiwan. Just as Taiwanese directors like Ang Lee are receiving international acclaim for their films, Taiwanese filmgoers are choosing movies from elsewhere. Although very popular, Taiwanese movies in the 1960s and early 1970s reeked of either melodrama or propaganda. But in the early 1980s, a generation of directors exposed to high-quality foreign films began producing realistic drama like *In Our Time*. This "New Wave" of serious, often historical cinema included directors Wang Tung, Edward Yang, and Hou Hsiao-hsien. A "Second New Wave" was initiated in the late 1980s by directors offering distinctive but more varied Taiwanese filmmaking. These films often dealt with contemporary issues satirically. Tsai Ming-liang's *Rebels of the Neon God* (1992) looked at teenagers in urban Taiwan. Stan Lai's *The Red Lotus Society* (1994) tells the story of a young Taipei dweller who wants to learn to fly as the old martial arts masters did. Among these Taiwanese directors, Ang Lee may be the best known in the West. Not only was his *Eat Drink Man Woman* a critical success in the West for its sensitive and humorous portrayal of a modern Taipei family; he also crossed new boundaries by directing Jane Austen's classic novel *Sense and Sensibility* with a British and American cast.[8] In Ang Lee's 1997 movie *The Ice Storm*, he looked at more contemporary Western family life—a dysfunctional, adulterous American family of the 1970s.

Despite of the critical acclaim of Taiwanese movies, in the early 1990s movies from Hong Kong were the biggest hits in Taiwan. Since 1994, restrictions on the import of films from China and Japan have gradually been loosened. As a result, movie theaters are more than ever concentrating on foreign films. Taiwanese filmmakers have responded by investing more in Hong Kong and Chinese movie deals. Increasingly, Taiwan has become part of an international audience for films.

As the Taiwanese watch more foreign films, the rest of the world is increasingly watching excellent Taiwanese films. International awards for Taiwanese films began in 1989 with the Venice Film Festival award given to Hou Hsiao-hsien's *City of Sadness*. The same award was given Tsai Ming-liang's *Vive l'Amour* in 1994. Ang Lee's hilarious story of a homosexual arranging a fake wedding to please his parents, *The Wedding Banquet* (1993), was nominated for best foreign film at the Academy Awards and attracted large audiences around the United States.

TELEVISION, MTV, AND KTV

Television and movies far outdistance other theatrical "art" forms in popularity and revenue. Interaction among operas, puppet theater, movies, and television has been complex. Although movies and television have replaced traditional stage arts in popularity, they have also transformed and modernized these old forms through cinematic and televised presentations. Taiwanese opera and glove puppet theater shows presented on television sport high-tech lighting and special effects. The most popular puppet shows are televised glove puppet shows of the *jinguang* (golden light) variety with special effects and fantastic battle scenes developed by Huang Hai-tai and his son Huang Chun-hsiung. Taiwanese and Mandarin soap operas and historical dramas on television and in movie theaters are much indebted to the narrative traditions and emotional values of older opera and puppet forms.

Taiwanese television also broadcasts shows wholly unrelated to the earlier performance arts. Silly game shows and colorful variety shows are probably indebted to American and Japanese television genres. Taiwanese television reflects recent rapid liberalization of society in Taiwan. Whereas only a decade ago television was dominated by three government-affiliated stations showing programming overwhelmingly in Mandarin Chinese, now most Taiwanese have access to cable television with programming from the United States, Hong Kong, Japan, and elsewhere. Cable stations began illegally in 1976, and not until 1993 did the government begin developing a legal structure for cable systems. By 1996, however, there were 150 cable TV systems. The provincialism of Taiwanese media is a thing of the past.

Traffic and long working hours of urban Taiwan have made access to many recreational activities difficult for most Taiwanese. Thus television is the most popular leisure activity. For those seeking entertainment outside the home, but still nearby, urban centers offer numerous MTV and KTV establishments. MTV refers not to the American rock television channel but, rather, to businesses that rent small rooms equipped with VCRs and a selection of videotapes. These establishments, extremely popular until the government started its crackdown on pirated videotapes, appeal primarily to young people, especially couples, who seek entertainment away from the cramped quarters of dormitories or the vigilant eyes of relatives.

KTV parlors are the Taiwanese version of Japanese *karaoke* television. *Karaoke* is a Japanese term that means "empty orchestra." These systems of microphones hooked up to videocassette or audiotape players make singing stars of anyone. Officials estimate that there are at least 1,500 registered KTV parlors throughout Taiwan. They appeal to anyone out for a good time and can accommodate those wishing to sing in Taiwanese, Mandarin, Cantonese, or English. The most elegantly furnished parlors with hostesses are expensive entertainment centers that serve business people and their clients.

SPORTS AND GAMES

For individuals with more free time, especially younger Taiwanese, outdoor adventure sports are increasingly popular: mountain climbing, sailboarding, surfing, and paragliding. Outdoor activities around the island are offered by the China Youth Corps.

The Taiwanese enjoy urban sports as well. Fifty-four different sports are represented in the ROC Sports Federation. Most popular are racquet sports such as badminton, tennis, and table tennis. Other sports originally from the West also flourish: baseball, basketball, golf, handball, rugby, volleyball, and track and field events. In addition, Chinese and other Asian martial arts thrive in Taiwan: *aikido, judo, karate, kendo, guoshu, taekwondo,* and *taijiquan.*

Professional sports have begun to thrive in prosperous Taiwan. Baseball, for instance, attracts large crowds. The Chinese Professional Baseball League has six teams, each playing 100 games per season. Now a new league, the Taiwan Major League Professional Baseball, with four teams, plays in competition with the older league. The popularity of professional baseball is also reflected in the high level of play among Taiwanese Little Leaguers. The excellence of youth sports bodes well for the future of professional sports, especially baseball.

Truly a U.S. import, professional basketball started up in Taiwan in 1994 with four teams and a seventy-two-game season. Also extremely popular in

Taiwan is professional golf, reflecting the high status of amateur golf in East Asia. The Asian Masters Tournament is held in Yangmei in Taoyuan County.

Taiwan has long been the recipient of a rich tradition of challenging strategy games from China: mahjong, *weiqi*, and *xiangqi*. Mahjong's history is a bit murky, but the game seems to have developed into its present form on mainland China in Ningbo. This form of mahjong played in Taiwan, Hong Kong, and China differs from that popularized in the United States after its introduction by Westerners who learned it in Shanghai in the early twentieth century. Although *weiqi* and *hsiangqi* have both been called Chinese chess, they are quite distinct. *Weiqi* is a game of elegant simplicity: It has few rules and endless possible strategies. The simple layout of the *weiqi* board consists of nineteen intersecting vertical and horizontal lines on which the black and white pieces move. The game starts with an empty board and ends with a board full of black and white stones whose placement gives evidence of failed and successful strategies for increasing territory at the opponent's expense. *Weiqi*, known as *go* in Japan, remains popular throughout East Asia. In contrast, *xiangqi*, or "elephant chess," is closely related to the Western game of chess that developed in Europe. Like *weiqi* and unlike Western chess, however, the play is on the intersections of the lines rather than in the squares. The basic goal of *xiangqi* is to capture the king, and there are restrictions on pieces not found in Western chess. Any good game that can be computerized, has been. *Weiqi, xiangqi,* and mahjong are no exception. Solitaire versions and networked versions are both available. Computer games derived from these are also popular, including a modern solitaire version of mahjong distributed by Microsoft called "Taipei."

Pachinko, a game that originated in Japan, is in a class of its own. This game encourages isolation and obsession. It is a cross between a slot machine and a pinball game. Players in brightly lit pachinko parlors watch steel balls bounce, fall, and disappear. Because gambling is illegal, only prizes are awarded inside the parlors. Outside the parlors, though, there are likely ways to exchange the prizes for cash. High-tech parlors offer the latest computer technology in pachinko gaming. On the streets, however, one may still see primitive pachinko boards of wood and nails—with a prize of sausage.

Leisure activities of the Taiwanese reflect their busy lifestyles. The average Taiwanese worker or student has little daily time for recreation. For city dwellers, traffic and congestion further limit access to recreation. Thus electronic entertainment fits the needs of these busy, modern people, which explains the popularity of video games, computer games, pachinko, KTV,

MTV, or just watching television at home. Traditional entertainments may well need to accommodate to these forms to survive. Televised puppet theater or computerized *xiangqi* may do well, but efforts to renew folk entertainment traditions such as Taiwanese opera or puppet theater as high-art traditions apart from their festival context are still awaiting a clear outcome. Some traditions remain alive and well without support from governments or foundations. When plenty of time is available for boisterous temple festivals or important family gatherings at New Year, the Taiwanese hold onto their cultural traditions remarkably well.

NOTES

1. Government publications such as the *Republic of China Yearbook, 1997* provide information about official government commemorative days.

2. Lunar calendars, called *nong li* (agricultural calendars), are widely available and frequently consulted in Taiwan. With the exception of New Year's holidays, lunar festivals are generally not official holidays and thus are not marked by the closing of banks, schools, or offices.

3. For an excellent treatment of the state of Hakka culture in contemporary Taiwan see Eugenia Yun, "The Hakka: The Invisible Group," *Free China Review*, vol. 43, no. 10 (October 1993), pp. 4–17.

4. For an interesting history of the military opera troupes in Taiwan, see Claire Liu, "Mothballing the Military Gear—The Kuo-kuang Opera Company," trans. by Brent Heinrich, *Sinorama*, March 1996.

5. A good overview of the character roles and symbolic techniques of Chinese drama is Celia S. L. Zung, *Secrets of the Chinese Drama* (New York: Benjamin Blom, 1964), especially pp. 37–58 and 77–148. Synopses of fifty popular plays are on pp. 151–292.

6. The primary source for the following discussion of puppet theater in Taiwan is B. Kaulbach and B. Proksch, *Arts and Culture in Taiwan* (Taipei: Southern Materials Center, 1984), pp. 47–55. Recent developments in puppet theater are found in the *Republic of China Yearbook, 1997*.

7. Recent developments in *xiangsheng* and dramatic theater in Taiwan are presented in the *Republic of China Yearbook, 1997*.

8. Information on the development of Taiwanese movies is found in the *Republic of China Yearbook, 1997*.

SUGGESTED READINGS

Ahern, Emily Martin and Hill Gates, eds. *The Anthropology of Taiwanese Society.* Stanford, CA: Stanford University Press, 1981.

Kaulbach, B. and B. Proksch. *Arts and Culture in Taiwan.* Taipei: Southern Materials Center, 1984.

Republic of China Yearbook, 1997. Taipei: Government Information Office, Republic of China.

4

Music and Dance

OLD TAIWANESE MEN play drums and horns in a funeral procession. A young child practices a Bach sonata on her piano. The ritual use of traditional Chinese music contrasts sharply with the popularity of classical Western music in contemporary Taiwan. The two traditions stand side by side, but for the most part exist in different realms. Taiwanese music serves ritual functions, but Western classical music functions as high art, as a form of personal cultivation, and as a middle-class status symbol.

Taiwanese music punctuates and narrates the action of Taiwanese opera and puppet theater. Taiwanese music accompanies the gods and goddesses on their processions; it accompanies the dead on their way to burial. And Taiwanese music celebrates weddings, birthdays, and any other festive occasions. Both Taiwanese and Western music can speak to people's emotions and transport them to a place of beauty, sadness, excitement, or tranquillity. Only with Taiwanese music, though, is there integration into the rituals and narratives of religion, theater, and the state.

Music is perhaps the most vulnerable of traditional arts. Whereas one can study the masterful calligraphy, poetry, or painting of past masters long dead, music can be studied only from living masters who pass on their technique and repertoire to students. Taiwanese ethnomusicologist Lin Ku-fang sees the end of the Qing and the early period of the Republican era on the mainland as a time of relentless assault on elite Chinese culture, an assault that seriously harmed the transmission of highly cultivated Chinese music.

The effect of this period of choosing Western culture over traditional Chinese culture is evidenced in Taiwan as well in the overwhelming preference for studying classical Western music.

HISTORICAL BACKGROUND

According to classical texts, the Chinese first discovered proper musical pitches under the legendary Emperor Huangdi in the third millennium B.C. The emperor sent the scholar Ling Lun to the western mountains to find bamboo pipes that would make the sounds of the legendary Chinese phoenix. His desire was to regulate music to create harmony between heaven and earth. Thus began the state's interest in music. As stated in the Confucian classic *The Book of Rites (Li ji)*, "Music is the harmony of heaven and earth while rites are the measurement of heaven and earth. Through harmony all things are made known, through measure all things are properly classified. Music comes from heaven, rites are shaped by earthly designs."[1] Chinese philosophers such as Mencius, Xunzi, and Dong Zhongshu were interested in the moral effects of good music, and like moral leaders in many cultures, they were often concerned about the possible demoralizing effects of "barbarian" music.

Following the tradition of the Yellow Emperor, classical writings describe a twelve-tone musical system based on the pitches of bamboo pipes. Chinese writers knew about producing harmonic pitches, in the manner of the ancient Greeks, by using the division of strings, but they emphasized the blowing of pipes to establish pitch. The size of the pipe, and thus the official imperial pitch, changed when the emperor's astrologists and musicians felt such alterations were necessary to align the imperial reign with the cosmos. The first pipe produces the "yellow bell" pitch. By overblowing the pipe, a pitch is produced that is an octave plus a fifth higher than the "yellow bell." Subsequent pitches are produced by blowing pipes alternately four-thirds and two-thirds the length of the previous pipe. Gradually, sets of tuned bells became important standards for establishing musical pitch. Sets of tuned bells from the fourth and fifth centuries have been discovered with inscriptions of their pitch names.

From the twelve pitches of pipes or tuned bells, scales are selected. Like Western music, Chinese music uses a scale of seven notes but focuses on a five-tone core and two changing tones. The five fundamental tones are related to the cosmological theory of the five agents: fire, water, earth, metal, and water. Music, like all things in the cosmos, is homologized to the human being and the natural world.

During the Han dynasty, rulers set up a music bureau to archive ancient and folk music. With the expansion of the Han dynasty came increasing contacts with other cultures. In the first century A.D., Buddhism and new musical instruments and styles entered China from India and Central Asia. Gandharan, Yueji, and Iranian cultural influences moved along the silk trade routes into China. During this period the popular *pipa* or plucked lute was introduced to China from Central or Western Asia. New instruments were introduced to accompany the rituals of Buddhism: the bronze basin-shaped bell (*qing*), for instance, that sits on a cushion to be struck. The military conflicts that followed the demise of the Han dynasty also brought new instruments and styles, increasingly encountering and using drums and double-reeded flutes to aid military communication.

During the Tang dynasty foreign musical influences reached a high point with instruments and styles arriving from Central Asia. In fact, Tang China may have had the greatest diversity of musical cultures in world history until the present century. Urban centers were full of foreign musicians and dancers popular with the Chinese of the period. Emperor Xuan Zong (reigned 713–755) became the greatest imperial promoter of the musical arts by founding the Pear Garden Academy (Li Yuan) troupe, which included large numbers of dancers and musicians. We have titles and some descriptions of the grand musical events of the Tang court. The texts tell of the instruments and costumes, but there is nothing resembling a musical score. For example, we know that in "The Imperial Birthday Music" for Emperor Wu Hou (d. 705) many colorfully costumed dancers line up to form the Chinese characters for "long live the emperor."

The Chinese classified their music according to the "eight sounds" (*bayin*), or more precisely according to the eight materials out of which the instruments were made: stone, earth, bamboo, metal, skin, silk, wood, and gourd. An example of a stone instrument would be the stone chimes (*qing*) used in ancient ritual music. The round clay ocarinas (*xun*) found in ancient archeological digs are of the earth category. The bamboo category includes the various flutes. The metal category included ancient bronze drums and gongs. The skin instruments are the various drums. The silk category includes all the stringed instruments because Chinese stringed instruments always use twisted silk rather than wire or animal gut. The wood category includes percussive clappers. The gourd category is represented by the *sheng* mouth organ—several bamboo pipes set into a gourd or wooden wind chest.

TAIWANESE MUSIC

Classical musical traditions supported by the imperial courts and urban wealthy people of China have their descendants in Taiwan. Modern

4.1 Classical music being performed in a hotel lobby by young woman in a *qipao*.

government-supported Chinese orchestras sport many different types of Chinese musical instruments. The Taipei Municipal Chinese Orchestra, the Chinese Orchestra of the Broadcasting Corporation of China, the Kaohsiung Experimental Chinese Orchestra, and the Experimental Chinese Orchestra of the National Taiwan Academy of Arts give public performances of adaptations of folk songs, classical Chinese music, and modern compositions. Their musicians have studied Chinese music in Taiwan's colleges and universities, but they may also have studied with folk performers as well.

Solo music existed in ancient Chinese culture. The *se*, a stringed zither with twenty-five strings and movable bridges, is often mentioned as a solo instrument in texts. More recently the *qin* and *pipa* were used for solo performances. The Taiwanese have developed solo instrumentation for a variety of instruments, including the composition of music for traditional Chinese instruments to be accompanied by Western orchestras.

Folk traditions of music, dance, and ritual have flourished without government support. Temple festivals and Taiwanese operas, weddings, and funerals would be incomplete without one or more of the wind and percussion ensembles of several amateur or professional musicians. These ensembles trace their roots to the military marching bands that accompanied high officials in imperial times. Now the ensembles are used to give ritual occasions a sense of solemnity and importance. The three ensembles described below differ in their constituent musical instruments, their repertoires, and their ritual functions.

The loud musical ensemble that accompanies most festive and funerary occasions is the drum pavilion or *guting*. The drum pavilion includes a large gong, a double-headed drum, a pair of cymbals, and one or more *suona*. The *suona* is a double-reeded pipe that looks a bit like a horn. The leader of the drum pavilion is the drummer who plays the drum while it is placed inside a seven-foot-high pavilion. The pavilion is carried either on a cart or in the back of a truck for temple festivals or funeral processions.

A necessity for Taiwanese temple festivals, the drum pavilion is usually a professional troupe hired by the temple to lead the procession that marks the temple deity's inspection of the area under his or her protection. Funerals also require drum pavilions. The sons of the deceased as a group are expected to hire the drum pavilion to accompany the deceased to the burial place. If there are no sons, someone else serves the role of the filial son, perhaps a nephew who is inheriting property and the obligation to worship the deceased as an ancestor.

The "eight sounds" or *bayin* ensemble have a lesser but nonetheless important place in Taiwanese rituals. For funerals, each married daughter, and sometimes married nieces and granddaughters, is expected to hire a *bayin* ensemble to follow the drum pavilion in the procession. The daughter's contribution of music to the funeral procession comprises part of the reciprocity between the family of the deceased and the son-in-law. It is related to the traditional wedding exchanges in which a *bayin* ensemble is given to the bride's family by the groom's family and then returned to escort the bride to the groom's family home. This ensemble, sometimes called the "daughter's pipe," includes at least the small-sized double-reeded pipe (called *ai-a* in the Minnan dialect) and the small *tongzhong* gong. Other instruments in the *bayin* ensemble might be the double-stringed lute, cymbals, and clappers.

A third folk ensemble, composed of amateur musicians, performs *beiguan* music. These amateur groups are often organized at the local temple to perform for the temple festival honoring the god's or goddess's birthday. At temple festivals, the processions include not only the drum pavilion hired by the local temple and the resident *beiguan* ensemble but also *beiguan* ensem-

4.2 *Suona* musicians performing as part of a religious procession.

bles sent by other temples to join in the procession. These ensembles also
play for the mutual benefit of their members and thus perform for the important ritual occasions of members' families: weddings, funerals, and birthdays. At funerals, the presence of the *beiguan* ensemble represents the network
of friends and associates of the deceased. Friends and organizations to which
the deceased belonged today hire *beiguan* groups rather than perform themselves. The *beiguan* ensemble has at least two double-reeded pipes (*suona*), a
woodblock (*bangzi*), a big gong (*daluo*), a small gong (*xiaoluo*), a single-
headed drum (*bangu*), a double-headed drum (*tonggu*), and a pair of large
and small cymbals.

Whatever its type, the folk music ensemble used in public rituals often
plays for long periods, throughout the funeral procession or throughout the
god's tour of his area. This means that a performance requires much repetition to fill the required time. Repetition is particularly needed in the funeral
procession because each type of ensemble has only a few songs reserved exclusively for funeral use. Each type of ensemble has a different method of
repeating a basic tune with variations. The drum pavilion repeats the commonly used "Great Restraints" (*Dajie*) in a method called "turning the pipe"
(*fanguan*). The *suona* pipe has seven notes in the scale, and the scale can be
played in seven different "melodic modes" (*guan*). As Ping-hui Li explains,

this change in mode "is not merely the transposition of the same melody into a different key, as is the case in Western music, for different *guan* may emphasize different scale degrees and melodic figures."[2] Another way to repeat the same song over and over is by using ornamentations commonly added to *bayin* melodies and occasionally to *guting* and *beiguan*. The tune may, for example, be repeated in different octaves or with additional flourishes.

A distinctive method for prolonging *beiguan* tunes is to insert percussion patterns between phrases. The player of the single-headed drum determines the type and placement of these insertions. *Beiguan* tunes are seldom prolonged by immediate repetition; players prefer to prolong the melody by adding percussion patterns or the tune "Wind in the Pines" (*feng ru song*). In addition to processional uses, *beiguan* music is also used to accompany Taiwanese glove puppet and shadow puppet theater and the less common *beiguan* theater (for human actors). Both make use of the loud and exciting drumming and gonging that *beiguan* does so well. The only professional *beiguan* opera troupe in Taiwan is the Hsin Mei Yuan Troupe.

Compared to *beiguan* music, *nanguan* is a calmer and less percussive sound. *Nanguan* music is more strictly composed. Its principal instruments are the melodic Chinese lute (*pipa*) and bamboo flute (*xiao*). The Taiwanese have become increasingly interested in this musical form, which developed in southern China and first appeared in Taiwan as early as the 1500s. The leaders in *nanguan* music are musicians Chen Mei-o and Lee Hsiang-shih and singer Wu Su-ching.

Taiwanese opera has a musical ensemble of five to seven musicians on both sides of the stage. The drum master plays the single-headed drum (*xiaogu*) and leads the other musicians. This drummer-conductor of the musical ensemble for theater must carefully time the music and percussion to accentuate the actors' movements and to convey information about the emotions and plot developments of the play. Musical performance for theater demands methods of interpretation other than the endless elaboration needed for processional music. But in both contexts, emphasis is on improvisation of a traditional theme rather than on composition of original music. In Taiwanese opera ensembles, the drum master is accompanied by gongs, the reed pipe, the *huqin*, the *erhu*, and the full-moon guitar (*yueqin*). Taiwanese opera music is based on *beiguan*, but it has developed into a distinctive style featuring local Taiwanese musical elements.[3]

Members of the orchestra (*changmian* or the "face of the show") of the Beijing opera look formal in their long, blue traditional gowns, sitting to the side of the stage. Their music accompanies singing but also accents gestures and provides musical passages after each phrase or speech. Four categories of instruments are used in Beijing opera music, with each category labeled according to how its instruments are played: blown, bowed, plucked, and struck. Blown instruments include the popular *di*, a wooden horizontal flute, and the *suona*, the reed-pipe so dominant in wind and percussion ensembles. The highest position of bowed instruments is held by the *huqin*, a two-stringed instrument with a bow permanently attached. The *erhu* is a two-stringed bowed instrument similar to the *huqin* but with lower pitch. The category of plucked instruments is surprisingly large compared to the same category in other musical cultures. The traditionally most important stringed instrument is the *pipa*, a four-stringed Chinese lute that has the sound of "large pearls, small pearls tumbling onto a plate of jade," according to poet Bai Zhuyi of the Tang dynasty. The percussion section of "struck" instruments is led by the drum master, who plays the *bangu* (a small drum) and serves as the conductor for the whole orchestra. The noisy sounds of drums and gongs is especially important for the fighting scenes of military operas. In addition to the *bangu*, this drum section includes the *danpigu* (a one-headed drum), the *huaigu* (breast drum), and the *tanggu* (large drum). Other important percussion instruments are the cymbals (*na* and *ba*), the large and small gongs (*daluo* and *luo*), and the *yunluo*, which is a group of ten gongs set in a wooden framework. The instruments include the reed pipe (*suona*), *haotong*, *huqin* (a two-stringed instrument played with the bow), *erhu* (similar to *huqin* but with a lower pitch), *yueqin* (full-moon guitar with four strings), *sanxian* (three-stringed guitar), *ban* (time beater), *danpigu* (one-headed drum), the *huaigu* (breast drum), *tanggu* (large drum), *di* (wooden horizontal flute), *xiao* (vertical flute), *sheng* (pan-style bamboo flute), *xing* (cup-shaped bells), *luo* (large gong), *xiaoluo* (small gong), *yunluo* (ten gongs hung in a wooden frame and hit with a wooden striker), *pipa* (four-stringed lute), and cymbals.[4]

Another important form of ritual music is the Taoist and Buddhist chanting of scriptures. Ordained and unordained Taoist priests perform funeral rituals, exorcisms, and elaborate rites of cosmic renewal called *jiao*. In all these the priest and his assistants provide chanting, instrumental music, and even dance. While chanting the priest stands before a brass bell and a wooden fish, both of which he strikes in accompaniment with his chanting. The brass bell is said to represent the principle of *yang* (and heaven); the wooden fish is said to represent *yin* (and earth). An assistant is in charge of the drum of the law (*fagu*). In many rituals, these instruments are joined by others of the *beiguan* group: *suona*, cymbals, block, and more drums. The music is powerful and mysterious: Exorcism of a spirit is marked by loud drumming;

petitions to the gods are preceded by the striking of the bell. At a certain point in the *jiao* ritual, the priest offers tea and incense to Laozi while dancing to a lively song by the wind instruments.[5]

Buddhist chanting conveys a solemn and peaceful feeling. Chanting is recitation of a sutra, hymn, or mantra. Chanting may involve repetition of a single phrase of praise to Amitabha Buddha or Guanyin Bodhisattva, or it may repeat words in praise of incense: "Incense is born of the mind. The mind through incense reaches out. Not remaining within the three Bounds (Heaven, Earth, Hell), it can travel throughout the Ten Regions."[6] Monks and nuns often chant selections from various sutras or from the entire, but very brief, Heart Sutra. Spectators and sometimes even participants in Buddhist chanting may not know what they chant because the words are in a classical Chinese form that includes many transliterated Sanskrit terms unfamiliar to most Taiwanese. Buddhist chants in temples are accompanied by percussion instruments, particularly by the "wooden fish" drum (*muyu*) and a brass bell. Other drums, sometimes a very large drum, punctuate the chanting. Cymbals, smaller bells, and clappers are also used. For temple rituals, "plucked" and "blown" instruments are not used, but these may play at funerary or death anniversary masses in private residences.

4.3 A "wooden fish" drum used to provide rhythm to Buddhist chanting.

MANDARIN AND TAIWANESE POP MUSIC

Until 1993, government regulations restricted the broadcasting of television and radio programming in languages other than Mandarin. This meant that Mandarin language songs filled airwaves and television variety shows. A generation of Taiwanese grew up with this popular Mandarin song tradition, an outgrowth of pop music culture from the Shanghai of the 1930s and 1940s. Mandarin pop music continues to be very popular despite the Taiwanization of pop music because it thrives in an international musical scene potentially more lucrative for singers seeking to reach the Hong Kong and PRC markets as well as overseas Chinese communities. Several Mandarin pop music stars have been from Taiwan. Teresa Teng, for instance, was one of the hottest Mandarin singing stars in Taiwan in the 1970s. She traveled to Japan in 1973 and began to record in Japanese as well as Mandarin Chinese. Born in 1953 to a mainlander military family in Taiwan, she often sang for the Guomindang armed forces. She also became a beloved singer in the PRC during the 1970s for her sweet, uplifting songs, becoming popular despite early PRC government bans on her songs as representing reactionary ideology. In fact, a common expression was "By day, Deng Xiaoping rules China. But by night, Teresa Teng rules." The PRC government lifted the ban on her songs in 1986 and reclassified her "reactionary" hit song "When Will You Come Back Again" as a "revolutionary patriotic song." Her popularity throughout East Asia revived after the 1989 Tiananmen massacre with her support for the democracy movement and the popularity of her songs among protesting students. Teresa Teng's death from an asthma attack in 1995 was widely mourned throughout East Asia.[7]

Whereas Teresa Teng was a Mandarin pop singer whose popularity moved from Taiwan to the rest of East Asia, the pop singer Jacky Cheung started in China and Hong Kong to eventually become a Mandarin pop success in Taiwan and other Chinese communities as well. His first albums were in Cantonese, but he is now most known for his slow Mandarin love ballads. The huge market for Mandarin pop music has made him a success; he was the first Mandarin singer highlighted in a *Billboard* magazine cover story. His 1993 hit album *Kiss and Say Goodbye* included seven Mandarin versions of Japanese love songs and three ballads by Taiwan-based songwriters. Fans love his voice and his sincerity, unconcerned that he lacks the gorgeous looks of the new breed of young singing idols of East Asia.[8]

Taiwanese language folk songs and ballads have become increasingly popular in Taiwan in the 1990s. Early Taiwanese ballads were influenced by aboriginal music and then by Japanese musical styles. In the early twentieth century, Taiwanese and Japanese folk ballads became popular genres. Taiwanese popular music, developed under the influence of the vocal style of Japanese folk songs, has a trembling, deep-throated style. The themes in this singing tradition tell of the hard lives of the Taiwanese. As Taiwanese singers have become more popular, their vocal styles have become more influenced by the Mandarin pop song styles more familiar to their younger listeners. They have added Western-style instrumentation more familiar to the new generation, but they sometimes retain the soulful sound of the traditional *erhu*. Popular singers such as Chiang Hui and Hung Jung-hung, known as the queen and king of Taiwanese pop music, still sing bittersweet lyrics about lonely and difficult lives with their updated musical styles. Chiang Hui knows of the hard times she sings about; she grew up poor and dropped out of school at age ten to begin earning money by singing in Peitou winehouses. Her hit song "My True Feelings Come Out After Drinking" is one of the most-requested songs at KTV parlors. Another KTV favorite is the very optimistic 1984 hit song by singer-legislator Yeh Chi-tien. Called "You'll Win Only If You Drive Yourself Hard," it was one of the first real hit songs in Taiwanese.[9]

WESTERN MUSIC

Western music has come to dominate much of the musical scene in Taiwan. Western classical music is the music of choice for most musicians who are formally studying music. The popularity of giving children piano lessons—with the usual emphasis on Western classical music—follows the middle-class model of the United States. Taiwan-born classical musicians increasingly play on international stages. Examples are violinists Edith Chen, Hu Nai-yuan, and Lin Chao-liang. Western orchestras such as the National Symphony Orchestra and the Taipei City Symphony Orchestra give regular performances to audiences larger than any classical Chinese musical group would attract. Even Western opera has made a move into Taiwan with the Taiwan Metropolitan Opera and the Taipei Opera Theater.

Western music was first introduced to the Taiwanese by Christian missionaries, but it was the Japanese who promoted Western classical music among the Taiwanese elites. Zhang Fuxing, a Taiwanese musician sent to Japan to study, was a major influence in the introduction of Western classical music when he returned to Taiwan. He organized the Association of Pleasing Tones in Taipei in 1920 as the first full Western orchestra. He also used Western musical notation to transcribe aboriginal music.[10]

Traditional folk songs continue to be popular, but Western pop music and Westernized Taiwanese pop music have attracted the attention of young Taiwanese. Westernized Taiwanese pop music has a great youth following in Taiwan, where Western singers and musical groups are popular, as are Taiwanese and Hong Kong singers who have embraced Western rock and pop. The openness of Taiwan's society since the late 1980s has enabled Taiwanese youth to follow international youth music trends closely. Performers from Taiwan and Hong Kong, and even ethnic Chinese from Southeast Asia or the United States, are becoming popular singing in Taiwanese, Mandarin, Cantonese, English, or some combination of these languages. The popular singer CoCo (Li Wen) represents well the international flavor of pop music in Taiwan. Born in Hong Kong, CoCo was raised in the United States, but chose to make her career in Taiwan. Another example would be the brothers and cousin calling themselves the LA Boys who brought rap and hip hop dance music from the United States to Taiwan. As overseas Chinese raised in Los Angeles, they saw great opportunities for a music career in Taiwan.

MOVEMENT AND DANCE

Dance and music followed similar lines of development in China. In fact, to separate dance, music, theater, and ritual in Chinese tradition is difficult. The dances and music of peoples of Central Asia mixed with the dances of the Han Chinese from the third century when non-Han peoples controlled northern China. Music and dance experienced further foreign influence and then strong imperial support during the Tang dynasty. The "ten movement music" dance of the Tang included dance elements from Central Asia, Persia, India, Xinjiang, Korea, and of course China. Elaborate costumes and intricate body movements combined with poetry, songs, music, and a dramatic narrative to form the ancestor of modern opera forms.

Chinese and Taiwanese dance traditions, seen in court rituals and folk celebrations, have emphasized formal movements of the bodies with feet close to the ground. With the exception of the acrobatic movements in operas or lion dances, traditions inherited by the Taiwanese do not emphasize the leaps and leg movements of Western ballet.

Taiwanese opera and other regional operas require training in highly symbolic body movements to convey emotions, changes in time and space, and the presence of unseen objects. In addition, many of the most popular dramas incorporate wild, choreographed acrobatic fighting-dancing. Elaborately costumed generals lead troops against each other with their swords swirling and their banners flying. Monks attack legions of demons as they leap and seem to fly through the air. This fighting is accompanied by the musical ensemble, which must carefully time drumming and gonging to coordinate with the actors' movements. It is said that if a drummer mistimes a beat, an actor could die.

The choreographed fighting of military operas closely relates to the martial arts of China. The *guoshu*, or "national arts" of China, are in many ways more like dance than sport. The many traditions of martial arts have been maintained in Taiwan much better than have been classical dance forms. Some styles of Shaolin martial arts are based on animal forms, for example, dragon, crane, snake, and tiger. The martial arts, whether Shaolin, *taijiquan*, or some other form, tend to employ highly choreographed movements and involve both internal training and external training. External training involves the bones and the muscles. Internal training, based on Taoist views of the body and the universe, disciplines the mind, the internal organs, and the flow of *qi* (life force) through the body.

Two folk dance traditions have been highly visible in Taiwan and in Chinese communities around the world: the colorful and rousing lion dance and the dragon dance. Traditionally, these dances were performed to bring the rain, to avoid the plagues, and generally to bring blessings to the community. Now they are performed to bring good luck and a lively mood of festivity to many celebrations. These athletic dance troupes with accompanying drummers can be seen at temple festivals and on television specials. Because the lion dance requires fewer participants, it is the most prevalent of the two dances. With one person animating the lion's colorful mask and front legs and another animating its rear legs, two people move in harmony to create the impression of a lively dancing lion. The lion jumps, rolls over, shakes its head, and generally conveys a wild, joyful movement. To avoid evil spirits, the lion runs in a zigzag movement. Sometimes there is a second lion or a person in a laughing Buddha mask romping with the lion.

The dragon mask and body is a long, elaborate work of folk art. When the dragon has been completed, the eyes are ritually opened to bring the creature to life. The dragon dance requires the carefully coordinated group movement of strong dancers. The first dancer carries aloft the large, elaborately designed dragon head, and the rest of the dancers carry the dragon's body in a curving, undulating line. The weight of the sections of the dragon's head and body and the speed of the dance require alternate dancers to replace those in line in a long procession.

Lions and dragons dance to the percussive music of the Taiwanese. Drummers accompanying the lion and dragon dances carry lion drums (*shigu*) and dragon drums (*longgu*) with bright red bases and tacked-on drumskins. The music and dance of the lion and dragon troupes dispel evil and celebrate auspicious occasions like the births of gods, New Year's, weddings, or na-

4.4 Dragon dance performed as part of a religious procession.

tional celebrations. The huge dancing dragon of the armed forces in Taiwan is 393 feet long and weighs about 220 pounds; it is carried by over 100 members of the armed forces. On national holidays this enormous dragon dances to celebrate the Republic of China in Taiwan.

Like much of Taiwanese culture, dance and movement traditions have been greatly affected by Western traditions. In the 1940s Western-style modern dance was performed in Taiwan by dancers who had studied in Japan: Tsai Jui-yueh and Lee Tsai-o. But Western modern dance did not make a major impact until the 1960s because the Guomindang government strongly promoted Chinese folk dance as a way to foster a sense of Chinese unity.

The most active Western dance form in Taiwan is clearly modern dance. Although several ballet schools and companies exist, the creative emphasis in Taiwan is on modern dance. Many dancers study ballet and Western modern dance, but they go on to develop distinctively Taiwanese dance pieces that draw on elements of their own culture in the context of a modern dance style. Development of modern dance in Taiwan is heavily indebted to Liu Feng-hsueh. She founded a dance studio in 1967 and began presenting modern dance to the public using her students in the physical education department at National Taiwan Normal University. She studied the dance notation system of Rudolf Laban in Germany in the 1970s. Using Laban's concepts of space, time, and direction, she choreographed some highly structural works. But she also draws on the dance and movement styles of Chinese opera and martial arts. She has also researched and choreographed ancient dances such as a seventh-century court dance.

The other highly influential person in modern dance is the founder of the acclaimed Cloud Gate Dance Theater, Lin Hwai-min. Lin studied with modern dance pioneer Martha Graham. When he returned to Taiwan, he combined modern dance techniques with the movements and stories of Chinese opera. In many of his best-known works he expresses the struggles of the Taiwanese. "Legacy" (1978) portrays the early pioneers crossing the Taiwan Straits. "The Rite of Spring" (1983) expresses concerns about urban life. "My Nostalgia, My Songs" (1986) looks at Taiwanese difficulties during the 1950s. Lin's early works explore issues of Taiwanese and Chinese identity. Later he expanded into more universal themes while still reflecting Taiwanese imagery. For the twentieth anniversary of his Cloud Gate Dance Group, he presented the highly praised "Nine Songs" production. This ninety-minute dance presentation was based on the 2,000-year-old poetry of Zhu Yuan. The first part of the production features beautiful lotus blossom imagery and the dancing of a shamaness, the god of the sun, the gods of fate, the river goddess, the showy god of the clouds, and the forlorn mountain spirit. After this dancing of nature spirits, the piece turns strongly political with a "Homage to the Martyrs." While the "martyr" dancers enter with baskets over their heads as if being led to execution, a voice recites the names of ancient fallen heroes, people killed during the Japanese period, and those executed by the Nationalists following the 1947 February 28th Incident. The Ju Percussion Group provides heavy percussion music that builds the tension as the dancers fall on the stage. At the end, a dancer evokes the televised image of the young man standing alone before the tanks at Tiananmen Square as he runs to the front of the stage to bravely face two bright lights. The political images are Chinese and Taiwanese, but the theme of the violence and oppression of the modern world is universal. The dance ends with a promise of rebirth as the dancers return to fill the stage with hundreds of lighted candles while the peaceful music of the Zou aboriginal people plays. The whole piece, from the music to the set design to the masked dancers, reflects the international influences of Lin Hwai-min, who spent much of 1988–1991 traveling to Indonesia, India, Europe, the United States, and elsewhere.[11]

The influence of the Cloud Gate Dance Theater can be seen in the founding of smaller dance companies by former dancers. Many of these smaller dance companies also combine modern dance technique with Chinese and Taiwanese narratives to present meaningful modern pieces to Taiwanese audiences. The Taigu Tales Dance Theater, founded by Lin Hsiu-wei, is known for dances that express a spiritual and poetic quality. Lin Li-chen's "Legend," a full-length production in 1995, captures elements of Taiwanese temple rituals. The Dance Forum Taipei has presented postmodern style in Sunny Pang's "Cadaverous Capers," which is based on the novel *The Journey to the West*.

The lively modern dance scene in Taiwan well represents the dynamic elements of Taiwanese culture today. Choreographers and dancers simultaneously explore their Taiwanese roots as they reach out to incorporate a wide range of international influences. They express the Taiwanese identity of a culture rediscovering and delighting in its cultural past while becoming part of an international community.

ABORIGINAL MUSIC AND DANCE

Music and dance traditions of the island's aboriginal peoples express their stunning diversity of languages and culture. Their songs and dances recount traditional legends, tell love stories, celebrate harvests, and accompany daily work routines. At major rituals the dance and singing traditions have been passed on, but now migration and the loss of their language among the young diminish these occasions.

The vocal music of the Ami is the best known. Their joyful song "Balafang" is about visiting friends and shouting for joy. This song is heard in two minutes of the two-minute and fifty-second 1996 Olympics theme song "Return to Innocence" by Enigma.[12] The Ami singers whose voices were heard around the world, the married couple and community elders Difag (Mandarin name: Kuo Ying-nan) and Igay (Kuo Hsiu-chu), were not credited with the beautiful vocals. Ami singing is polyphonic, that is, several voices sing together or consecutively at different pitches. One distinctive aspect of Ami singing is a call-and-response style that uses meaningless syllables at points to carry the melody. The leadership of the singing reflects social status. The lead singer is usually a high-status elder who improvises lines to which the younger groups musically respond. The Ami live an agrarian lifestyle in eastern Taiwan. In song, they urge themselves on in their work; for weeding the paddyfield, for example, they sing, "Friends, we need this hard work, we the people of the land, let us not despise it! Friends, we will undertake this difficult task with joy, so that we may live off the fruits of our labors. Friends, have no fear of the difficulties, nor the burning sun, for we are only doing our duty."[13] The primary festival for the Ami, as for many indigenous peoples, is the Harvest Festival in July or August. The festival consists of all-night dancing and the call-and-response singing for which they are known. The elders of indigenous groups lament the decline of their traditional culture in the younger generations. As Ami elder Difag says, "Kids today can't even speak their mother tongue, and they don't participate very much in the harvest festival, so how will they be able to sing the songs?"[14]

The Bunun of central Taiwan have a highly developed harmonic musical tradition. Like those of the Ami, their songs are often call-and-response style, yet they also have choruses with three-, four-, or five-part harmony. Traditionally political authority was held by shaman healers, as shown in the following meeting song of the shamans:

> May our hands be strong.
> They have been straightened by these mystical chantings.
> May they acquire the power of healing.
> Is that not what Itudihanin [paradise] taught us?
> He taught us how to pray, how to carry out the hunting ritual.
> Whatever the sickness, may our hands know how to heal it!
> May they soothe pains of the chest and stomach.
> May they reduce fractures.
> What does it matter if you are in the grip of madness,
> when we are able to cure you.
> What does it matter if your ribs are cracked, if we can set them.
> Our hands are floating above your head.
> Let us join them together, giving them their healing power.[15]

The Paiwan and Rukai groups, both in the far south of Taiwan, are agricultural communities that live in walled or fenced-in villages. Their festivals are related to the agricultural calendar. Their grandest festival, called *maleva*, which takes place once in five years, includes singing, dancing, feasting, and games with the ancestor spirits. In addition to ancestor spirits, worshipped are the god of thunder, the goddess of creation, and the sun. Paiwan and Rukai vocal music is distinctive in its use of a drone in the chorus.[16] The Paiwan instrumental music is known for an unusual double-piped flute played by nose.

Because of their relative isolation, the Yami people of Orchid Island off the southern coast of Taiwan have retained more of their language and culture than have most surviving aboriginal people. They make highly decorated canoes without nails or glue, painting their crafts white, red, and black. Every year they perform ritual music and dance when they launch new canoes. They also celebrate the flying fish with ritual and the "hair dance" in which women rhythmically swing their long hair through the air.[17]

The Taiwanese have shown increased interest in the music and dance traditions of aboriginal peoples, realizing that it is their cultures that are most closely tied to the beautiful island that is their common home. Taiwanization has fostered a love for the beauty and distinctiveness of the island and thus brought about greater appreciation for those who first knew and loved the land.

Taiwanese history is reflected in the island's music and dance traditions. Whereas the earliest songs and dances of aboriginal peoples have survived to give evidence of the island's life before widespread immigration from the Chinese mainland, the popularity of modern dance and Western classical music reflects the push for modernization and westernization under the Meiji-era Japanese government. The popularity of Mandarin songs reflects both the legacy of the Guomindang's language policies before 1993 and the current forces of an East Asian music market, and the growing popularity of Taiwanese songs and increasing appreciation for traditional instrumental music reveal the current robust pride in all things Taiwanese.

NOTES

1. *Li ji, The Li Ki,* trans. by James Legge, The Sacred Books of the East, vols. 27 and 28 (Oxford: Clarendon Press, 1885), translation adapted by author.

2. Ping-hui Li, "Processional Music in Taiwanese Funerals," in Bell Yung, Evelyn S. Rawski, and Rubie S. Watson, eds., *Harmony and Counterpoint: Ritual Music in Chinese Context* (Stanford, CA: Stanford University Press, 1996), p. 144.

3. See B. Kaulbach and B. Proksch, *Arts and Culture in Taiwan* (Taipei: Southern Materials Center, 1984), p. 73.

4. For descriptions and illustrations of these musical instruments, see Cecilia S. L. Zung, *Secrets of the Chinese Drama* (New York: Benjamin Blom, 1964).

5. Recording by John Levy, *Chinese Taoist Music* (New York: Lyrichord Discs), LLST 7223.

6. This and another hymn to incense were recorded in Taiwan by John Levy, *Chinese Buddhist Music* (New York: Lyrichord Discs), LLST 7222.

7. Ku Lin-hsiu, "Teresa Teng Forever," trans. by Phil Newel, *Sinorama,* July 1995, pp. 6–19.

8. Michael Wester, "Making Waves in Mandarin," *Free China Review,* June 1994, p. 10.

9. Eugenia Yun, "A Place on the Pop Map," and Michael Wester, "The Queen of Taiwanese Music," *Free China Review*, June 1994, pp. 5–19.

10. Jackie Chen, "Images of a Century of Taiwanese Music," trans. by Phil Newell, *Sinorama*, June 1995, pp. 124–29.

11. For a description and photographs of Lin Hwai-min's "Nine Songs," see Sarah Brooks, "Songs of the Universe," photos by Liu Chen-hsiang, *Free China Review*, March 1994, pp. 65–73.

12. The group Enigma used the recording of the Ami on the CC *Polyphonies Vocales des Aborigenes de Taiwan* (Paris: Maison des Cultures du Monde et Chinese Folk Arts Foundation). These recordings were done in 1988 during a European tour of indigenous Taiwanese singers.

13. *Polyphonies Vocales des Aborigenes de Taiwan.*

14. Jackie Chen, "Ami Sounds Scale Olympic Heights," *Sinorama*, vol. 21, no. 9 (September 1996), p. 15.

15. English translation of these Bunun lyrics are from the liner notes of *Polyphonies des Vocales des Aborigenes de Taiwan;* no translator listed.

16. *Polyphonies Vocales des Aborigenes de Taiwan.*

17. *Republic of China Yearbook, 1997* (Taipei: Kwang Hwa Publishing, 1997).

SUGGESTED READING AND LISTENING

Levy, John. *Chinese Taoist Music.* New York: Lyrichord Discs, LLST 7223.

Levy, John. *Chinese Buddhist Music.* New York: Lyrichord Discs, LLST 7222.

Polyphonies Vocales des Aborigenes de Taiwan. Paris: Maison des Cultures du Monde et Chinese Folk Arts Foundation.

Articles on popular, classical, and aboriginal music in *Sinorama* and *Free China Review.*

5

Art and Literature

ARTISTS PRODUCING STUNNING visual and verbal images in Taiwan today are the inheritors of glorious cultural traditions. They live on an island where people of Chinese ethnicity, representing the world's longest continuous culture, came to dominate. This cultural tradition of mainland provenance flourished during the Dutch (1642–1661), Cheng Ch'eng-kung (1661–1684), and Qing (1644–1912) periods and has provided great inspiration for Taiwanese artists of the twentieth century. The work of nineteenth- and twentieth-century Western artists also came to exert considerable influence on the visual and literary artists of Taiwan. Here the Japanese colonial government played a considerable role, sponsoring select Taiwanese students for study at Japanese universities, where Western culture, technology, and science figured greatly in curricula. Taiwanese artists of the twentieth century have fashioned unique expressions of thought, sentiment, and vision, drawing upon Chinese and Western traditions with mounting attention to the Taiwanese turf upon which they practice their art. In the work of both visual artists and literary artists, themes close to the Taiwanese experience have grown ever more important, frequently touching base with the splendid tradition of crafts and folk arts on the island and increasingly attentive to the island's aboriginal heritage. Taiwanese artisans and craftspersons have traditionally worked their colorful magic upon the themes of everyday existence on an island frontier where life was tough, belief comforting, and dashes of vivid color invigorating to people who spent so much time knee-deep in rice paddies. Taiwanese artists today work in the context of a society that has gained unprecedented freedom in its creative expression and that is in the midst of an energetic search for identity. That search conducted now with all the persistence and time that prosperity allows, makes the contemporary artistic and literary scene on Taiwan an exciting place to inhabit.

North of the frantic commercial center of Taipei, perched on an impressive, verdant hillside, lies the greatest museum of Chinese art in the world: the National Palace Museum. This museum stands as a powerful reminder to Taiwanese artists of the grand Chinese tradition that represents part of their cultural ancestry. Appearing as if the fundamental Chinese statement of a civilization that came to stay, endure, and triumph, bronze drums of the Shang and Zhou dynasties stand on the first floor of the National Palace Museum, heavy, solid, eternal. A bronze ceremonial vessel known as the *yu* seems to express an enduring Chinese faith in the human spirit: A zoomorphic creature, reminiscent of the famous *taotie* design found on so many Chinese bronzes, holds a man in its mouth; the man peers out at the observer, smiling and undaunted. Han dynasty bronze mirrors, wall reliefs, clay figurines, and tomb tiles demonstrate a Confucian belief in the possibilities of humanity, the proper conduct of people in a harmonious social order, and the central place of China in the cosmos. Buddhist statuary demonstrates the impact of that Indian faith on the Chinese, particularly those of the sixth to the ninth centuries A.D., figures becoming ever more Chinese of appearance and given to Mahayana objects of worship. And in many different art forms the Taoist influence is pervasive, helping to relieve creative spirits of the tight strictures of Confucianism, suggesting a mystical force that unites humankind with nature. This is a cultural heritage breathtaking in scope, one of several streams of inspiration from which Taiwanese artists may draw.[1] The arts of the brush are part of the heritage brought from Fujian and Guangdong, then other mainland provinces. The Chinese revere brush and ink as the tools of their highest artistic expression.

Explored in the pages that follow are the realms of this exciting world and their cultural context. Special attention is given to Taiwanese calligraphy, painting, other contemporary visual arts, poetry, prose, crafts, and folk arts.

CALLIGRAPHY

Calligraphy (the artistic rendering of the Chinese character with brush and ink) and painting surpassed the other arts of China in the centuries after the Tang (A.D. 618–906). No other art forms rival these for permanence and degree of influence on the Taiwanese visual artist of today. Of these two, calligraphy has priority of place. The intimate connection of these two supreme arts and their relative status is indicated in the Mandarin term *shuhua* (calligraphy-painting). As early as the Han dynasty, calligraphy was recognized as highly revelatory of a person's refinement and character. In subsequent dynasties there were officials who made sure that documents were written with proper strokes of the brush; in the Tang this official was known as the "master of calligraphy." In Ming and Qing times calligraphy was considered so important as an indicator of quality in a civil service candidate that some judges concentrated more on the strokes of the examinee's brush than on insightful analysis or mastery of the classics themselves. Calligraphy developed as an independent art featuring numerous styles, evolving from the early elongated, curved lines of the "official seal" (*zhuan*) script; to the square, flat style of the "clerical" (*li*) script; to the graceful lines of the cursive or "free-flowing" (*cao*) script; to those popularized in contemporary times, the "standard" (*gai*) and semicursive or "running" (*xing*) script, the latter a hybrid of the "free-flowing" and "standard" styles.[2]

"Four treasures" are necessary to the art of the calligrapher: the calligrapher's brush (*maobi*), paper, ink, and inkstone.[3] The *maobi* combines a long, straight handle of wood or bamboo with a round tip that comes to a point. Made of rabbit, wolf, or deer hair, the point is soft yet firm and responsive. Silk makes an elegant canvas, but paper more readily reveals the speed of the brush, the level of skill used in its handling, and the judgment used by the calligrapher in deciding how much ink should be used. Paper is more unforgiving, a calligrapher's greater challenge, much as an actor finds greater challenge on stage than in movies or television. The calligrapher's ink originates in a dry stick made from lampblack mixed with glue; to the stick a bit of water is added, then the stick is rubbed into an inkstone. Grinding the ink is a slow ritual that calms the calligrapher and focuses her or his attention so that an inner spirituality reveals itself as the artist creates.

Tradition set high standards for the very most ideal implements of the calligrapher's art. Superior brushes would be made with the pelt of an animal captured during the first weeks of March. The best inkstone would grind ink quickly and would be "cold" enough to keep the fluid wet for long periods; it might come from a famous mountain far away. The choicest inks were made from the smallest particles of smoke, gathered from the burning pine wood of *tong* oil, and then beaten thousands of times to improve quality. The finest papers were made using the cleanest water, capable of washing all impurities from the pulp.[4] Once in the hands of the calligrapher, these best of materials were handled with all the care they deserved. Every dot was rendered as if it held a world of meaning; indeed, for all they contributed to the whole of the work, the dots, lines, all marks that went down on the calligrapher's fine paper, were intended to stand on their own.

Fine calligraphy is thought to be a product of character and dedication, making a strong emotional impact upon the admirer. Wu Tsia-luan was no conventional calligrapher; a person of Tang times, she was at once a great artist in a form dominated by male scholars and a paragon of feminine virtue: She reputedly went to work every day for ten years to support her ailing husband, becoming so honored in the folk tradition that she gained deification as an immortal believed to have flown to the heavens on the back of a tiger. Wang Xizhi's characters are said to have an aural effect, a "sound like being on the verge of tears." Yang Xiong of the Western Han described calligraphy as "pictures of the heart." Great calligraphers are keen observers of nature. Wang Xizhi's teacher taught him to watch rocks falling off mountains in order to draw a dot; to observe clouds stretching flat across the sky in order to draw a horizontal line; and to meditate upon a 10,000-year-old vine so as to draw a vertical line. Wang also thrilled at the sight of geese, whose graceful necks found their way into his fluid calligraphy. Wen Youge found in his witnessing of combatant snakes inspiration of sufficient power to take him to new levels in his art. *Cao*-style master Zhang Xu of the Tang got revelations from the "swordplay" of the sun and the "hooting horns" of the owl. Another Tang master, Huai Su, studied the fantastic shapes of summer clouds to capture the majesty and mystery of mountains with proper emotional impact.[5]

Calligraphy necessitates both "composition" (*jieti*) and "feeling" (*biqing*). The long practice required to produce calligraphy with the grace of the masters resulted in treasured tales of dedication. Reputedly, when Wang Xizhi sat by a pond practicing calligraphy, all the pond's water became ink. The monk Ji Yong spent fifteen years in his attic without coming down in order to perfect his calligraphy. Erudition and wisdom were thought essential to the fine calligrapher. Said Song-era calligrapher Hong Tingjian: "The aura of a learned man's brush will show he has read a myriad of books; otherwise, he is just an unartistic bureaucrat."[6]

Calligraphy offers as interesting a challenge to one seeking the soul of contemporary Taiwan as any cultural realm. Taiwan is now one of the most highly computerized societies in the world; when people are not at their keyboards, they use a ball point, not brush, to execute the tasks of the pen. Children receive rudimentary training in the arts of the brush in elementary school, but by the time they reach high school they practice calligraphy as an extracurricular activity, if at all. Such organizations as the Republic of China Calligraphy Association and the Ho Chuang-shih Calligraphy Foundation, though, are at the forefront of an effort to sponsor contests and classes making calligraphy more accessible to the Taiwanese public. Taipei's Minchu Elementary school has attracted wide notice for the special emphasis it places on calligraphy in the curriculum. Parents of older students, too, are finding that even in an exam-driven educational system the mental focus required by calligraphy has practical utility as well as aesthetic and cultural value.

Devotees of calligraphy practiced with full attention to proper steps and rituals argue forcefully that calligraphy has much to offer the contemporary Taiwanese: heightened patience, emotional control, artistic appreciation, mental focus, spiritual insight, and physical relaxation. As in traditional times, students of the art of calligraphy hold the firm belief that the strokes of the brush reveal the character of the person who produces them. Buddhist master Hung Yi is held to reveal in his calligraphy the high degree of self-cultivation, mental discipline, and spiritual focus for which he is known. To students of contemporary calligraphic art in Taiwan, Chi Pai-shih reveals with the sweep of his brush that cordiality and sincerity that echoes his personality.[7] Practitioners of the traditional art in contemporary Taiwan start with the time-honored step of imitation, only gradually proceeding to develop a personal style. Many of those who have dedicated themselves to the art of calligraphy have found the hours of time devoted to their craft have their economic rewards. Taiwan has a number of calligraphers notable for their work on newspaper mastheads, restaurant signs, and bank "chop" (a specially carved Chinese stamp for fixing official signatures) designs.

Some calligraphers in Taiwan are not content just to practice the traditional form or even to find a unique style within the tradition. Those who search for a more contemporary spirit in calligraphy take note of current forms in Japan, which have attracted international attention. Japanese calligraphers emphasize "manifestations of ink" (*bokusho*) controlled by the ink's concentration and moisture to achieve imposing structure and intriguing feeling in their brushwork, giving great attention to form and shape. Characters are deconstructed, becoming very abstract: The rendering of "dragon" in a calligraphic work frequently features the actual form of the mythological beast rather than the Chinese character itself. Inspired by such innovations, Taiwanese artists of the "Ink and Wave Society" have taken their own liberties with the Chinese character. Lien Te-sen became famous for his rendering of the character *xing*, meaning "motion," into several disconnected pieces, surrounding the character *gui*, "turtle," written in ancient script, all of which was meant to mock Taipei's clogged traffic and slow construction of the city's long-awaited mass transit system. Hsu Yung-chin wrote the four large characters for the "Republic of China" (*zhonghua minguo*) on paper and brushed over them with light ink, pasting strips of red paper symbolizing the ROC flag in the blank spots; entitled the "Unfocusable Republic of China," the work demonstrates a very contemporary combination of calligraphy and painting in an artistic search for societal definition, as well as a freedom in political and social commentary that would have been unthinkable well into the 1980s.[8]

More traditional calligraphic artists find this liberal use of the Chinese character disturbing, and in general there seems to be an unsettled state among the community of calligraphers in Taiwan that yet awaits a contemporary synthesis. Renewed public interest, artistic skill, and fervent will are there, but the definition is in the making, not yet attained. Taiwanese painters have in the course of the twentieth century more confidently embraced the themes of modernity, referring in their work to tradition while expressing themselves on contemporary issues.

PAINTING

Although traditional Chinese painting is associated most with the great work of landscape artists, the human figure attracted the initial interest of the Chinese painter. One of the earliest extant examples of Chinese painting is a Warring States (the fifth to the third centuries B.C.) period work, "Lady with Bird and Dragon," featuring a woman in profile with dragon and phoenix in front of her. Artists of later generations such as Gu Kaizhi (A.D. 344–406), Yan Liben (d. 673), and Gu Hongzhong (mid-tenth century) developed a great tradition of figure painting on handscrolls, conveying Confucian themes of gentlemanly restraint and loyal self-sacrifice and capturing a wide variety of personalities: the robustly military, the pensively literary, the highly gregarious. A famous work of Zhang Zetuan of the Southern Song period uses the handscroll format with similar interest in human activity but on a much more panoramic scale, showing the teeming life flowing into and dwelling within the Northern Song capital of Kaifeng. In a sense this human activity in panorama provides a bridge between the figure painters of the early dynasties and the landscape tradition that became dominant during the Song and forever changed the way the Chinese thought about art. Painters such as Fan Guan, Xia Gui, and Zhao Mengfu produced elegant work of sophisticated composition; their works purposefully moved the viewer's eye through particular levels of their paintings, ultimately calling attention to mountains that encompassed humanity, mist that suggested the mystery of the Tao, or verdant forests "far," as Buddhists would say, "from the din of the dusty world." In the Yuan dynasty Ni Zan and other painters developed a school of painting quite different from that of the Song masters. "Literati" painters in this style sought to reveal the personal taste, spirit, experience with nature, classical education, and yearning for freedom among scholar-bureaucrats at a time when the alien Mongols were in control at the highest levels. This style could feature whimsy as well as solemnity. It put a premium on economical brushwork of a quality that shows with great clarity the kinship of Chinese painting and calligraphy.[9]

Chinese painters on the mainland and Taiwan during the late dynastic period took their cues from the great Song landscape and Yuan literati painters. Twentieth-century painters on Taiwan have painted with ample reference to those traditions but have shown at least as much interest in Western styles and in the unique culture and social experience of the island of Taiwan. Chen Cheng-po (1895–1947) used oil paints, rather than the ink medium of the Song landscape and Yuan literati styles; his subject matter, though, was not foreign but very close to home: the idyllic Taiwan of fifty years ago.[10] His series on the old port town of Tamsui reveals old-fashioned red tile roofs stretching lazily along the bank of the river that is the town's namesake, the townspeople ambling up and down the winding road as they go about their daily chores. His *Suburbs of Chiayi* shows an old grandmother keeping busy in her backyard. Laundry hangs from bamboo poles behind her. Chickens peck the ground for food. Chen's art is classified stylistically as Taiwanese impressionism, revealing the influence of years spent in study of modern Western art at Tokyo Fine Arts College during the colonial era. As to content, he is revered by young back-to-roots artists in Taiwan today for his seminal contributions to Taiwan's first generation of Nativist painting. Chen painted outdoors, directly from nature, employing quick, distinct dabs of color with swirling, vigorous brushstrokes reminiscent of Van Gogh. A painting like his *Fresh Flow* (1929) also reveals an ochre-based color scheme and precise structural composition influenced by Cezanne.

Despite the considerable influence of Western painting on Chen's style, one discerns in his art references to traditional Chinese painting. The mountain peak rising through mist on a hazy Taiwan morning in the background of *Fresh Flow* shows at once a respect for the Song landscape tradition and energetic brushwork to make a Yuan literati painter proud. His scenes and subject matter are most frequently those of his native land. Numerous sun-baked landscapes painted by Chen glow with the colors of central Taiwan. Hot air steams forth from the yellow soil. Dense green foliage echoes the red brick walls. Modern forms, social history, pride in tradition: These create feelings of exquisite nostalgia not only in Taiwanese folk but also in foreigners who have caught precious glimpses of these scenes in travels through rural

Taiwan. Chen Cheng-po's death in 1947 came in the roundup and execution of notable intellectuals that accompanied the February 28th Incident. An aura of martyrdom therefore further endears him to young Nativist painters in Taiwan today.

Pan Chaur-sen, a former art teacher, provides another example of a Taiwanese oil painter in whose work one observes the life of the island. In his long teaching career he experimented with surrealism and abstractionism and with still life, rural scenes, and foreign landscapes. He arrived ultimately at a unique, symbolic style, the striking effect of which is amplified in his bold use of color. He says that in his days as a teacher, he learned much from children's open-minded use of color. There is a concern for unity in many of Pan's paintings that subtly harks back to the neo-Confucian quest for order that so informed the work of the Song masters. His *Wanting to Fly* (1994) pictures a young nude in close-eyed dreams of birds in flight, suggesting a Taoist flight of fantasy, particularly the 10,000 *li* that the imminent philosopher Zhuangzi traversed through the medium of mind. Pan Chaursen's work has a universal quality about it, yet it contains numerous personal and cultural references. A frequently recurring personage in his paintings is based on a young woman with whom he had a fleeting, memorable romance before losing touch. She is identifiably Chinese but rendered in a style that owes much to Western expressionism. Pan presents a trademark rendering of her with crossed arms and mouth shut. In *A Day of Selling Fish* she appears amidst the clutter and crowding of Taiwanese houses that provide a suggestion of cultural flavor that Pan, unlike Chen Cheng-po, incorporates into rather than focuses upon in his oil paintings.[11]

Discerning viewers of the work of ink painters Peng Kang-lung (b. 1962) and Lee Ku-mo (b. 1941) find large doses of the mystery and the whimsy that characterized Yuan literati painters. Peng uses traditional ink, brushes, and mineral pigments to achieve a unique, heavy style focused on the principal subject of a painting. He frequently employs exaggerated shapes and individualistic composition to impose his personal will on the viewer. His *Fine Snow* (1986), *Autumn Wilds* (1993), and *The Chill of Spring* (1990) characteristically show strong, dry brushstrokes and the prominence of a massive mountain that relentlessly squeezes secondary objects into a bottom corner. The disquiet, even desolation, that the viewer feels when gazing at *Autumn Wilds* echoes the similar effect frequently found in Yuan literati paintings. His restlessly twisted brushstrokes portray an irrepressible nature made ill-tempered by the habits of humanity. Lee Ku-mo uses similar tools to portray the whimsy that frequently found its way into literati landscapes. One of his paintings, *On the Point of Feeling Something about This Inscription*, amounts to a playful dig at the famous calligrapher Wang Xizhi, he of the claim that his understanding of art was the product of a flash of inspiration triggered by watching geese swim and move. Lee reverses the arrangement in his painting, showing the geese peering at a wall filled with Wang's famous script, apparently finding in the master's calligraphy the inspiration that he found in them.[12]

Tseng Yu-wen (b. 1954) and Kuo Chuan-chiu (b. 1960) are painters who have experimented their way to highly personal statements in their art. In the late 1970s Tseng utilized ink and watercolor in focusing on rather traditional subjects: houses, mangroves, egrets. But he came to discover that oil paints best suit the intensity of the folk motifs that had filled his childhood and to which he was turning increasingly for subject matter. His paintings in one sense represent a kind of update on Chen Cheng-po's Taiwanese countryside, showing folk forms that Tseng remembers from the late 1950s and 1960s. His experimentation gradually brought him to a distinctive style showing closeup folk motifs in raw contrasts of emerald green, indigo blue, bright yellow, and vermilion. The titles of Tseng's paintings reveal the subject matter that has come to dominate: *Blackroofed House, Door Gods, Window, The Eight Immortals, Temple Lanterns*. Clearly, this is a painter with strong Nativist leanings: "My paintings must have a strong Taiwanese flavor, so when people see them they can feel Taiwan immediately. . . . I've always wanted to show the happy, peace-loving atmosphere of the old Taiwan."[13]

Kuo Chuan-chiu is most notable for her sophisticated utilization of crayon. She is another artist of relative youth but old enough to remember fondly a rural upbringing, in her case a fishing village near Keelung. Critics have received her meditative, romantic, imaginative, delicate work such as *Lamp, Silent Music, Yellow Blossoms on Child's Hill, Music of Light, A Threatening Silence*, and *Rock Garden* with enthusiasm. She believes in delivering a massive image with understated power, framing the work in the "simplest but finest structure." Toward that end, she crops many of her paintings to about twelve-by-sixteen inches, eliminating all but the essential elements, arriving finally at just the right economy of expression. This sense of power in the apparently small reveals an ongoing influence of Taoism in Chinese painting, and as unique as her images appear, her focus on nature with a diminished role for humankind echoes the style that dominated the work of most post-Tang painters in the days of the emperors.[14]

Given that many of these painters focused their work on Taiwan, on fond memories of a simpler time, and on the search for the island's contemporary identity, the interest attracted by the painter Yu Cheng-yao (1898–1993) in the latter years of his life seems poignant. Yu was a mainlander, a lieutenant general who fought in the Guomindang army against the Japanese, then against the Communists. But he hated the business of war and retired in 1946, at the formal start of the civil war. A native of Fujian Province, he was on business as a trader in medicinal herbs in Taiwan when the Communists achieved their victory; speaking the language, not wishing to live under the rule of those he had fought, he stayed. He quickly tired of business, though, and in the grand Chinese tradition of the world-weary, thoughtful soul, he retired to the life of a recluse in a rural hovel. He took up painting after deciding that the landscapes in the National Palace Museum did not reflect accurately the scenes that he had witnessed on his extensive travels on the mainland. He found them "too mild, too flat—not energetic or changeable enough, and lacking in the necessary tight structuring and shade." Using cheap brushes, inkstone, and pigments as befitting his humble economic circumstances, Yu gave unique renderings in a form reminiscent of the Song, Ming, and Qing masters that eventually caught the eye of Kansas City University professor Li Chu-chin. Wealth had little appeal to Yu, but today his work sells at astronomical prices. Taiwanese art enthusiasts seem to find very appealing some combination of Yu Cheng-yao's withdrawal from officialdom and then commerce for the pure life of the secluded artist; the exquisite work he did in isolation; and the symbolic connection of disparate, even contending, forces inherent in his mainlander but Fujianese status. The old man's life speaks to those engaged in the contemporary Taiwanese search for rootedness, identity, and meaning.[15]

Arts of the brush dominate, but other forms of visual expression are gaining attention in the increasingly cosmopolitan universe of the Taiwanese.

Photographer Cheng San-hsi has received considerable fame for his straightforward, unpretentious photographs of old Taiwan, some taken nearly forty years ago. At the Taipei Fine Arts Museum, founded in 1986, an array of modern visual art can be found on display. In 1996 the museum featured a Taipei Biennial exhibit indicating four sources of Taiwanese culture that await synthesis: traditional Chinese culture, aboriginal culture, the cultural legacy of the Japanese colonial period, and the local manifestations of Western culture. A recent exhibit entitled "Mutant Materials in Contemporary Design" featured items of international commercial design utilizing a host of materials including wood, metals, ceramics, glass, plastic, fibers and composites, rubber and foam, gels, and recycled materials.

Creative artists employing the written word as their mode of expression evidence in their work that respect for tradition, together with a desire to convey a contemporary spirit, that one sees in the visual arts of Taiwan. This search for a culturally valid contemporary literature is clearly seen in the work of Taiwanese poets.

POETRY

Poetry was a traditional art that all cultivated Chinese gentlemen were expected to practice skillfully. For guidance, they could draw upon a long and glorious literature produced by those who practiced the art at its height. That literature begins with the collection of poetic songs of the early Zhou dynasty known as the *Classic of Odes* (*Shi jing*). Rendered in four-character lines, the even numbers of which rhymed, the poems featured frequent refrains and occasional alliteration and internal rhyme. Another collection featuring pre-Han poetry was the *Songs of the South* (third century B.C.), compiled in the state of Chu in the Yangtze Valley; these poems were freer in form than those of the *Classic of Odes*, and though making a stab at didactic themes, they were more given to flights of fancy and magical deeds.[16]

Three major forms of Chinese poetry evolved in the course of the Han dynasty. The *fu* was a demanding form that featured prose introductions building rhythmically into the poem proper. The *yuefu* was rendered more simply, with more direct imagery, focused thematically on the daily life of the people. The *shi* form featured either five-character lines with a caesura (a stop in the midst of a line to stress meaning) after the second character or, alternatively, seven-character lines with a caesura after the fourth character in each line. This became the most influential poetic form in the Chinese tradition and gave to modern Chinese the character meaning "poetry." During the Tang dynasty significant innovations upon this basic style were made, in particular a highly regulated, eight-line version and a somewhat less demanding four-line rendering. Although the Song and later dynasties would produce fine poets, the Tang is considered by the Chinese to be their great age of poetry. Of many fine poets during the Tang dynasty, Li Bo and Du Fu stand out. Li Bo employed lushly colorful language evoking drunken, romantic, and sometimes even childlike visions. Du Fu is generally regarded as the greatest poet in all Chinese history, packing allusion, word play, and themes of Confucian responsibility into the demanding eight-line *shi* form, with its elaborate requirements for verbal and tonal parallelism.

May Fourth–era intellectual ferment resulted in the call of Hu Shi, Cai Yuanpei, and others at Beijing University for a colloquial style of writing that could expand the Chinese reading public and usher in a modern age of social reform. Xu Zhimo and other mainland writers ushered in an age of modern

Chinese poetry that employed "plain speech" (*baihua*) capturing the ca-
dences and phrasings of everyday conversations in freer poetic forms than
those of the classical era.[17] This modern style of Chinese poetry revealed
considerable Western influence at the same time it reflected a search for the
soul of modern China. On Taiwan, poets studied Western styles but produced a literature highly unique because of the impact of the Japanese education Taiwanese intellectuals received prior to 1945. This poetry frequently
focused thematically on Taiwan's predicament but utilized the language of
the colonizers.

Lin Heng-tai is to Taiwanese poetry what Chen Cheng-po is to Taiwanese
painting.[18] The course of his life and art constitutes an overview of the development of Taiwanese poetry in the twentieth century. Born in 1924 in
Taichung in the heart of the Japanese colonial era, Lin wrote all his early
material in Japanese; yet early on his poetry took up Nativist themes that
today make him a hero in the eyes of young Taiwanese writers, just as Chen's
painting endears him to young painters. At the age of sixteen Lin moved to
Taipei, where he gained introduction both to modern Japanese poetry and
to classical Chinese poetry in Japanese translation. He also discovered modern
Chinese writers such as Hu Shi, Lu Xun, Guo Moro, and Lin Yutang. His
poems of the early 1940s mingle youthful introspection with insights into
the pain felt by the Taiwanese during the tough wartime years of the Japanese
occupation. After the war, at the urging of fellow poet Chu Shih, Lin Heng-
tai joined the Silver Bell Poetry Society. This society had been founded in
1942 at Taichung First High School by three students who published a
mimeographed magazine, *Green Grass*, with their poetry written entirely in
Japanese. The publication continued under the name *The Tide*, following
Retrocession. Lin and other young writers in the society came under the
influence of Yang Kui, who frequently published his Minnan dialect poems
and folk songs in *The Tide*. Lin frequently visited this mentor at his home
near Taichung, taking to heart Yang's injunction that poets should seek the
reality of experience among the people themselves, to produce his poem
"Walls":

> Some rich and influential families
> Have been building the walls all year round
> But it's sad the neighbor is a thief
> They talk business all year round on the street
> But a graveyard is just off the street
> Intelligent people
> Do you know

What will grow
From the seeds you are sowing?

Lin's poem was meant to point out the economic injustice existing in Taiwan during the 1940s. "Walls" targeted families that had been content to prosper under Japanese rule or under the Guomintang, caring little for the needs of those less fortunate.

Guomindang authorities were not enamored of this kind of social criticism. In the aftermath of an islandwide crackdown that began on April 6, 1949, the Silver Bell Society was decimated. Lin caught a fleeting glimpse of Yang Kui as he stood on a railroad platform awaiting his transport to Green Island Prison, where he would spend twenty years. At least one member of the society was executed, and another fled to the mainland; the lucky ones, including Lin Heng-tai, were merely detained, harassed, and eventually released. The legacy of the Silver Bell Society, was huge. It embodied the realist spirit that characterized much of occupation-period literature: Anti-imperialist, socially engaged, infused with Nativist spirit, the publication introduced Taiwanese intellectuals to the ideas of Pushkin, Tolstoy, Baudelaire, and Verlaine and featured expositions of European symbolism, surrealism, and neo-realism. The biting social satire of the mainland's Lu Hsun appeared frequently in *The Tide*, and movement toward the "plain speech," vernacular style was evident. There was also the fighting spirit that pervaded the magazine, typifying a people who have come through times of enormous adversity to outlast many of those who would use their bountiful physical and intellectual energy for their own purposes.

Martial law took effect in May 1949. The Guomindang government banned writing in Japanese, overtly a patriotic act but also designed to undermine a generation of intellectuals who were most comfortable with the language of the colonizers. In 1950 the government established the Chinese Literature and Art Awards Committee and the Chinese Literature and Art Association, seeking to promote anticommunist and antileftist ideas and to remove anything it deemed smut. Lin and others outfoxed the authorities by mastering written Chinese and channeling expressions of lonely inner dissent into pieces the authorities would be hard pressed to ban. Lin's work of this period—exemplified in his haiku-like testimony to day's end at the height of summer in Taiwan—foreshadows the Nativist interest that would burgeon in the 1970s:

mosquitoes
in the banana grove
harassing

In 1956 the poet Chi Hsien took the lead in establishing the Modern Poetry Society; he successfully sought the participation of Lin Heng-tai and other major poets, who in an intellectually repressive atmosphere turned to stylistic experimentation as the main focus of their creative energies. Lin Heng-tai's famous paired "Landscape No. 1" and "Landscape No. 2" provide salient examples of the modernist experimentation going on in the late 1950s and early 1960s. The former goes as follows:

> crops next
> to more
> crops next
> to more
> crops next
> to more
> sunlightsunlight shone upon the ears long
> sunlightsunlight shone upon the neck long

The second in the "Landscape" pair reads:

> windbreak
> outside   another
> windbreak
> outside   another
> windbreak
> outside   another
>
> but the sea   and the arranged waves
> but the sea   and the arranged waves

Trees and waves achieve symmetrical resonance and offer the silent mystery of nature in between. The first poem in the pairing expresses a farmer's hope; the second shows the power of nature lurking behind human attempts to mitigate its awesome force.

By 1963, modernist experimentation had lost its vigor; the following year Lin joined twelve others in forming the Li Poetry Society, with the avowed goal of returning to the realism of Taiwanese poetry of the 1930s. Lin's "Dirty Faces" (1972) shows a return to concerns about social injustice; the last stanza reads:

> At night the world changes, everything changes.
> Isn't there more dust on the window sill this morning?

Won't the road be even rougher tomorrow?
And won't it all happen while everyone is sound asleep?

By the late 1970s, Taiwanese society had reached a point in its postwar development at which young poets were straining to break free of the noose the government had placed on intellectuals. "Native soil literary debates" raged: The government argued that Nativists were veering into proletarian literature all too reminiscent of the social realism of the communist mainland; Nativists replied that they were returning to a form that harked back to the 1930s and reflected the legitimate political and social concerns of the writer. Lin Heng-tai believed both arguments were overwrought, but political commentary in his work of the 1980s and 1990s has revealed greater sympathy with the Nativist position. His "One Party System" reads as follows:

the toy piano
on the table
has just

white keys
black keys

all having but
one sound

And in 1988 he expressed at once his love for the island of his nativity and his concern about the price of contemporary economic success:

Painted in green
O, Taiwan, beautiful island
I've lived here for sixty years
This is the first time I've left you
Looking down from the clouds proves further
O, Taiwan, that you are lovely

Rocky coast inlaid among white waves
O, Taiwan, beautiful island
Away from you for a time
I come back
Leaving the airport, I discover to my surprise
O, Taiwan, that you are a filthy mess

In retrospect, poets and poetry critics now appreciate the efforts made by the Blue Sky Poetry Society in the 1950s to defend less abstruse, more emo-

tional verse against the stylistic experiments of modernists.[19] Inspired by the
passion, vitality, and social conscience that Lin, noted poet Luo Fu, and the
Nativists brought to Taiwanese poetry from the 1970s onward, young poets
in Taiwan today are seeking to make poetry more accessible and relevant to
the public. In 1974 National Taiwan University student Yang Hsien set
poems by Yu Kuang-chung to music and held a concert in Chungshan Hall
as part of Yang's efforts to create "modern folk music." Particularly well
received was Yu's "Nostalgia for My Hometown":

> When I was small, nostalgia for my hometown was a tiny postage
>   stamp
> I am here and my mother is there
> After growing up, nostalgia was a very thin boat ticket
> I am here and my bride is there
> Later, nostalgia for my hometown was a small gravestone
> I am outside, my mother is inside
> Now nostalgia for my hometown is a shallow strait
> I am here and mainland China is there[20]

In the mid-1980s the poet To She-sun released *Spoken Poetry of To She-
sun* and produced a reading of his works by Chao Tien-fu. Set to the sound
of mining shovels, trains, and heartbeats and backed by the music of a traditional instrument, the *erhu*, the poem "Coal," lamenting a recent mining
accident, struck an especially responsive note with the audience:

> Child, it is fixed that the colors of our lives are
> Dug up from the blackness of the earth
> The green vegetables and white rice on our dinner table
> The colorful second-run movies in the street
> Mother's red slippers
> All of these require father's sweat, and are dug up from the blackness
> after today father will no longer be spending time with you[21]

In 1992 poet Chang Shang-hua began hosting a radio program in which
she enthralls listeners with her engaging voice, reading her own and others'
poetry, introducing the writers, and explaining the imagery, meaning, and
aesthetic value of the poems. Chang has also recorded a CD entitled "Tea
Does Not Speak," an enchanting synthesis of her poetry with the music of
composer Weng Chih-heng. Traditional instruments such as the *erhu* and
the *nanhu* appear on many of the pieces; modern piano and guitar accompany

others, producing styles ranging from Chinese and Western classical to jazz. A guitar accompanies Chang on "A Sheet of Blotting Paper":

> I am a sheet of blotting paper
> Lightly pressed against the page
> you've written on
> Absorbing the drops you left there[22]

At times with great courage in the face of government disapproval, poets such as Chen Ming-jen and Li Min-yung have pioneered poetry readings in the Minnan (Fujianese) dialect. During the 1990s the government has made an about-face on the dialect question and in general has supported efforts to bring poetry to the public. In 1995 the Council for Cultural Planning and Development sponsored a program of poetry and music featuring Chang Cheng-chieh's violin in accompaniment to the noted poet Hsiang Yang.[23] Poetry seems to be attracting a genuine public following in today's Taiwan, as people assess the state of their lives and the meaning of life outside of economic success.

Perhaps this public response to poets literally giving voice to their art holds promise for the fate of poetry rendered in another vein, namely, through the poetry societies that exist in towns and cities around the island, the membership of which is comprised mainly of older people who have long been interested in amateur poetry composed in styles rooted in the Ming and Qing dynastic periods.[24] The custom of old was to tie a coin above a bronze bowl and attach an inch-long stick of incense to the middle of the thread, lit when the topic was given. When the stick was used up and the thread burned, the coin would fall to the bowl with a "dong" and the contest would be over. Thus, the poems rendered by these societies, though their composition is now timed with watches, are to this day known as "hitting the bowl" poems. The associations have long histories on the mainland and in Taiwan, and as a rule they have a close association with local Taiwanese culture and temple fair activities.

Just as Taiwanese poets have drawn from multiple sources available to creative spirits on the island, those Taiwanese who take up pen to create works of contemporary prose find ample inspiration both in the great Chinese tradition and in the triumphs and turmoil of a rapidly changing society.

PROSE

As valued as poetry is in the Chinese cultural tradition, writers of prose were even more voluminous in their output. As indicated by the esteem in which calligraphy is held, few people revere the written word as do the Chinese. Prose writers used ink generously in their production of works emphasizing history and social philosophy.[25] Since Song times, scholars who strove to pass the civil service examinations had to master the Four Books, the Five Classics, and the respected commentaries on those texts that gained a kind of canonical status, chosen for their emphasis on the moral cultivation and social harmony stressed by Confucius. Great Han historians Sima Qian (c. 145–90 B.C.) and Ban Gu (A.D 32–92) demonstrated straightforward stylistic grandeur unequaled in later dynasties, but court-sponsored, detailed dynastic histories have given the Chinese the reputation of being the most history-minded people on earth.

Over the centuries preceding the Tang dynasty, a style known as "parallel prose" (*pianwen*) developed. Used for memorials, letters, and most other prose forms, the style featured parallel phrases tailored in equal units of four, five, or six characters, with occasional rhyme and tonal euphony. In time this style became highly formalized and pretentious. At mid-Tang the writer Han Yu (768–824) ushered in a more straightforward style so clearly modeled on the work of Sima Qian and Ban Gu that it became known as the "ancient style" (*guwen*). Writers in the Song dynasty used this style so effectively that the tenth through thirteenth centuries became the great age of contemporary Chinese prose. In succeeding dynasties scholars reverted to more florid, convoluted written expression, and by Qing times candidates were expected to answer examinations in the highly contrived "eight-legged essay" style. All these forms were rendered in phrases so terse and formalized as to be unrecognizable to mere speakers of the language. Collectively these styles were known as the "language of the literary word" (*wenyanwen*).

Colloquialisms did, however, creep into Chinese fiction. Fiction developed from Taoist tales of fanciful journeys of the mind, alchemy, supernatural and mythological lore, Indian tales carried by Buddhist monks, and popular biographical accounts focused on recluses and eccentrics. Such sources provided the material for "wonder tales" (*chuanji*), "popularizations" (*bianwen*), and storytellers' "prompt books" (*huaben*) that in turn influenced the authors of great Ming-era novels: *Water Margin, Romance of the Three Kingdoms, Journey to the West, Golden Lotus,* and *Dream of the Red Chamber.* Not until the May Fourth Movement of the 1920s, bringing the New Culture emphasis on "plain speech" (*baihua*), did written works truly reflect the ordinary speech of the people.

Twentieth-century mainland "plain speech" writers such as Lu Xun, Guo Moro, and Lao She were well read in their own tradition as well as in the works of great Western fiction. In their short stories and novels these fine authors probed tradition and modernity in search of a new identity for China. The search for a contemporary identity also figures heavily in the work of Taiwanese authors. Taiwanese writers of prose literature probe for the soul of a society that has its own currency, passports, military, and flag yet still engages in energetic political discussions over whether it is a country, a province, or forever destined to be a special political entity. Much like today's painters and poets, many Taiwanese short-story writers reveal a longing for a simpler time, lost forever. In his "Rustic Quandary," Shu Kuo-shih uses a rhythmical style recalling a proud Chinese tradition of poetry-influenced prose to capture the atmosphere and comforting routines of the old society, where everyone knew who she or he was and where she or he belonged:

> One thing after another, there were endless things to do. When you had finally finished everything that needed doing, and your hair was properly combed, a whole life had been used up.[26]

In Shu's story, a stranger appears on a ridge looking out at farmers hard at work in the fields rimming their village. Neither the stranger nor the farmers venture an introduction, but one at a time the farmers turn to stare at the stranger. Their thoughts are made known to the reader, and what they reveal in their perceptions and dreams says much about the fuzzy identity of Taiwanese people at the close of the twentieth century.

In "Everybody Needs Ch'in Te-fu," Huang Fan provides several signposts of contemporary Taiwanese society: a son living in America, a virtual stranger to his family; an ingeniously run, "wild chicken" (illegal) bus company; a mistress who deftly maneuvers a bequest from a recently deceased lover without attracting the attention of his wife. In describing the protagonist of the story, the narrator says:

> He was one of the few truly rich and powerful figures in upper-class circles in Taipei. They really despised him, mocked his background, his wife who dressed like a cabaret girl, and his lavish, extravagant, but utterly purposeless and tasteless parties. Nevertheless Ch'in Te-fu remained popular and was welcome everywhere. He was the perfect representative of this rapidly changing society which is getting more and more difficult to understand.

Huang Fan is a writer with fond memories of a saner, calmer Taipei before motor vehicles, entrepreneurs on the make, and multisource pollution clogged its streets. In "Tung P'u Street," he bemoans the latter development with this passage:

> The house was directly opposite a filthy little park. The neighborhood dumped its garbage in a place originally designed to be a fountain.

Chang Hsi-kuo's "The Policy Maker" is an innovative, gloomy tale of warring factions among scholar-technocrats. With the focus on the hero's invariably wrong answers to a computer questionnaire, the story illuminates the communication gap between what people say and what they mean when they feel alienated and friendless in a hostile political environment. In "The Scholar of Yanghsien," Chang trains the writer's lens on greed, lust, and overfascination with technology, welded awkwardly onto folk remedies and a considerable dose of traditional thinking. The main character is the wife of a man consumed by business matters, leaving her chief social outlet a membership in the Cockroach Protection Society, her only dependable companion a talkative robot that leads her, upon her persistent urging, to the Scholar of Yanghsien. With ample allusions to the classic *Dream of the Red Chamber*, Chang Hsi-kuo presents this scholar as "a purveyor of gourds that can shrink the object of one's desire, bringing whoever or whatever to the person's side." Explanation for this capability is not to be sought in the supernatural, as in the great Ming novel, though, but in the world of modern physics and Big Bang. The story is a funny, twisted tale conceived in a society where odd juxtapositions abound.

Hard upbringing of a girl in a village near Taichung is the focus of Liao Hui-ying's emotionally wrenching, memorable "The Rapeseed." The story is a wonderful examination of a mother-daughter relationship that offers insight into a troubled marriage and women caught on the cusp of change:

> Mother still talked the way you chopped kindling—splitting the wood with one sweep of the ax, mercilessly and uncompromising . . .
>
> A woman's fate is like the seed of the rape plant: it grows where it falls. As far as she was concerned, a daughter was only a daughter, no matter how good.
>
> Only sons could keep the . . . family incense burning.

When mother will not come to the wedding because it conflicts with her horoscope, the young woman flirts with anger that melts into sympathy:

> When I looked at that face reflecting the countless sorrows of years past and saw how it had aged, I could only cry, Mama, Mama.

Positing the notion that the mainlander portion of Taiwan's population has struggled no less with its identity than has the Taiwanese segment of longer provenance on the island, in "The White Jade Ox," Ah Sheng focuses on a brief, transforming relationship that develops between an old Taiwanese man, who appears mysteriously day after day outside a luxury apartment building, and the mainlander doorman who discovers him.[27] The doorman asks a young man to bridge the Mandarin-Taiwanese language gap for him with gentle queries as to the elderly gentleman's purposes. It turns out that the old man bemoans his lack of attention to his family's ancestral grave site that has long since been buried beneath the towering building. The old man is haunted by dreams in which his father chastises him for selling their rice paddies to developers under pressure from his sons. His father's demands, issued through nocturnal visitations, have brought him to Taipei:

[He said that] I failed to retrieve all his bones when the body was disinterred. His shoulder blade ... one bone was missing from his shoulder blade. In my dreams, I would assure him that I would go and find it.

Mainlander and Taiwanese strike up a friendship given to lengthy conversations over tea and wine. Linguistic and subethnic barriers are bridged as the doorman reveals his own sorrows in

... stories about farming in his native village, about joining the army, the prolonged war, running from the enemy, and his separation from his folks.

Ultimately, the doorman delights in the old man's startling suggestion: He would like to adopt the doorman as a son. The adoption ceremony is held; then, only ten days later, one of the old man's two natural sons arrives with the sad news that he has died. With tears streaming down his face, the doorman listens to the man's son address him as "Third Brother." The tears continue to fall as the son opens a parcel revealing the doorman's inheritance: a white jade ox and a round flat piece of jade, half the size of his palm, with a hole in the center, and three imperial silver coins dating to the turn-of-the-century reign of Qing Empress Dowager Ci Xi. The moment is full of symbolism, and emotions run high:

It was only when the man ceremoniously addressed him as "Third Brother" that the doorman came back to his senses.
Third Brother ... My father told me to address you in this manner.

He wanted you to wear the round jade piece around your neck. The white jade ox is a family heirloom. He said you were born in the year of the ox.

Another example of the poignancy of family relationships in a quickly changing society comes in Chen Fang-ming's literary remembrance "Unexpected Encounter at Yuraku-cho."[28] The remembrance is Chen's tribute to a father who was educated during the Japanese era and spoke using a blend of Japanese and Taiwanese. Chen regrets the gulf that came between their generations, the one surviving on the borderline separating the Japanese era from the toughest years of Guomindang rule, the other raised entirely in the post-Retrocession era:

> Like all Taiwan men after the war, they sold their souls to their work, they toiled day and night. In the dead of night there were occasional house checks, and whole families plummeted into pits of terror. . . . to maintain a shred of self-dignity, Father never missed a minute of pouring himself into his labor . . .

> If he had any hopes, the insane rush of history and the trickling down of the sand pebbles that belonged to that era surely must have wiped away every dot, every trace of them . . .

> I fear that my generation and I cannot picture so very easily the turmoil and chaos caused by the fires of the war, and then the anxiety and dread that followed in its aftermath. . . . After I was sent off for my education, I can say that I no longer had any connections with Father's world. I would even go so far as to say that as a result of my education I learned to look down upon my father's generation. . . . I learned how to stretch out my hand and point the finger, to point to the people of that time who had worn the clothes of the colonizers, and who spoke the language of the colonialists.

Years later Chen Fang-ming gained a greater understanding of the dashed hopes and the terror of his father's time. Yet in the end he knew that no trip to that place of which his father frequently sang in a tune called "Accidental Meeting at Yuraku-cho," or any other posthumous search for his father's soul, could ever close the generational gap between them:

Along the way of finding a path which could bear fruit in a respectable society, he stumbled upon the webs of a social fabric in which value structures were inexorably tinged with hostility and suspicion. . . . He saw the future in optimistic and progressive terms, but in an abrupt turn it was to became a pile of gloom and ashes, a journey without hope. It was only in 1947 after the Great Incident of February 28th that Father knew for certain that after the struggle, all the earlier promise had come to absolutely nothing.

Perhaps as a means of escaping from pressures brought from living on an island of uncertain political status, where economic success has become the measure of a person, a place where entrance exams hover over young people like a hurricane promised by August, a still younger generation than that of Chen Fang-ming has turned to the romance novel as a means of relief.[29] Approximately one hundred of these novels are churned out every month, some writers priding themselves in their ability to toss off one a month. Ninety percent of the readers are young women aged seventeen to twenty, most of them students seeking escape from disappointing, boring reality. Whatever their literary merit, these romance novels provide a fascinating glimpse into the reigning tensions felt by young people in contemporary Taiwan: the pressure to succeed in exams, the push to succeed economically, the fear of being left behind in a dynamic, fast-paced society. No wonder, given these tensions, that Taiwanese people at century's end find in their vigorous folk tradition a sense of that rootedness and meaning for which they long.

CRAFTS AND FOLK ARTS

Five crafts of the Chinese tradition have been particularly popular on domestic and international markets: jade, lacquerware, cloisonné, ivory, and porcelain.[30] Fine work in all these forms is showcased at the National Palace Museum and can be bought in many hotel arcades. The ceramics industry encompassing porcelain is most vital on Taiwan today. The town of Yingko, fifteen miles south of Taipei, is the center of Taiwanese ceramics.[31] Some 800 factories continue to turn out such items as toilet seats, wash bowls, and plates; owners and managers have plans to take ever greater advantage of the industrial market. But these factories also carry on a magnificent tradition in porcelain, turning out Qing-style underglaze blues and red, Tang tricolor glazes, Tienmu black glazes (favored by the Japanese for fine tea services), finely inscribed ware with calligraphy or intricate designs, and ware born of the particular experiments of Yingko ceramics artisans with exquisite crystalline glazes. Yingko artisans have maintained attention to the demands of the marketplace and to an aesthetic that finds its ware sought by customers in Europe and the United States.

Paper making is another fine craft that has known the hands of highly skilled Taiwanese artisans. In the central Taiwan town of Puli, the children of Chen Su-ho, who died in a 1990 plane crash, carry on the tradition of handmade paper making in the Chang Chuen Cotton Paper Company, which he established in 1968.[32] Workers first wash bark now imported from Thailand and Malaysia, boil it for five to six hours, then rewash, bleach, and finally pulp it. These highly skilled workers next mix the pulp with more water and sap from the Malabar chestnut tree, which brings the pulp to the surface and holds it in an even film in a "forming" vat. A worker lowers a bamboo screen into the vat and "dips" the paper, shaking the screen back and forth until a thin layer of pulp appears on the screen's surface, forming the sheet. Big stacks of paper are then pressed for several hours, after which each sheet is baked on a flat dryer. The company maintains a branch factory in the Philippines to compensate for a shortage of labor in Taiwan. Chen Su-ho's children have demonstrated aesthetic taste and business acumen in running the company their father started. They have also fulfilled Chen Su-ho's dream of opening a museum in Taipei to explain and preserve the island's heritage in handmade paper.

Taiwanese temple culture and religion inspire a great deal of folk art on the island; to create a temple requires collaboration among architects, woodcarvers, stone carvers, and painters. Carvers fashion stone into detailed images, symbols, and portrayals of stories passed down through the ages. Green stone (*qingshi*) and Quanzhou white (*Quanzhou baishi*) imported from the mainland have traditionally been favored. Taiwanese artisans have also carved Guanyin stone (*Guanyin shi*) found at Guanyin Mountain close to Taipei, and marble from Taiwan's east coast.[33] Dragon columns at temple entrances, stone panels carved in flower and animal designs, and scenes from popular legends carry high symbolic value. Woodcarvers produce panels featuring similar subject matter and occasionally create pieces of special importance, such as an octagonal window in Taipei's famous Lungshan Temple thought to encapsulate the spirit of the *Book of Changes*.[34] These enormously talented craftspersons apply their skill to create ornate roofs, altars, and impressive statuary. The exterior of temple walls is often decorated with colorful glazed frescoes, with woodcarvings coated in real gold. A particularly notable Taiwanese woodcarver is Lee Sung-lin of Lukang, still active in his nineties. Lee is a fine furniture maker but gained his reputation by carving almost all the figurines that grace his town's Tienhou Temple and Sanhsia's Tsushih Temple, the latter still in the process of meticulous renovation after five decades.[35]

Paintings and woodblock prints of the folk tradition are also most often produced under the religious impulse. Painted scrolls enliven the existence of people celebrating the New Year, childbirth, weddings, and religious festivals. They also are in evidence at funerals. Woodblock print images can be found everywhere in Taiwanese homes, shops, and temples.[36] In producing woodblock prints, the artisan carves the image in wood, applies different colors a layer at a time, starting with black and then proceeding to brighter colors such as red, green, and indigo. Subtle colorings sometimes benefit from touchups with rouge and eyebrow pencil. Common images include bright and decorative door gods on the main and bedroom doors of the house and on each of the double leaf doors to the ancestral hall during the lunar New Year; they bring good luck and happiness to household members, assuring the birth of sons and hence continuation of the family line.

Lukang is the island's center for temple-based folk art featuring symbolic images such as these. It houses a splendid folk arts museum and numerous fine craftspersons plying their trade near some of the most significant temples of Taiwan. Here, in this same town where the eminent woodcarver Lee Sung-lin lives, another master craftsperson, seventy-one-year-old Wu Tun-hou, practices the centuries-old craft of lantern making.[37] Although he had only a primary school education, at an early age Wu Tun-hou revealed enormous talent and keen interest in painting, calligraphy, and handicrafts. In making his lanterns, he fashions a bamboo frame by weaving and tying strips into basic round or oval form. Wu then covers the frame with at least two layers of fine gauze or high-quality paper, carefully gluing the edges in such a way as to render them virtually unnoticeable. He then brushes on a layer of rice flour paste to seal the material and leave a smooth surface for painting. Turning painter, he brushes human figures, animals, calligraphy, and nature symbols in blue, vermilion, and other bright pigments common to Taiwanese folk art, mixing the paints with glue made from cowhide. Even in Taiwan's humid climate, this paint can withstand heat, wind, and rain for more than fifteen years. The winner of numerous awards, Wu has shown that a consummate artist can prosper making traditional lanterns. Two of his sons plan to carry on the tradition.

Youthful people such as the Wu sons provide encouragement that Taiwan's brilliant folk art heritage will remain vital. In the town of Hsinchuang another young man, Wang Hsi-kun, is at the forefront of an effort to keep the art of drummaking alive.[38] He has established a reputation that has brought him orders from Chinese overseas communities all over the world;

he has even produced made-to-order drums for customers in India and Japan. To make a small drum, Wang hammers and chisels a block of cedar to shape the drum's shell. For larger drums, up to one and a half meters across, he cuts wooden strips, planes them until smooth, and then carves and fits them together to form a barrellike shell. He reinforces the shape with metal collars running the length of the drum, sands the shell, and places the drum in a smoke room where the wood dries for a day. For the top of the drum, Wang pours hot water over a large piece of leather, shaves off any hair left on the surface, cuts the leather to proper size, calls upon considerable strength to scrape the layers of fat from the inner side, and then fits it over the drum, temporarily tying it down to stretch it into shape. When the outer side of the hide is dry, it is removed so that the inner side can dry. Finally, Wang undertakes the most crucial step: restretching the shaped and dried leather over the drum. Wang is inspired by the *Book of Rites* instruction that a drum will be loud and deep like thunder only if it is covered while it is thundering. But to turn out sixty or seventy drums a month, his wife says, they don't wait on thunder; to achieve the crucial tautness, she says, "We stand on top of the drum and push it taut with our feet."

Temples continue to inspire folk art such as this in response to the very active faith of many contemporary Taiwanese. The important part played by incense in temple worship, together with the large quantity demanded by Taiwan's dense and affluent population, has created an intense competition among makers of incense for attractive package design.[39] Incense makers employ creative artists to capture scenes that will attract customers to their product. These artists emphasize lucky sayings and symbols from Taiwanese tradition: the "Dragon Boy," Maitreya Buddha, cloud-striding deity Jigong, auspicious dragons, bamboo (symbol of durability and upright conduct), plum blossoms (faithfully taking on the chill of early spring), enduring pine trees, mounted sages, the *qilin* (Chinese unicorn, symbol of benevolence, rectitude, and longevity), the phoenix (symbol of peace, prosperity, and fertility), the red-faced deity Guan Gong, Mazu (goddess of the sea), Guanyin (female incarnation of the Bodhisattva Avalokitesvara), and Shou Lao (god of longevity). Incense focuses the mind and spirit with smoke "flavored" by spices, engaging senses of sight, taste, touch, and smell. Package design has turned into a popular art in its own right, conveying much cultural information.

Taiwan's current generations keep the folk arts vital not only by practicing the traditional arts but by collecting items significant to their heritage and by moving forward into new realms of fine handicraft. Vice-president Lan Lin of Les Enphants, a maker of clothes for children, has drawn attention to the exquisite folk craft of hat making, practiced by adoring mothers in Taiwan over the centuries.[40] Freelance writer Chang Yen-feng has amassed a collection of 600 commercial posters that serves as a veritable overview of twentieth-century Chinese social history as it underwent enormous changes.[41] Echo Publishing Company, a respected magazine and book publisher dedicated to cultural preservation, has published a two-box set entitled *Old-Style Calendar Advertising* (*Lao yuefenpai guanggao hua*) featuring Chang's collection.

Forging new paths with traditional methods is Cheng Hui-chung, designer and maker of "fashion-resistant" alternative clothes.[42] Cheng eschews trendy synthetic fibers for cotton and wool. He draws inspiration from aboriginal clothing and from the robes of Buddhist monks, admiring these for the combination of high aesthetics and simplicity to which he aspires in his own minimalist clothing. A latter-day philosophical Taoist in retreat from artificial complexity, Cheng seeks simplicity in beauty on his own journey through life. Glass maker Wang Chia-chun (known internationally as Heinrich Wang) studied various methods in the United States during the late 1980s.[43] He learned lampworking (a process of sculpting glass by twirling thin coloring rods over a gas-oxygen burner), blowing, fusing, cutting, grinding, and *pate de verre* (a technique whereby liquefied glass takes shape as it hardens in a plaster mold). His Heinrich Crystal Company has made Taiwan world renowned for fine crystal, producing items that constitute a statement of the cultural resources upon which Taiwanese artists can draw. Some draw inspiration from Western abstract art. Others recall mainland and Taiwanese porcelain and ceramic designs. Still others are unique creations from Wang's own imagination; these, too, are informed by the folk art tradition, featuring many auspicious titles and images in relief. In the major city of Taichung an area anchored by a thoroughfare known as Art Street has become a magnet for people showing the combined attention to tradition and progress reflected in Wang Chia-chun's life and work.[44] Retailers on Art Street express in their attitude and in the items they feature a cultural vision that combines Taiwanese tradition with contemporary progressivism.

Among the elements considered heavily in the avid search for a contemporary identity in Taiwan is the aboriginal heritage. There is now an excellent center in central Taiwan featuring reconstructions of traditional aboriginal dwellings and material culture, and in 1994 Shung Ye Museum of Formosan Aborigines opened in Taipei, fulfilling the vision of business magnate Lin Ch'ing-fu (Safe C. F. Lin) and housing his extensive collection of aboriginal art.[45] The museum structure is modeled on an aboriginal longhouse, bisected vertically by a single pillar, completely white except for footings paved with the iron-colored slate favored by Taiwan's Paiwan tribe. Items include a Paiwan stone carving with snake motif used by shamans to determine the propitious time and place for tribal hunting; a Paiwan nose flute; a tin chest ornament with bead decorations; an Ami tribe chief's cap; silver and stone bracelets; Paiwan rings and carved wooden boxes; knives with distinctive tribal designs on the handles; colorful clothing, armor, and helmets; a wooden wedding cup; a Paiwan clay pot used for divination and ceremony; and distinctive woodcarvings revealing individual styles by tribe. Currently giving predominate space to the Paiwan art to which Lin Ch'ing-fu was most attracted, museum curators plan to feature the work of other tribes more prominently in the future. They would do well to consider finely woven and sewed embroidered items of the Bunun, Tayu, and Plains aborigines; the unique carved dugout boats painted in distinctive red, white, and black design by the Yami; and the abundant woodcarving items inspired by the human form and Taiwan's diverse fauna, rendered in highly particular styles by each of the aboriginal tribes.[46]

Wishes for good fortune and material prosperity abound in the calligraphy and symbols of Taiwanese art. The god of literature and culture smiles on many a Taiwanese artist at the close of the twentieth century, granting material prosperity in some cases and good fortune, in the form of cultural inheritance and current context, to all. Cultural inheritance and social context have graced the Taiwanese artist so abundantly that the greatest difficulty lies in sorting, choosing, and innovating upon the themes presented by history and modernity. So graced and so burdened, Taiwanese artists and craftspersons can take great pride in their ability to sort through the vast tools of their inheritance and context, choose those appropriate to themselves, and construct statements of individual skill and vision.

NOTES

1. For concise overviews of the Chinese artistic heritage, see Chu-tsing Li, "Chinese Art," in John Meskill, ed., *An Introduction to Chinese Civilization* (Lexington, MA: D. C. Heath, 1973), pp. 418–61; and Michael Sullivan, "The Heritage in Chinese Art," in Raymond Dawson, ed., *The Legacy of China* (London: Oxford University Press, 1964), pp. 165–243.

2. Chang Chiung-fang, "A Brush with Immortality: The Long and Twisted Tale of Chinese Calligraphy," *Sinorama*, August 1996, p. 31.

3. For good descriptions of the "four treasures" and the uses to which they were

put in Chinese calligraphic art, see Jim Hwang, "Brushing up the Brushwork," *Free China Review*, July 1996, pp. 61–65; Chang, "A Brush with Immortality"; and *Insight Guides: Taiwan* (Boston: Houghton Mifflin, 1997), pp. 77–81.

4. *Insight Guides: Taiwan*, p. 80.

5. Chang, "A Brush with Immortality," p. 33.

6. Ibid., pp. 35–36.

7. Ibid., p. 37.

8. Ibid., pp. 37–39.

9. For an overview of Chinese figure painting, see Chu-tsing Li, "Chinese Art," pp. 440–47; for an overview of Chinese landscape painting, see the same work, pp. 447–60. See also Sullivan, in Dawson, pp. 193–205, for another good summary of the Chinese painting tradition.

10. Wang Fei-yun, "Nostalgia in Oils," *Free China Review*, March 1995, pp. 62–73.

11. Eugenia Yun, "The Painting Employee," *Free China Review*, June 1997, pp. 57–65.

12. Eugenia Yun, "Painting, Not Starving," *Free China Review*, February 1997, pp. 56–65.

13. Winnie Chang, "The Colors of Taiwan," *Free China Review*, October 1995, pp. 64–73.

14. Winnie Chang, "Paring down to Essentials," *Free China Review*, October 1996, pp. 54–65.

15. Anita Huang, "Make Art, Not War," *Free China Review*, pp. 56–65.

16. For overviews of the Chinese poetry tradition, see Burton Watson, "Chinese Literature," in John Meskill, ed. *An Introduction to Chinese Civilization* (Lexington, MA: D. C. Heath, 1973), pp. 618–42; and David Hawkes, "Chinese Poetry and the English Reader," in Raymond Dawson, ed. *The Legacy of China* (London: Oxford University Press, 1964), pp. 90–115.

17. By the late 1960s noted Taiwanese poet Lin Heng-tai and others had come to feel that these Chinese poets had not been entirely successful in adapting "plain speech" to Western models in the service of twentieth-century Chinese poetry. He and others led the search for a more authentic Taiwanese poetry rooted in the history and culture of the island. See John Balcom, "Modern Master, Native Son," *Free China Review*, December 1995, p. 70.

18. Our summary of Lin Heng-tai's long and illustrious career is based on the Balcom article, pp. 62–73.

19. Li P'eng, "The Rise of the Well-Versed Society: A Poetry Renaissance in Contemporary Taiwan," trans. by Vincent Chang, *Sinorama*, December 1995, p. 129.

20. Ibid., p. 127.

21. Ibid.

22. Ibid., p. 126.

23. Ibid., pp. 124–26.

24. Liu Lan-fang, "Taiwan's Living Poets' Societies," trans. by Jonathon Barnard, *Sinorama*, April 1996, pp. 40–53.

25. For an overview of traditional Chinese prose, see Watson, "Chinese Literature," in Meskill, pp. 618–42. For a treatment focused entirely on fiction and drama, see Patrick Hanan, "The Development of Fiction and Drama," in Raymond Dawson, ed. *The Legacy of China* (London: Oxford University Press, 1964), pp. 115–43. For a focus on history writing, see E. G. Pulley-Blank, "The Historiographic Tradition," also in Dawson, pp. 143–64.

26. This quotation and those appearing on the succeeding pages for short stories by Shu Kuo-shih, Huang Huang Fan, Chang Hsi-kuo, and Liao Hui-ying are from Ching-hsi Perng and Chin-kuei Wang, eds., *Death in a Cornfield* (Hong Kong: Oxford University Press, 1994), as reviewed by John Tremble in "Fuzzy Logic," *Free China Review*, February 1996, pp. 58–63.

27. Ah Sheng, "The White Jade Ox," trans. by May Li-ming Tang, *Free China Review*, March 1995, pp. 58–61, reprinted from *The Chinese PEN*, autumn 1994.

28. Chen Fang-ming, "Unexpected Encounter at Yuraku-cho," *Free China Review*, July 1995, pp. 36–40.

29. Anita Huang, "All for Love," *Free China Review*, October 1996, pp. 48–53.

30. For a discussion of these Chinese crafts, see Sullivan, in Dawson, pp. 179–93. For a very good, succinct treatment, see *Insight Guides: Taiwan*, pp. 86–89.

31. Huang Wen-ling, "Yingko: Making Money from Muck," *Free China Review*, December 1996, pp. 54–65.

32. Jim Hwang, "Paper Tigers," *Free China Review*, pp. 64–73.

33. B. Kaulbach and B. Proksch, *Arts and Culture in Taiwan* (Taipei: Southern Materials Center, 1984), p. 83.

34. Huang Wen-ling, "Symphonies in Stone," *Free China Review*, July 1996, pp. 28–33.

35. Ibid., p. 32.

36. Ibid., pp. 78–81.

37. Virginia Sheng, "Lighting the Way," *Free China Review*, March 1995, pp. 50–56. See also the accompanying article, "A Beacon from the Past," focused on lanterns for the Lantern Festival holiday.

38. Jessie Cheng, "The Sound of Thunder," *Free China Review*, April 1995, pp. 66–73.

39. Roger Meyer, "Celestial Sales Force," *Free China Review*, July 1996, pp. 40–45.

40. Eugenia Yun, "Hats in Hand," *Free China Review*, March 1997, pp. 58–65.

41. Roger Meyer, "Revaluing the Popular Past," *Free China Review*, August 1995, pp. 62–73.

42. Eugenia Yun, "Alternative Clothing," *Free China Review*, May 1996, pp. 60–63.

43. Jim Hwang, "Taiwan's Crystal Maze," *Free China Review*, April 1997, pp. 58–65.

44. Wang Fei-yun, "Utopia, Ltd.," *Free China Review*, July 1996, pp. 50–55.

45. Wang Fei-yun, "Tribal Treasures," *Free China Review*, May 1996, pp. 64–73.

46. See discussions of these aboriginal folk crafts in Kaulbach and Proksch, pp. 83–85 and pp. 99–101. For an excellent review of the current interest in aboriginal culture on Taiwan, among both the Chinese and the aboriginal populations, see Eugenia Yun, "The Great Awakening," *Free China Review*, April 1997, pp. 4–29.

SUGGESTED READINGS

Chang Chiung-fang. "A Brush with Immortality: The Long and Twisted Tale of Chinese Calligraphy," *Sinorama*, August 1996.

Free China Review for frequent articles on contemporary Taiwanese artists and craftspersons.

Li P'eng. "The Rise of the Well-Versed Society: A Poetry Renaissance in Contemporary Taiwan," *Sinorama*, December 1995.

Meskill, John. "Chinese Art," in John Meskill, ed., *An Introduction to Chinese Civilization.* Lexington, MA: D. C. Heath, 1973.

Perng, Ching-hsi and Chin-kuei Wang, eds. *Death in a Cornfield.* Hong Kong: Oxford University Press, 1994.

6

Architecture

HOUSING

HOME IS MORE than just shelter from the elements. Taiwanese homes express ideals of family relationships, hope for family prosperity, and the desire to live in harmony with the natural world. The materials used show a pragmatism and an adaptation to the local environment. The structural values and meaning of the structures demonstrate concepts dating back over 2,000 years.

The earliest homes in Taiwan were those of indigenous peoples. Their constructions varied according to environment, family structure, and mythological beliefs. Few traditional aboriginal structures have survived. When immigrants from China began building shelters on the island of Taiwan, they brought with them radically different views of family and the cosmos. For the most part, their homes reflected the architectural style and family structures of southern Fujian Province.

Early Chinese immigrants probably built simple shelters out of available materials, but these houses could not be called homes. The earliest immigrants were single males who planned to return to their mainland homes. Only after they established family units through marriage with a Sinicized indigenous woman or the coming of a new wife from the mainland did they build homes. These homes then began to reflect the Chinese traditions of structure.

To be secure in nature and provide well-being for the family within, homes were sited in harmony with their surroundings. Location and orientation of a home was chosen according to *fengshui* principles, many of which simply reflected common sense concerns to avoid flooding, to make the best use of the sun, and to protect from strong winds. Expressed in terms of the flow of *qi* and the balance of *yin* and *yang*, these concerns resulted in homes with southerly or southeasterly orientations. Even early settlers sited their homes according to basic *fengshui* principles; only with later wealth did the immigrants consult trained specialists to help them in siting their domestic architecture.

Homes had to be built on auspicious days. Traditional almanacs listed auspicious and inauspicious days for various of activities, including breaking ground for a new building and raising the ridgepole. To ensure successful completion of a building and its protection from evil spirits, rituals and charms were used. Most Taiwanese built their own homes, but the wealthier hired artisans and builders who relied on oral and written traditions of technique and ritual. The fifteenth-century manual *Lu ban jing* is supposedly written by the patron saint of carpenters and bricklayers. According to this text, carpenters used a special measuring device to determine proper harmonious dimensions of rooms, doors, windows, courtyards, and stoves.

Folk tradition also offered various means of protecting a home and its inhabitants after completion. Some charms protected against possible curses built into the home by disgruntled construction workers. Other charms brought general good fortune. Red strips of paper were hung outside the home, particularly at New Year. On each side of the door, vertical red banners painted with couplets expressed hope for the coming year. Red paper charms of single characters communicated the hope for happiness, position, long life, joy, and wealth. Sometimes woodblock prints of door gods dressed in warrior attire were placed on the front door to protect against unwanted evil presence.

The Taiwanese use many means to bring good fortune into their homes. Near the stove, the Kitchen God's image is pasted to symbolize the unity and the desired harmony of the family. On the family's altar, ancestral tablets and the images of gods and goddesses bring divine protection into the home.

The structure and shape of Taiwanese homes began to follow Chinese custom as soon as immigrants from the mainland first established permanent homes. Although Chinese immigrants adapted their construction to local materials, they did not accept the building traditions of the aboriginal peoples. In a 1717 gazetteer *Zhuluo xianzhi*, a drawing of a town on the western coastal plan of Taiwan shows the striking contrast between the aboriginal thatch-covered buildings on raised piles and the Chinese houses set on the ground and facing south or southwest.[1]

Traditional Taiwanese dwellings follow mainland styles, emphasizing symmetry and balance. The basic structure is a single story rectangular room, with the door placed in the middle for symmetry and balance; this rectangular room can be partitioned on each side to provide sleeping rooms. The central or perhaps only room of the house is the *gongting*; this room serves multiple purposes: reception room, altar room, family room. As the ritual center of the family, this room contains the family's domestic altar, which can be a simple high table or an elaborately carved piece of ritual furniture. Stage right on this altar family members place wooden tablets representing their ancestors. Stage left they place any images of gods, goddesses, Buddhas, and Bodhisattvas that are worshipped by family members. Modern altars use painted glass images of gods as the focal point behind the table. Guanyin Bodhisattva, Mazu, and Guandi are popular presences. Candles and incense holders are placed on the altar to be used when making offerings to ancestors or deities. This ritual center belongs to the whole family. Even after brothers divide the family property, this room would continue to belong to all brothers.

The sleeping rooms or storage rooms on either side of the *gongting* are assigned according to family hierarchy. Hierarchy of space is determined along an axis by the distance from the ritual center and the left-right difference. To the immediate left of the *gongting* is the "great room," the ritually highest space outside the *gongting* and thus the bedroom for the parents. Children are assigned rooms according to a hierarchy of gender and seniority, with the oldest sons placed closest to the center *gongting*. With the marriage of the oldest son, the parents might move to the room immediately to the right of the *gongting* to give their son and daughter-in-law the "great room" and thus the position of ritual responsibility.

When Taiwanese families grow, additional buildings are added to the main rectangular building. Sometimes the original homes are built with a bricked-up door on each side wall to facilitate the hoped-for later additions. These newly attached structures are added perpendicularly to the sides of the main building. New additions are added first to the left and then to the right to create a U-shaped structure with a courtyard inside. In northern Taiwan the courtyard is usually left open, whereas in the southern part of the island the courtyard is enclosed with a low wall. The courtyards constitute important living space for the family because unlike the dark interiors of the home, it is a bright space to work in. In this space the agricultural products of the family are dried and bundled.

A wealthy family that develops into a stem or joint family sometimes needs

6.1 Traditional rural housing with symmetrical wings and open courtyard.

to enlarge its compound even beyond the U-shaped basic structure. These large Taiwanese families accomplish this by building new additions parallel to the original wings of the home. These are ideally built in pairs to preserve the symmetry of the building. The original wings are called the "inner protectors," and the outer wings the "outer protectors." Many large residences in Taiwan have as many as six pairs of "protectors."[2]

Following mainland traditions, Taiwanese homes are built on packed, raised foundations to provide some protection from flooding. Some homes pile a layer of stones on top of this foundation to further raise the house above flood level. Most interior floors were made of packed earth until the relative prosperity of the 1960s and 1970s.

Wooden frameworks support the grand, sweeping roofs of temples and large buildings, but many Taiwanese rural homes are built with brick or adobe brick walls that support the roofs. Temples and homes that rely on frameworks use one of two different systems: a pillar-and-beam system (*tai-liang*) or a pillar-and-transverse tie beam system (*chuandou*). Neither system uses nails to construct the framework. The flexibility of these structures allows for greater survival of earthquakes.

Walls of Taiwanese houses were made from plentiful bamboo even into the mid-twentieth century. Because houses made of bamboo last only about twenty years, however, those with the means to use other materials abandoned bamboo. Thus sun-dried mud bricks were often used to construct walls. These mud brick walls were topped with kiln-dried brick or stones so that the damp mud bricks would not cause rotting in the wooden roof. Walls made entirely of kiln-dried bricks were rare until the mid-twentieth century, though. Kiln-dried bricks were brought as ballast by ship from Fujian. Beginning in the late seventeenth century these imported bricks were used in wealthy homes, temples, and government buildings. Indeed, most of the large homes surviving from the nineteenth century are made of the red bricks imported from southern Fujian.[3]

The most visually striking feature of Taiwanese domestic architecture is the roof. The earliest homes built by Chinese immigrants had roofs of grass or rice straw, but by the late 1600s the roofs of homes in town were tiled. The rural Taiwanese kept their thatch roofs for a long time. In 1952 45 percent of rural homes still had thatched roofs. With the increased rural prosperity following the Land-to-the-Tiller program, tiled roofs soon increased dramatically among farm family homes. Such roofs used either curved red tiles (*hongwa*) or tiles that look like rows of bamboo (*tongwa*). The profiles of these tiled roofs were in the "saddle" shape (*mabei xing*) or the "swallowtail" shape (*yanwei xing*). The "saddle" shape is a steep sloping roof common throughout Taiwan. According to laws of the Qing dynasty, the "swallowtail" shape, an elegant upswept design, was supposed to be used only on temples and official buildings, but the Taiwanese frontier dwellers felt safe from the enforcement of these laws and often violated them, especially in the northern areas. Also on Taiwanese homes are a variety of gable styles. Many gables are highly decorated with auspicious symbols.

Brick farmhouses with sloping roofs are no longer the norm in modern Taiwan. Most farmhouses are rectangular structures made of reinforced concrete often covered with ceramic tiles. Many are now two-storied "Western-style" dwellings. A few families have chosen to build new homes that draw on traditional Taiwanese styles, however. For example, an Ilan County program encourages custom-built homes that reflect the landscape and traditions of the area.[4]

Urban houses developed differently. In densely populated areas such as the early mercantile center of Lukang, narrow and deep row houses were built. Commercial activities took place at the front of the buildings, on the street, and the family residence took up the rear.[5]

In the 1990s the Taiwanese increasingly live in high-rise condominiums. Swallowtail roofs and enclosed courtyards are an impossibility for most urban Taiwanese given the population density and real estate prices. Although *fengshui* cannot be directly applied to the location and orientation of a particular apartment, buildings may draw on *fengshui* practices to increase their appeal to buyers. More and more urban Taiwanese are applying *fengshui* principles

6.2 Urban housing: the multistoried apartment building.

to interior decoration as they seek consultation on the placement of furniture, mirrors, and symbolic objects to increase the harmony and auspiciousness of their urban dwellings.

TEMPLES

The most exciting buildings in Taiwan are temples, which are everywhere. (The government gives a conservative estimate of 12,000 temples on the island.) Temples are highly ornate structures. With their sweeping swallowtail roofs and ornate roof decoration, temples are immediately recognizable as the most important structure in a community. They are built like palaces to house the deities within. The numerous Buddhist and Taoist temples appear similar on the outside. Moreover, they usually house deities of both traditions. The truly orthodox Buddhist temples contain fewer ornate decorations of the folk tradition, and Confucian temples are somewhat austere by Taiwanese standards.

Temples are located and oriented according to *fengshui* principles. A *fengshui* master determines the most auspicious and harmonious location for the temple. The height of the roof pillars is guided by the surrounding landscape. According to master carver Huang Kwei-li, it is also important for carvers to

6.3   One of the many Mazu temples.

incorporate a knowledge of *fengshui* and the system of the five agents (*wu xing*) to create a fully harmonious structure. If, for example, the temple is near the ocean, then the overwhelming presence of the water agent should be balanced by the fire agent in the form of recurrent flame motifs in the woodcarving.[6]

There are two central foci for the temple: the incense burner and the statue of the enshrined deity. Of these two, the incense burner is the more important. Even without a temple, members of a community can organize themselves and their ritual lives around an incense burner whose location rotates among the families of the community. The family with the incense burner becomes responsible for organizing the ritual offerings and festival for the community. New temples either incorporate the incense from its "mother" temple or provide a new home for an old, spiritually powerful statue.

Statues of the oldest and most honored gods and goddesses are blackened by several centuries of incense burning. The earliest statues were brought by immigrants to Taiwan. Since there were no skilled woodcarvers among the earliest immigrants, carvers were brought from the mainland to carve new images and to teach apprentice carvers. The carving of an efficacious statue requires artistic skill as well as ritual knowledge. Before carving begins, a Taoist priest selects an auspicious day to make offerings and invite the spirit into the wood. The wood block, usually camphor or pine, is carved from the bottom up in order to revere the deity's head. After the carving is completed, the statue is covered with sizing, paper, and a thin coat of yellow clay. It is then sanded smooth. Gold relief filigree and painted colors are then added. Like the temple itself, the statue must represent a balance of the five agents of wood, earth, metal, fire, and water. The statue is wood, the clay covering is earth, and the gold, red, and blue pigments of the paint represent metal, fire, and water. After the carving and painting, a small hole is cut into the back of the image to add symbolic materials. Recently the most commonly used materials have been the "five kernels" to ensure good harvests or special incense. Then a Taoist priest conducts the dedication and dotting ceremony in which the god or goddess enters into the statues. Offerings are made and spells are chanted. The priest dots various parts of the statue with a red mixture according to the ritual texts. Finally the statue is put into its sedan chair to await the actual arrival of the deity.[7]

Some of the newer temple complexes of Taiwanese popular religion are so large that they are more like temple cities. The Mazu temple at Luermen outside of Tainan claims to be the largest temple complex in Asia. There are three major temples in this complex. The first two temples are two-storied temples, with the second temple serving as the main altar for the goddess Mazu. The third temple is an enormous three-storied temple housing Buddhist images on the lower two floors and the Jade Emperor on the third floor. The complex also include pagodas, gardens, ponds, and almost every other element of Taiwanese temple structures.

An older style of temple is the Lungshan Temple of Lukang. Traditions say it was built around 1653 but rebuilt on its present location in 1786. It also consists of three temples, each separated by a courtyard. The front temple has five doors, which indicates the high status of the enshrined deity. The center doors depict the guardian deities, Weiduo and Zhailan. The other doors have Buddhist guardians, each holding a special object: a sword, a *pipa*, an umbrella, and a snake. Thus these four guardians hold objects that represent to the Taiwanese the qualities of good weather: wind, harmony, rain, and smoothness.[8] The central temple at Lungshan temple houses Guanyin Bodhisattva, whose compassionate image presides over the central altar. On either side of her are two Taoist deities: the goddess of childbirth and the guardian of the temple precincts. Along the sides are the eighteen *luohan*, early disciples of the Buddha. There is also a large temple bell weighing 500 kilos. In front of the rear temple is another courtyard; this is where the local religious associations meet to chant scriptures and the various committees meet to plan temple events.

The stone and wood carvings on temples are intricate works of art. Taiwan has few skilled carvers now. It is easier and much cheaper to use concrete pillars made from molds than to employ carvers. Some newly built and restored temples have brought woodcarvers and stone carvers from the mainland in order to save on labor costs. Traditionally carved temples are museums of the folk art of woodcarving. The ceiling beams, the pillars, the panels, and almost every other wooden surface of the temple interior are intricately carved with auspicious symbols, animals, and scenes from historical tales. Many of the carvings are not explicitly religious, however. The carvers draw on their knowledge of traditional stories, sometimes visualized through the scenes of Taiwanese operas, to create their art. Popular subjects are scenes from novels such as the *Romance of the Three Kingdoms* or the *Legend of Deification.* The short wooden beam called *yuan guang* is one of the highest forms of the woodcarver's art. Because this beam can be seen from both sides, the carver must create a three-dimensional scene to be viewed from both sides. The Taiwanese would sometimes hire two different woodcarving teams to work on different parts of the temple; this would initiate competition to see who could produce the most elaborate and beautiful carvings.[9]

Temples serve the religious, social, and political needs of the community. Community temples are built by the community and for the community. The temple committee allows religious, musical, and social groups to use their facilities, making them something like community centers. At times temples serve as a focus of political and communal rivalries. A good example of this is the old Longshan Temple of the Wanhua district of Taipei. The temple was first built in 1738 to house an image of Guanyin Bodhisattva brought from the Longshan Temple in Anhai Township in Quanzhou, Fujian. Immigrants from the three Quanzhou districts of Chinjiang, Huian, and Nanan (collectively referred to as Sanyi), took charge of the temple. The temple was used for worship, for guild meetings, for hometown association meetings, and for socializing by the San-yi people. In 1853 during one of the frequent conflicts over trading rights on the docks, the Sanyi people used the Longshan Temple as the strategic base for attacking the rival Tongan people.

Taipei's Longshan Temple—like many Taiwanese temples—has been used to promote the interests both of rulers and of opposition groups. During the Japanese period the governors-general came to Longshan Temple to attend festivals and to ritually begin their terms of office. Later the Guomindang government tried to control activities here during their long period of martial law. Control was never complete, and in a period of strict media censorship the speeches given at Longshan Temple were an important means of spreading opposition during the 1980s. In 1986 opposition activists held a sit-in at the temple to protest the continuation of martial law. When a leading advocate for Taiwanese independence, Cheng Nan-jung, burned himself alive as a form of protest, his supporters set up a memorial altar at the temple to maintain a vigil in his memory. After the lifting of martial law more and more outsiders came to the temple, which became known as a dangerous area. This prompted the temple committee to hire security guards to deal with the problems of the homeless, mentally ill, and con artists who increasingly made the temple their home.[10] The close relationship between political leadership and community religious leadership has always made separating religion and politics difficult. From the very beginning, Taiwanese temples have served as a center for politics as well as religion. At times the central government—whether Qing, Japanese, or Guomindang—has tried to pressure the temple committees to support them and their policies.

CITIES: PUBLIC SPACES AND PUBLIC BUILDINGS

The city of Taipei is chaos. Traffic is unbearable despite a belatedly built urban mass rail system. Buildings are illegally constructed on public ground. Motorcycles cover almost all the available sidewalk space. Remaining sidewalk areas are filled with street vendors. Residents of Taipei complain about the congestion, the pollution, and the lack of green spaces. Other cities in Taiwan share these problems, but to a lesser extent. Taipei is the height of creative mess.

Taipei was originally a planned city. In fact, the Qing government, the Japanese government, and the Guomindang government each had plans for the city. A succession of governments disregarded earlier plans; to compound the problem, the most recent planning by the Guomindang was never implemented.

The Qing dynasty drew on the long tradition of well-planned Chinese cities. Urban plans from the Zhou dynasty described the planned city as a square walled city with three gates on each side and nine roads running parallel horizontally and vertically. The great cities of the Qin, Han, Sui, and Tang dynasties had underground sewers made of fired clay. The carefully planned city of Changan was laid out with the imperial city at the center surrounded by a grid of north-south and east-west roads. The central road leading to the imperial city from the south of the city was more than 100 meters wide. Eastern and western districts were designated for business; residential areas were separate. South of the city was the Qiujiang pond and hibiscus gardens. This careful zoning for residential and commercial uses

6.4 The old city gate (East Gate) decorated with Chiang Kai-shek's portrait and surrounded by modern skyscrapers.

combined with the inclusion of green spaces represents a model of urban planning envied by modern city dwellers.

The capital city of Beijing was another carefully planned city. The Yuan dynasty built the underground channels of Beijing before the rest of the city was planned. Beijing's tree-lined streets were accomplished by imperial orders that encouraged the planting of trees but prohibited residents from cutting them down.

The capital city Taipei was founded by the Qing dynasty in 1879 as an administrative center between the commercial centers in Ta-tao-ch'eng and Wan-hua. In 1884 the walls of the city were completed. The Qing governor's palace was built to the north of the modern center of the city. However, the construction of a city according to Chinese traditions did not proceed very far. Only a few government buildings were finished before the Japanese took control. Although the city walls of Taipei were torn down by the Japanese, the gates to the city of Taipei remain as incongruous testaments to early Chinese urban planning. The gates were built in the architectural style of Fujian. Whereas the North Gate remains in this Fujianese form, the East and South Gates were renovated by the Guomindang government into northern palace-style architecture after Retrocession. The East Gate is at the center of a traffic circle near the Japanese-built structure housing the Presidential

Palace. The West Gate is no more—the Japanese tore it down along with the walls.[11]

The Japanese came to Taiwan in 1895 with the intention to stay. They planned to build a modern administrative center that would serve as their headquarters as they moved into Southeast Asia. When they began implementing their plans for a new city after 1900, they tore down the four walls surrounding the city and used the salvaged stone to build public buildings. Initially the Japanese may not have had a comprehensive city plan. A 1905 plan was concerned primarily with landscaping the city environs, including the addition of wide boulevards lined with camphor and maple trees. A true city plan was not announced until 1928. This plan showed Japanese concern for building a clean, modern city. The Japanese installed underground pipes to bring water into the city. In 1932 the Japanese announced a comprehensive urban plan for its administrative center—the "Greater Taipei Metropolitan Area Plan." The plan for a city of 600,000 included the renovation of Chinese residential areas and the development of Japanese residential districts.[12] The slow growth of Taipei allowed for reasonable development in terms of the Japanese plan.

The Guomindang government's move to Taiwan in 1949 radically changed the city of Taipei. No plans were drawn for the new capital of the Republic of China because the move was to have been temporary. Because the Guomindang hoped to retake mainland China quickly, they merely took over the Japanese public buildings. They also occupied much of the public space reserved for parks. Only in 1954 was there sufficient interest in city planning even to translate the Japanese documents for Taipei's planned development. Increased population and skyrocketing real estate prices led to continued chaotic growth in the city. The government failed to plan ahead. According to Deng Tsung-de of the Building and Planning School of National Taiwan University, "Taipei's urban policies bent to the prevailing winds, allowing commercial activities to spread into residential areas, turning a blind eye to illegal structures, and implementing the law 'flexibly.' "[13]

The primary government buildings in Taipei thus date from the Japanese period. They reflect the Meiji government's desire to modernize along Western lines. For Japanese architects trained in new Western techniques, Taiwan was a place to experiment with their new style. The buildings dating from 1900–1920 reflect the "Second Empire" style of France under Napoleon III. This style draws on eighteenth-century neoclassical styles, which used the pure geometric shapes of classical architecture. This style was called "pattern architecture" by the Japanese builders because they could draw from a wide selection of classical patterns and use them as they wished.[14]

The most important Japanese era building was the office of the governor-general, which now functions as the Presidential Palace. At first the governor-general worked out of the Qing dynasty government offices. But the Japanese desired a more majestic and non-Chinese structure to symbolize their rule. According to architect Li Chung-yao, a technical officer in the governor-general's office during the later years of Japanese rule: "At that time, Japan's power was in the ascendancy and the Japanese planned to build up Taiwan as their main base from which they would push south into southeast Asia. This imposing building was the symbol of this ambition."[15] Competition for architectural designs began in 1906, but work did not begin until 1912. The winning designer was Nagano Heiji, who created a symmetrical five-storied building with a central tower. To build it, the Japanese removed the ancestral shrines of the Lin and Chen clans, relocating the Lin shrine to an area north of the train station, and the Chen shrine to Ta-tao-ch'eng.

The style of the Governor-General's Office, now the Presidential Palace, is the Renaissance-baroque style popular during the Japanese Meiji Restoration period. The building faces east, reflecting its original loyalty to Japan, the land of the rising sun. The floor plan is in the shape of the Japanese character for the sun, thus representing the Japanese emperor. The building was built with steel reinforcing bars with walls of stone and brick. The stability and durability of the structure was proven during American bombing of the district during World War II. With its high tower, this building continues to tower over the government district of the town. In fact, the ROC government prohibited building any structure in the district higher than the Presidential Palace. Outside the district the high skyscrapers of modern Taipei soar above the tower.

The second most important Japanese-era building, the residence of the Japanese governor-general, was completed in 1901 as an impressive baroque-style building. Designed by Japanese architect Nomura Ichiro, it was the first "pattern style" building in Taiwan. When the wooden roof was devastated by a termite infestation, the building was rebuilt by another Japanese architect, Moriyama Matsunosuke. The building is now the Taipei Guest House, a place to entertain guests of the government. This is the only remaining building designed by Moriyama, who was notable for his French-style roofs and elegant pillars.

Another important Japanese era building was the Kodama Goto Memorial Hall, built to honor Governor-General Kodama Gentaro and Senior Minister Goto Shimpei. This building, designed by Nomura Ichiro with Arkai Eiichi, was completed in 1915. This "pattern style" white building has Doric columns and triangular gables. Inside is a domed ceiling and marble imported from Europe. During the Japanese era, Western classical music was performed regularly on the outdoor stage of this hall. To build this memorial to honor Japanese leaders and to promote modernization, the Japanese tore down the Mazu temple that had served as the religious center of Taipei. Today the building serves as the Taiwan Provincial Museum.

The two Japanese government buildings on either side of the Governor-General's Office were the Bank of Taiwan and the High Court. These buildings represented the economic and police powers of the Japanese rulers over the Taiwanese. When the Nationalist government took over the buildings, they took over these powers as well. The High Court building is a good example of the eclectic Japanese architecture of Taipei after 1920. After a serious earthquake in Tokyo in 1923, Japanese architects began to rethink their construction methods; they abandoned brick construction in favor of steel and concrete. The High Court, built in 1934, uses this steel-and-concrete exterior covered with tile facing. The second and third floors have light green tile exteriors. The building is notable for its central tower capped with a helmet shape that marks the building as "Imperial Crown" architecture. The most modern of Japanese buildings is perhaps the Directorate-General of Telecommunications, completed in 1938. This building is closely linked to modern European architecture with its bright colors, horizontal lines, rounded corners, rectangular windows, and striking lack of decorative embellishment.[16]

For the enjoyment of the Japanese rulers, the Japanese designed a park near the Governor-General's Office. Renamed New Park by the Nationalists, it now symbolizes yet another stage of political development as it houses a memorial for those killed by the Nationalists during the February 28th Incident. The Japanese-era park has become a symbol of the new openness and democracy of Taiwan.

The Japanese left to Taiwan numerous government buildings, roads, and the beginnings of a modern infrastructure. It was the Japanese who introduced to Taiwan modernization and Westernization in architecture and urban planning. The Guomindang took over the Japanese buildings but later worked to impose a Chinese look on the city of Taipei. To create a more auspicious Chinese look, during national holidays the exteriors of the Japanese era government buildings are covered with red and yellow partial façades celebrating the birth and development of the Republic of China. The Nationalists built the grand halls in exuberant northern Chinese style. Completely rejecting the Japanese Westernization, ROC leaders built monuments to traditional Chinese culture. The grandest of these monuments are two

6.5 Chiang Kai-shek Memorial in Taipei.

memorials in honor of Republic of China leaders Sun Yat-sen and Chiang Kai-shek.

The Chiang Kai-shek Memorial Hall is an enormous hall inside expansive, formally landscaped grounds. It was dedicated in 1980, five years after the death of Chiang Kai-shek. White with a blue roof, the hall is an imposing 250 feet high. Inside, the place of honor is reserved for a twenty-five-ton bronze statue of a seated Chiang Kai-shek. On either side of the memorial hall are the National Concert Hall and the National Opera Hall, both resembling Chinese palaces. Carefully landscaped grounds are enclosed by a white wall with eighteen different styles of Chinese windows. A Ming-style archway with five openings serves as the main entrance to the expansive memorial area. Through much of the 1980s the Chiang Kai-shek Memorial seemed a rather austere place whose overpowering presence, expense, and military guard were resented by many Taiwanese, but in the 1990s the place has become a popular communal center for early morning *taijiquan*, evening jogging, romantic walks, fireworks, and various public gatherings.

Taiwan's primary memorial to Sun Yat-sen, known as the father of modern

China, is a large red Chinese-style building with a sweeping roof of glazed yellow tile. Inside the hall is a 200-foot bronze statue of Sun Yat-sen. The hall has served to honor the founder of the ROC and also to house cultural exhibits. Another memorial structure is the Revolutionary Martyrs' Shrine, which is built in Ming dynasty palace style. The shrine area contains drum and bell towers, guest pavilions, and a main shrine with murals depicting the accomplishments of Chinese heroes who died in events leading up to the Revolution of 1911. The structures in the Martyrs' Shrine are based on the designs of Beijing halls and pavilions. The Martyrs' Shrine and the memorials to Nationalist leaders were attempts to tie the island of Taiwan more closely to mainland China both politically and culturally. Imitation of Ming dynasty styles expresses hope for a unified China that may not represent the desires of the Taiwanese majority.

The best representative architecture for Taiwan in the 1990s might be the fifty-three-story skyscraper called the Shin Kong Life Tower. This towering modern structure was built in 1993 by a private financial consortium. Throughout the cities of contemporary Taiwan stand similar monuments to modernism and capitalism. One of the great towering structures of modern southern Taiwan is the fifty-story Grand 50 Tower of Kaohsiung. The city center of Kaohsiung is made up of this and other towering office blocks indistinguishable from those of many modern cities of the world. Crowded clusters of modern multistoried condominiums circle Taiwanese cities. Glass-and-steel office buildings line the traffic-filled streets of the newer commercial developments. New industrial parks of modern industrial design expand outside the densely populated cities. The norm is the sleek line of glass, steel, and concrete.

Traditional architectural styles in Taiwan drew primarily from styles of southern Fujian for inspiration. This was true for homes as well as for temples. With the coming of the Japanese, the Taiwanese were introduced to Japanese style homes and to modern Western architecture as interpreted by Japanese designers. The Japanese esthetic as reflected in traditional Japanese homes continues to have some influence in modern Taiwanese culture, but in recent decades it has been the modern, efficient style of Western architecture that has had the greatest influence as the Taiwanese build their homes and businesses. Sleek high-rise buildings house families and businesses in urban Taiwan. Those with wealth and land in the countryside have occasionally experimented with a combination of traditional Taiwanese style and Western efficiencies for their own homes.

Taiwanese architecture, as developed from southern Fujian styles, continues to be a powerful presence in ritually oriented buildings in modern Taiwan. Numerous new, newly restored, and expanded temples continue to prefer sweeping roofs with elaborate ornamentation from the Taiwanese folk tradition. Occasionally other Chinese architectural styles are used, but in general only in government-financed buildings have the northern styles of architecture been fostered. Architecture reflects Taiwanese culture. A love of Taiwanese traditions dominates in those areas requiring ritual, but there is an embracing of all things modern for business and efficient housing. Although enjoying government support, the northern Chinese culture imported by the Guomindang is rarely embraced by the majority of the Taiwanese. In matters of Chinese style, the Taiwanese preference for things of Fujian origin has outlived government attempts to impose northern forms.

NOTES

1. Ronald G. Knapp, *China's Traditional Rural Architecture: A Cultural Geography of the Common House* (Honolulu: University of Hawaii Press, 1986), p. 90.

2. Ibid., 93.

3. Ibid., 102–3.

4. Jackie Chen, "Architecture Down on the Farm," *Sinorama*, vol. 20, no. 12 (December 1995), pp. 40–57.

5. B. Kaulbach and B. Proksch, *Arts and Culture in Taiwan* (Taipei: Southern Materials Center, 1984), p. 108.

6. Emma Wu, "Carving a Life," *Free China Review*, January 1994, p. 64.

7. Hsü Shih-hua, "God Statues, Past and Present," *Sinorama*, vol. 9, no. 8 (August 1984).

8. Huang Wen-ling, "Symphonies in Stone," *Free China Review*, July 1996, pp. 28–33.

9. Emma Wu, "Carving a Life," *Free China Review*, January 1994.

10. Jenny Hu, "Sacred Battle Ground—The Lungshan Temple," *Sinorama*, April 1995.

11. Jane Wang, "A Legacy to Build On: Japanese Architecture in the Po Ai Special District," *Sinorama*, January 1995, p. 29.

12. Chang Chin-ju, "If Taipei Had Been Designed in the Tang Dynasty" and "Modern Problems, Ancient Strategies," *Sinorama*, vol. 20, no. 4 (April 1995), pp. 6–17 and 18–25.

13. Chang Chin-ju, "Modern Problems, Ancient Strategies," p. 15.

14. For a discussion of Japanese-era building of Taipei, see Jane Wang, "Space and Power in the District of Universal Love," *Sinorama*, January 1995.

15. Jenny Hu, "The Presidential Palace Opens Its Doors," *Sinorama*, January 1995, p. 11.

16. Jane Wang, "A Legacy to Build On," p. 31.

SUGGESTED READINGS

Knapp, Ronald. *China's Traditional Rural Architecture: A Cultural Geography of the Common House.* Honolulu: University of Hawaii Press, 1986.

Sinorama and *Free China Review* articles on housing, public buildings, and temples.

7

Cuisine and Fashion

CULTURAL BORROWING is one of the fascinating processes of international exchange. When one area of the world comes under heavy influence from another, to what new cultural features do people prove most responsive, and to what features of their own culture do they hold most firmly? In the first section of this chapter we consider an aspect of Taiwanese life to which its people have held very firmly indeed: the glorious heritage of Chinese, Fujianese, and Taiwanese cooking. In the second section we turn to a Taiwanese cultural feature that has been much more overwhelmed by the Western alternative: the elaborate, classy, but less convenient styles of fashion typifying traditional Taiwanese society.

CUISINE

Our strongest memories of first arriving on Taiwan in 1980 are associated with smells. The most glorious of those emanated from the countless eateries that dot the capital of Taipei. Food is everywhere, from the humble to the fancy and all manner of gradations in between. The enticing aromas of Taipei food drift down alleyways, where some enterprising vendors make a mint producing select specialties with artful simplicity under conditions of very low overhead. Smells sweet, pungent, piquant, seduce the sense of olfaction. They welcome the stroller and the patron as they waft from small restaurants whipping up noodle dishes, soups, roast duck, steamed dumplings, or menus of wide choice and stylistic variety. Delectable culinary fragrances come as well from gourmet restaurants, where chefs from around the world gather to learn the high art of Chinese cooking in places that have few rivals in the height of culinary art.

Western fast food has made a regrettable invasion into Taiwanese thoroughfares in the course of the last decade, and Western-style restaurants of commendable quality can be found at international hotels and independent establishments in Taipei, Kaohsiung, and more rarely other major cities. For the most part, though, food in Taiwan and Taiwanese food are the same as Chinese food. There is, however, a distinction between the food of Taiwan and Taiwanese food, the latter representing a variant of the highly regarded Fujian school of the mainland, the former reflecting the Sino-cosmopolitan nature of the island generally and Taipei especially, resulting from the mainlander immigration into Taiwan from the late 1940s. All four of the major Chinese cooking styles now have ample representation on Taiwan.

Four Styles of Chinese Cooking

Chinese cuisine is divided most logically into four broad styles, beginning with the fundamental distinction between Northern and Southern styles, then classifying the southern style in three separate categories.[1] Northern China is a land of wheat and a variety of grains such as millet, barley, and sorghum; rice dominates south of the Wei River. Pork and fowl have been preferred meats traditionally in China, but mutton has been important in the North, and the South has acquired for China a reputation for consuming dogs, cats, and snakes—all considered off-limits to astounded Westerners. The farmers of the North grow fruits such as peaches, jujubes, apricots, and pears; whereas Southern farmers produce citrus fruits, litchis, and bananas. Similarity among Northern cuisines is sufficient to maintain a single Northern designation. In this region the poorer soils and people of Shanxi and Shaanxi have tended to produce less imaginative fare than have the wealthier people of Hebei, Henan, and the Muslim Northwest. The Southern cuisines sort into three major branches of Chinese cooking: the West, Far South, and East. Cooks in the West make generous use of the chili pepper and thus turn out spicy dishes that stimulate the palate and challenge the tongue. The Far South has numerous adherents and makes claims for being China's finest cuisine, noted for chefs who at their best insist on only the freshest ingredients—fish fresh caught from the bays; vegetables and fruits just harvested from fields and groves. The best chefs of the South maintain split-second timing and fastidious temperature control, and they use an astounding variety of ingredients meticulously blended for both main dishes and sauces.

Taiwanese cuisine is a variant of the Fujianese style, in its turn a highly regarded subcategory of the Eastern style of Chinese cooking. The Eastern style prevails in the mainland's lower Yangtze Valley and the coasts north and south of it. Cooks of this region excel in their preparation of crab, shrimp, water plants, and varieties of seaweed that live close to the confluence of land, fresh water, and the water of the salty seas. They cook with generous amounts of oil, sugar, sweet bean paste, and rice ale. Also used abundantly is vinegar, and that which is produced in Fujian is arguably the finest in the world. Shellfish, fish, and the more tender vegetables find preference in a large variety of dishes; and from a long tradition of Buddhism in this area has evolved excellent vegetarian fare. The great city of Shanghai provided a meeting ground for various eastern Chinese cuisines and a variety of Western cuisines. During the late nineteenth and early twentieth centuries the French, British, Germans, Russians, and others overseeing spheres of influence in China introduced numerous Western foods to Shanghai residents. Thus, Shanghai cooks and chefs gave attention to bread, cakes, pies, candy, and other snacks unusual in other areas of China. Russian influence on the production of fancy cold appetizers reinforced a local tradition based on a similar idea. Some Shanghai chefs learned to master full-course Western meals as well. On the northern extreme of the territory encompassing the Eastern style, Shandong is especially notable for contributing delectable wheat products, including the small dough-wrapped dumplings called *jiaozi* or *shuijiao*, filled with chopped meat, vegetables, leeks, or some combination thereof.

Fujianese variants on the Eastern theme have proponents who advance a claim for this coastal region as having the finest cuisine of the Eastern school and one of the best in all China. Likewise, the Fujianese culinary art finds one of its finest expressions on the island of Taiwan.

Fujianese and Taiwanese Cuisine

Fujianese practitioners of the culinary art offer several unique features in their dishes and the manner in which they are prepared.[2] Among the emphases of Fujianese cooks is that placed on soups. At a banquet, three to five soups are conventionally incorporated into the meal. The thinnest of clear soups, the pure essence of chicken or fish, is highly prized, but thick delicious soups grace Fujianese banquet tables as well; in addition, shark's fin and bird's nest soups are especially well turned out by Fujianese cooks, and a unique soup known as *guobian* (wokside) is produced by cooking a batter at the bottom of the wok, then simmering the soup inside the soft crust.

Unique within the broad tradition of Chinese cooking is the Mongolian chafing dish, which was invented in the North but presented in its most delectable form by the Fujianese. This delightful item in the Chinese repertoire gained fame as a warming dish in the wintertime and remains especially associated with the cold season. A central chimney stoked with fire is featured, ringed by a shallow, doughnut-shaped pan. This pan is filled with stock; diners pick up raw food placed on plates before them and use their chopsticks to hold the morsels in the stock. Thinly sliced, the food cooks rapidly and is dipped in one of several sauces presented for the choice of the diner. In a singular process unique to a cuisine notable for multiple courses and plates, firepot diners drink the stock at meal's end to complete a sumptuous, self-contained meal. Also very popular and superbly developed by Fujianese cooks is Mongolian barbecue, consisting of combinations of meats (venison, mutton, pork, chicken, and beef); vegetable, root, herb, and fruit items (green peppers, onions, leeks, mushrooms, coriander, mint, tomatoes, and pineapple chunks); and sauces: These items are selected by the diner, placed in a large bowl, and then grilled to perfection by cooks wielding yardstick-sized chopsticks; once cooked, the foods are returned to the bowl for gustatory eating. Accompanied by sesame seed–covered *shaobing* bread, Mongolian barbecue as presented on Taiwan is one of our very favorite dining experiences.

Fujianese cooking is unique in China and East Asia generally for its use of lard as cooking oil. This is traceable to the mountainous terrain of the region, where fodder for pigs was plentiful but oilseeds were in short supply; today former necessity has become present preference. Fujianese culinary artists distinguish themselves in other ways from the standard approaches of Chinese cooking. They incorporate more slow-cook methods into their techniques than do the renowned fast-cook artists of other regions; this is a matter of degree, of course: Among the great international cuisines, Chinese food is notable for the exquisite items emphasizing limited cooking duration and split-second timing. But Fujianese cooks have extended the slower process required for simmering stews and soups to other dishes, allowing some vegetables to simmer in the wok longer and thus to gain a softer texture than southern cooks would consider ideal. Steamed and roasted foods are similarly allowed to cook longer. Deep-fat frying is popular among Fujianese chefs and diners, though it is a quick process by Western standards: Fujianese cooks raise the heat high and plunge the food into the bubbling lard so as to sear and seal the food against the intrusion of fat, gaining when properly done a crispy, nongreasy taste.

Dip sauces are popular accompaniments in Fujianese dishes, which tend to have their particular varieties: garlic crushed in vinegar for poultry, sweet malt syrup for fried fish balls, and the wonderful array customary for Mongolian firepot and barbecue dining: soy sauce, wine, vinegar, sugar, chili peppers, garlic, fish essence, sesame oil, and ginger water. Fujianese cooking is similar in its choice of ingredients to other eastern Chinese cooking styles but is peculiar in its fondness for blood, eaten in the spirit of avoiding waste. The preferred method of preparation is coagulation in the manner of soybean milk; it is then sliced and steamed or stir-fried with alliums. Whereas pig's blood is considered common fare, fresh poultry blood served along with the boiled or roasted bird is a delicacy.

Rural Taiwanese cooks maintain the Fujianese lard and noodle heritage, but the Taiwanese variant of the Fujianese style evidences more use of vegetable oil and an even greater emphasis on seafood, along with a number of Japanese influences, than is true of eastern and Fujianese styles generally. Particularly fine editions of *shuijiao* (boiled dumplings) in Taiwan feature crabmeat in addition to the more traditional pork and leek ingredients. Cookbooks filled with particularly admired delicacies in Taiwan are heavy on seafoods, featuring, for example, oysters with black bean sauce; squid centered inside egg yolks; prawns wrapped around seaweed, eggs, pork, lettuce, and carrot slices; garlic puree abalone; cucumber crab rolls; fish-flavored cabbage; and clam and winter melon soup.[3] The Japanese influence can be seen in the Taiwanese preference for lighter, more delicate, and less oil-heavy foods than other Fujianese styles, with the Japanese love of seafood having reinforced that tendency on the Beautiful Island.

Some of the finest fruits in the world come from Taiwan. Citrus fruits produced on the island are especially delicious. Taiwan produces succulent mangoes, papayas, pineapples, watermelons, lemons, and limes and respectable oranges, pears, cantaloupe, and musk melon, as well as other melons. Vegetables are raised with great care. Asparagus and Western mushrooms were raised with high success for the export market during the 1960s and 1970s, but on Taiwanese tables it is the Chinese cabbage, various leafy and spinach-type vegetables, Chinese mushrooms, pea pods, four-season beans, broccoli, carrots, and eggplant that are most in evidence. A typical city street market will display in all over 100 species of fruits and vegetables. Especially notable in Taipei's East Market are family-run *tofu* (bean curd) stalls, where *tofu* settles in large wooden tubs and is sold slightly warm, just the right amount of liquid still in the product, compared favorably by one international cuisine writer to *creme caramel*.[4] Seafood stalls feature live shrimp, crabs, fish, dried and soaked cuttlefish, and soaking seaslugs (sea cucumbers), seven times larger thoroughly soaked than they are when dry. The biggest carrot that we have ever seen (eighteen inches long and eight inches in diameter) appeared before us in a market of the Shihlin district of Taipei.

Bean curd is popular in Taiwan, especially the dried presentation, often pressed to remove the fluid. Buddhist temple restaurants present imitation meat dishes using bean curd to great effect. Fast-food purveyors simmer bean curd, tea, and soy sauce stock along with eggs. Eggs cooked in this way, to absorb other delicious flavors into the eggs, are also common in other Chinese cuisines. A fun outing in the greater Taipei area is a trip to Peitou, where visitors cook their eggs in hot sulfuric springs to putative favorable health effects. Also popular in Taiwan are soybean milk, "soybean curd flowers" (undrained bean curd made into a pudding-textured edible) and soybean skin. Gary's personal favorite among the delightful preparations of this versatile item in the Taiwanese cook's inventory is the stinky *tofu* served up with delicious soy and vinegar dip sauce on Tainan's Tungning Street.

Certain foods in Taiwan are sold at particular times of the day or year. Bread, fruit, and stinky *tofu* are sold mostly in the late afternoon and evening. Soybean milk, steamed buns, and clay-oven rolls (*shaobing*) are sold only in the morning. Spring rolls are sold mostly during April; moon cakes during the Mid-Autumn Festival; rice dumplings (*zongzi*) during the Dragon Boat Festival. "Red Turtle Cakes" are prepared for birthdays and temple worship. Snake meat and blood are mostly served in night markets, most notoriously in "Snake Alley" of southwestern Taipei. The Taiwanese eat snake, tiger, and dog particularly for their medicinal value. Because these are expensive, no one would drop them into one's soup, noodles, or fried rice as a replacement for beef. The likelihood of being served dog meat has been further reduced in recent years because preparing and serving this fare has become legally proscribed.

As Taiwanese society has become ever more sophisticated, and as the island's decision makers have liberalized the economic, social, and political life of the island, Taiwan's profile in matters of international culture has risen accordingly. Taiwan now has a number of people, many known by Anglicized names, who have gained fame on the international culinary scene.[5] Theresa Lin, consultant to the Chinese Gourmet Association, served as chief adviser on matters of food preparation and presentation for Ang Lee's well-received film *Eat Drink Man Woman*. A language major at Taiwan's Fujen Catholic University and a student of design and nutrition, Ms. Lin served 750 kilos of food for the film's opening night party at the Cannes Film Festival; she also coordinated the efforts of six master chefs toward production of the 1,000-person banquet in Los Angeles to promote *Eat Drink Man Woman.* Jason Ong, director of food and beverages at Tien Hsiang Lo, one of the best West Lake (Hangzhou) style restaurants in the world, delights international visitors with his drunken chicken; preserved duck; pickled radish; fish smoked over brown sugar, rice and tea leaves; water lily soup with handmade fishballs; and the famous dish West Lake Fish, served with cucumbers and edible flowers. Chef Yang Chi Hua at Taipei's Din Tai Fung Restaurant makes dumplings filled with a chicken and jellied consommé mixture that turns liquid when cooked; the result is such a delectable example of the culinary art that two foreign chefs once came to study with him for a full week but failed in their attempts to learn how to make the dumplings. Mary Yang presides over kitchens at her architecturally splendid Fu Yuen Restaurant in Taipei that produce such delectables as sautéed duck liver; jellyfish wrapped in vegetable leaves; squid and leek bundles; fried, stuffed bamboo shoots served with slices of roast goose, roast duck, and cucumber; *tofu* formed in the shape of a small fish surrounded by pea pods cut to look like fishtails and fins, accompanied by crabmeat sauce; and a molded almond gel dessert with sliced kiwi, honeydew melon, starfruit, and fruit sauce.

Accompanying dining experiences as extraordinary as those offered up by these chefs, and those of a more humble nature as well, is a code of etiquette fastidiously observed by the people of Taiwan.

Manners and Customs of Dining

Taiwanese people maintain the Chinese preference for chopsticks. Somewhere between the ages of five and seven a Taiwanese child becomes comfortable with using chopsticks. Until then, she or he has made do with the aesthetically pleasing deep, curved Chinese spoon, which adults use almost exclusively for consuming soup. Using chopsticks is not nearly so difficult as most Westerners suppose and is one of those skills best learned through observing experts and application of what one learns with personal practice and adaptation. What one does, fundamentally, is hold the bottom chopstick stationary in the crook between the thumb and the index finger while positioning the corresponding bottom utensil for pinching the morsels of food between the two chopsticks. Taiwanese folks never use a knife unless they venture into a Western-style restaurant in the big cities or, much more rarely, towns. Because the cutting is done at the preparatory stage, fowl, pork, beef, and other meats come in small chunks, as do vegetable pieces, with which they are often tossed together. In general, Taiwanese people do not like huge amounts of meat and would even find the eight- and certainly sixteen-ounce beefsteaks coveted by many Westerners an intimidating, wasteful, and even revolting proposition. Traditionally a luxury in Taiwanese society, meat was to be savored in small amounts as a flavoring for and accompaniment of rice, noodles, and vegetables. Larger chunks of meat in the form of pork chops and chicken legs, breasts, and thighs do make it onto the serving table at a number of the economical and occasionally quite good cafeterias that dot Taiwanese towns and, especially, cities. In these cases there still is no recourse to knife and fork; rather, the whole piece is held between the chopsticks, a bite is taken, and the entire piece is put down until by further repetition of this procedure the pork chop or chicken part is consumed. More tradition- ally, this same sort of technique was used with larger items such as spring rolls. It is a matter of observation, practice, and adaptation; our little boy, Ryan, surprised us on a return visit to Taiwan (the place of his birth) at the age of six when, after only observing us and playing around with chopsticks in previous years and months, he picked them up and used them like a skilled veteran.

Other matters of Taiwanese meal customs are notable for the Westerner. A Taiwanese diner holds her or his rice bowl close to the face rather than leaving the bowl on the table. Plates do remain on the table, however; in the traditional style, diners reach for the morsels from common platters and with their chopsticks take just enough to go directly into the mouth. Fish, chicken, pork, and other bones are spit out onto the table; this may rankle the Western sense of propriety and hygiene but is much preferred by Taiwanese to placing the bones in the rice bowl or on a small plate, and of course putting these back on the common platter would never do. Chopsticks should never be placed pointed down into the bowl; they should, rather, be placed across the top of the bowl or on the table. Leaving chopsticks sticking vertically into the bowl is reminiscent of incense sticks placed in a bowl of ashes at a temple, an inauspicious signal of death. Use of the toothpick likewise differs from the Western style. One hand is used to operate the toothpick, the other to block another person's view of this operation. Allowing another person to witness one's toothpick between one's teeth removing food is considered unseemly.

Special banquets in Taiwan such as that occasioned by the New Year, temple worship, or a wedding will feature at least ten courses. Unless diners pace themselves, they will feel a post–Thanksgiving gastronomic misery as they face most of those courses still awaiting consumption. Even at the most sumptuous feast, the host will respond to a guest's compliments with the return, *"Mei shemma cai"* ("This food isn't anything [worth complimenting]"). The claim of having presented a humble spread is understood by all in attendance to be a *pro forma* exhibition of humility, even though the recognition on the part of the guest tendering the compliment is much appreciated and the host actually takes great pride in the feast that she or he has cooked, arranged, or paid for. Commonly, if a number of people have gathered for a special meal at a restaurant and the exact responsibility for payment is indefinite, the male family heads or other individuals bearing potential financial responsibility for the meal rush to the cashier to pay the bill. In most such situations a pattern of reciprocity has evolved from the group's history of mutual celebration, and thus the person whose turn has arrived will emerge as the payer. The offer to pay, the ultimate willingness of all but the payer to back off, and the arrival at the correct payer according to the rules of reciprocity are part of a very important social ethic in Taiwan whereby people try to maintain balance in mutual obligation, payment of debts, and at all cost avoidance of being one over whose head a social obligation lingers.[6]

Taiwanese people take particular delight in certain beverages, especially tea and a variety of alcoholic drinks. The consumption of these beverages entails other rituals particular to Chinese and Taiwanese culture.

Beverages and Drinking Rituals

Taiwanese folk have no lingering guilt over the consumption of alcoholic beverages, and booze can flow freely at celebratory occasions. Traditionally women were expected to be discrete about alcohol consumption, and if they declined would be respected for doing so. A devout Buddhist would likewise be released from the social pressure to imbibe. But for males in general, though random and chronic drunkenness is frowned upon, participation in liquor consumption at banquets and such is expected, and the pressure to drink is intense. Domestic alcohol production in Taiwan is a government monopoly, and imports are expensive. Taiwanese beer is cheap, though, and enjoys a good reputation for quality. It is labeled by the straightforward name "Taiwan Beer." By all accounts Taiwan also produces a good sweet red grape wine, a plum wine, and a white grape wine appreciated by some Westerners. The liquors, however, are in general strong and harsh tasting, reputedly best for mixing with other beverages. Taiwanese rum reportedly mixes well with Coca-Cola.[6] The Taiwanese, though, prefer to drink their liquors straight. The strongest of a muscle-bound lot is Kaoliang, which takes its name from the locally grown *gaoliang* (Chinese sorghum) from which it is made. NASA would do well to examine its potential as rocket fuel: It contains 65 percent alcohol; a little goes a long way as a liberator of social inhibitions. Also quite popular is Shaoshing wine (rice wine), plenty potent at 15 percent alcohol content.

Attendance at a feast or dinner party will lead to invitations to play *hua-jiuquan*, a finger game that obliges the loser to empty his glass. Repeated losses create for the unlucky player the demeanor of a boxer down for the count and ultimately out, being dragged from the ring by, in this case be-mused, handlers. Most difficult of all for the nondrinker to refuse is the toast, with its attendant calls for *gan bei*, "dry glass." If the party finds great num-bers of people and matters to toast, the result is a field day for Taiwanese herbal medicine shop proprietors visited when light returns and heads are pounding. A possible out during such occasions comes in the form of the phrase *sui yi*, "as you like," which sets up a sipping maneuver as a surrogate for the bottoms-up approach. Gary holds to the more stubborn teetotaler's refusal, which calls forth an initial response of astonishment, momentary hurt, and mild ill-feeling that ultimately gives way to respect and admiration from the male participants in the drinking rituals.

On the stimulant side of things, tea is a product of literally more uplifting qualities in Taiwan.[7] With its mostly subtropical and occasionally tropical climate and abundance of hillsides and upper elevations, Taiwan is an ideal place for growing tea. The black tea preferred by Westerners for iced tea and, perhaps by inertia, for hot tea is called "red tea" in Taiwan. Fully fermented at twenty-seven degrees centigrade for several hours then heated at ninety-five degrees for drying, the local product is of high quality. Green tea is also grown. This variety is steamed rather than fermented; then the leaves are rolled, crushed, and dried. Perhaps enjoyed most by older folks who acquired a taste for this variety of tea from the Japanese, who imbibe it enthusiastically, this is not the usual Taiwanese preference. Jasmine, a mixture of green tea and flowers, has some adherents, but the greatest popular following goes to oolong (*wulong*, "black dragon"), a fine tea produced at arguably the highest level of quality in the world on the island of Taiwan. Oolong is a partially fermented tea that has variations including *longjing* (dragon well), a relatively mild version; *tie guanyin* (iron goddess of mercy), a rather strong blend; and *dongfang meiren* (Eastern beauty), a relatively heavily caffeinated mixture.

Drinking tea in Taiwan involves a whole aesthetic. A classy way to prepare and drink tea is sometimes known as "old man style." A tiny teapot is stuffed full of tea leaves, then scalding hot water is poured inside; before steeping for very long, the tea is poured into a small flask to cool; it is then served in tiny cups, allowing the tea to finish cooling quickly. More water is poured into the teapot, and a second brew is prepared. As the tea gets weaker, the water is left to steep the leaves longer. At an artfully judged point beyond which the leaves no longer provide excellent flavor, the steeped leaves are discarded, the pot stuffed with leaves again, and a new brew prepared. A number of teahouses can be found in Taiwan for tea, conversation, and reading. One pays between N.T. $130 and N.T. $360 (U.S. $5–$15), then can sit for hours refilling the pot with hot water at will. Tea in Taiwan is never taken with milk and sugar; this would be an aesthetic abomination ruinous of the pure taste of this product that commands such local pride. Herbal teas are not usually sold in tea shops but can be purchased in grocery stores, supermarkets, and pharmacies. Hibiscus tea is rather good. Wheat tea is reminiscent of coffee. Ginger tea is spicy and strong but has enthusiastic adherents; the unusual taste of chrysanthemum tea would, in contrast, find few Western enthusiasts.

Taiwanese people consider tea to have a variety of healthful benefits, some of which can be substantiated by scientific research. Tea is high in fluoride, which benefits the teeth. It also contains polyphenol, which some residents think has cancer-fighting properties. Green tea is particularly high in both of these substances. The Taiwanese are highly conscious of the impact of food and drink on their health. This is in fact part of a long tradition originating on the mainland and continuing to this day on Taiwan.

Food and Drink as Medicine

Taiwanese people have traditionally not made a rigid distinction between food as sustenance and food as medicine.[8] The two functions of food consumption are in the Taiwanese conception closely related, although certain foods are particularly valued for their medicinal value. Illnesses great and small in Taiwan are occasions for alteration of the diet, the first thing done by the patient or family at the onset of sickness. The Taiwanese react to physical distress of any kind by changing what they eat. Diet and medicine are closely related, one shading into the other with minimal distinction. Ginseng, white fungus, birds' nests, and stewed wild birds are foods but among those edibles reserved mainly for medicinal use.

Taiwanese traditional doctors follow the Chinese science of nutrition based on the observation that foods provide corporal energy. Energy takes different forms, found in different foods. Some foods build strength, others weaken the body. The term for energy is *qi*, "breath," "spirit," or "invisible energy." This same *qi*, or life force, is the essential energy behind the internal combustion engine and is prevalent in all matter associated with air or gas. The forces behind the cosmic *qi* are *yang* and *yin*. *Yang* is associated with the sun and thus represents the bright, dry, warm aspect of the cosmos, whereas *yin* is associated with the moon and represents the dark, moist, cool aspect of the universe. *Yang* is thought to be the active, potent, male force, whereas *yin* is thought to be the positive, receptive, female force. Both are necessary and equally instrumental in bringing things into existence, sustaining them during their earthly tenure, and governing those processes by which things die, pass on to other forms, or are regenerated. Incorporated into the Taiwanese philosophy of medicine is the Chinese attachment to the number five, which describes the five phases (earth, metal, wood, fire, and water), the five directions (north, east, south, west, center), the five smells (rancid, scorched, fragrant, rotten, putrid), and the five flavors (sour, bitter, sweet, pungent [piquant, "hot"], and salty). Seminal Han dynasty medical texts linked each of these flavors with the particular region of China that at the time emphasized the particular flavor or taste in its cooking.

Great herbal and agricultural texts appeared on the Chinese mainland during the fifth century A.D. Sometime before then the idea of humoral medicine, shared by the Hippocratic-Galenic, Vedic, and Near Eastern medical traditions, entered China, introduced by Buddhists, who first came to China in significant numbers after the fall of the Han dynasty and the reunification of China by the dynasties of Sui and Tang. The humoral theory holds that the body is affected by the paired opposites of hot-cold and wet-dry. In the Chinese dietary system, certain foods are accordingly productive of heat or cold, wetness or dryness. Heating foods include ginger, pepper, chilies, meat, fat, and sugar. Foods considered heating are also taken to have properties that strengthen the body. Among these, foods considered especially strengthening are chicken stew, pig's blood, internal organs, dog meat, snake meat, guava, and Chinese wolfhorn berries. These foods are particularly valuable in treating diseases in which the body temperature falls to a low level: tuberculosis, shock, pallor, chills, wasting, anemia, and diarrhea. This association of heating foods with strengthening qualities was based on principles that we today recognize to be sound: The foods designated as heating and strengthening are in general those high in iron, protein, and other minerals enhancing bodily strength and energy levels. Some foods are considered beneficial to those in good physical condition but dangerously heating to those not in good shape; those who are in a weakened condition should, in the Taiwanese medical conception, stay away from such dangerously overheating consumables as strong alcoholic beverages and all foods that are fried, long-baked, or spicy hot. In contrast, milder heating foods are considered strengthening and restorative to those suffering from, or given to, chronic illness; they are particularly good for those possessed of too much cool energy. These foods include most meats, red beans, ginger, many varieties of ginseng (although some kinds are considered cooling), and a few vegetables; an especially notable example of a mildly heating, restorative vegetable is chrysanthemum, the edible greens of which are spicy, but not overly so.

Cooling foods according to the Taiwanese medical tradition include especially vegetables: Chinese cabbage, watercress, carrots, green radishes, green beans, and all manner of other vegetable fare. Cooling foods are considered appropriate for treating conditions such as chronic sores, dry skin, redness, fever, rash, overheating, burns, and constipation. Since vegetables tend to be high in fiber, minerals, and vitamins, the traditional Taiwanese medical view again followed generally sound principles. Certainly there were gut level associations that were logical in their own way but not in accord with modern nutritional science. Bitter foods were considered heating, as were foods with vivid, striking colors: red, orange, or brilliant yellow. Icy white and green foods were considered cooling, whereas pale brown and chalk white foods were considered neutral. Even many of these associations, though, were formed in the presence of confirming experience. Many protein-rich, or heating, foods, for example, do have a red color; the so-called cooling vegetables are frequently green; and neutral staples such as rice, noodles, and fish do tend toward bland coloration. Some foods present question marks, arising from certain contradictions between color and substance: Are plums heating or cooling? They have the heating property of red coloring but the cooling characteristics of sour taste and watery texture. Such contradictions were often resolved on the basis of opinions prevailing in the village or marketing area.

Categories of wet and dry also held sway in the traditional Taiwanese medicinal foods system. Many kinds of shellfish and watery fruits offer particularly salient examples of foods considered wetting. Coffee, dry-roasted peanuts, and most foods dry in texture and received as such on the tongue are considered drying. The wet-dry continuum is not as important as that of hot-cool, but it does affect the kind of treatments prescribed and fits well into the logic of the system, grounded in the Confucian worldview emphasizing balance, order, and harmony.

Taiwanese nutritional medicine includes a category of foods known as *bu*—"supplementing," "patching," or "strengthening"—closely associated with certain warming foods but distinct from the humoral polarities of hot-cool and dry-wet. The *bu* foods are held to be particularly effective in promoting tissue repair, restoring proper blood flow, and producing general tonic action. Foods considered *bu* are generally easily digested, high-quality protein; thus, this category has in the main been deduced on rational bases:

The foods included do have qualities that promote bodily strength, blood cell proliferation, and iron buildup. Some foods are considered *bu* because their appearance or color suggests qualities pertinent to the category: The edible contents inside the walnut shell resemble the brain, for example, and red jujubes and port wine have the color of blood. Other foods are considered *bu* because of some obvious, direct association: Stewed lungs of animals are held to be good for human lungs; the blood of pigs, chickens, or ducks is thought to bolster the contents of human blood. The most popular source of *bu* is fowl; the wild fowl that roam the hills and mountains of Taiwan are considered especially *bu*. Certainly it is very *bu* to the pocketbooks of restaurant owners in the hills of Tainan County: We came away gastronomically delighted but economically humbled after a dining experience at an establishment specializing in wild fowl, boar, and rabbit. Frequently plants, animals, and parts thereof that have particularly striking appearances are considered to have very potent *bu* action; thus sea cucumbers, ginseng (cooked in foods or taken in powdered or tinctured form), birds' nests, raccoon, dogs, deer antlers, bear gall, snake meat, rhinoceros horn, shark fins, white tree fungus, abalone, unusual-looking fish (such as the giant grouper), pangolins, and other wild animals are considered highly effective in their supplementing and strengthening capacities. Although Taiwanese medicine and traditional Chinese medicine in general are not overly attentive to foods with reputed aphrodisiac properties, the genitalia of the buck is considered to enhance sexual functioning of the human male; a wide variety of foods rich in minerals and protein likewise are held to heighten potency and male sexual functioning. *Bu* foods frequently have moderately stimulating effects, as with the panaquin and panaquiline found in ginseng; such substances are energizing but not "wiring" in the manner of caffeine. Ginseng is usually considered to fall in the "heaven and ruler" class of substances that promote overall strengthening of the body and increase of energy rather than helping a particular condition, as with other tonic *bu* drugs. Foods considered *bu* are generally found at the low-calorie, low-fat, low-irritant end of the hot scale; they are heating, but gently so, producing a soothing warmth rather than a sudden shock. Great *bu* effect is thought to be produced by steaming or simmering animal foods slowly with herbs; calcium is in fact leached in significant quantity from chicken bones stewed in enough vinegar.

Certain foods are held to be *du* (poisonous). This category of foods can introduce poison directly into the body, but more commonly such foods cause poisons to arise within the body through chemical reactions of foods in combination. Uncastrated male poultry is thought to be capable of causing cancer. Sometimes beef, lamb, mutton, several kinds of fish, nuts, and seeds, and even certain vegetables produce hives, rashes, and allergic reactions. These are caused by the heating and wetting properties of particular foods in combination: Rashes appear when internally produced poisons break out at the surface of the body. In this conception of Taiwanese traditional medicine, susceptibility to venereal disease results from similar internal chemical reactions productive of overheating, excessive wetness, and the manifestation of those conditions in rashes and sores. There is a close association between *du* items and *bu* substances. The seeming paradox gains some resolution when it is understood that *bu* items have a broad pharmacological effectiveness that in a given individual and in given combinations can give rise to internal poisons: they are powerful in their curative capability but under certain prevailing conditions difficult to control. People in Taiwan commonly consider crab to be ill-combined with pumpkin, port to be a bad companion of licorice, and mackerel potentially dangerous in combination with plums.

Foods sometimes provide *qing* (cleaning), *xiao* (dispelling), and *jiedu* (poison-freeing) functions, as well. Such foods can cure inflammation and edema by clearing away excess wetness, "wind," and accumulating ill humors. According to the traditional Taiwanese medical view, licorice and honey are particularly effective in freeing the body of poisons. Other foods having *qing, xiao,* and *jiedu* capabilities are brown sugar, sugarcane juice, and some vegetables and herbs. Taiwanese pharmacies sell an herbal mixture known as *qing bu liang* (named for its ability to "clean," "strengthen," and "cool"). Variously containing herbal tea or a soup mix, *qing bu liang* can reputedly at once flush out extraneous substances, gently strengthen the body, and provide a kind of cooling relief from excessive internal heating.

"Taiwanese people really like to eat stuff" (*Taiwan ren zhen xihuan chi dongxi*), goes a popular recognition of reality on this island of our fascination. No wonder. Most people on Taiwan are descendants of Fujian folk who created one of China's greatest culinary traditions. Taiwanese people, surrounded as they are by ocean and expert as they have proven themselves at fish farming, have in turn developed a magnificent variation on the Eastern and Fujianese styles of cooking. On top of that wonderful inheritance and innovation, historical events have found people from all mainland provinces immigrating to Taiwan, bringing with them the culinary artistry practiced for thousands of years by people for whom food as sustenance, health, and art is a prime feature of their culture. The people of Taiwan have held firmly to their own cultural heritage of food, even as other aspects of Western culture have made significant inroads into this island's modern life. The comfort and convenience of Western clothing, by contrast, have for the most part turned the preferences of today's Taiwanese away from a very rich tradition of Chinese and Taiwanese fashion, toward the less encumbering styles of the West.

CLOTHING AND FASHION

Taiwan inherited the rich, millennia-old Chinese tradition of textile making, embroidery, and symbolism. Despite its richness and beauty, traditional Chinese clothing is one of the cultural traditions most completely abandoned in everyday life in Taiwan. Modern Western clothing has been thoroughly embraced in school and business life as appropriately modern and efficient. Young urban Taiwanese dress in cosmopolitan clothes not significantly different from what you might see in Tokyo or Milan. In fact, Italian and Japanese designers are particularly popular in stores in Taipei and Kaohsiung. More traditional Taiwanese clothing can still be seen on older rural Taiwanese people and for special ceremonial occasions.

Clothing Traditions

Until the manufacture of synthetic fabrics in this century, Taiwanese clothing was made of hemp, cotton, and silk. Cultivated in China since the third millennium B.C., hemp dominated Chinese clothing until the mid-thirteenth century, when cotton became the most popular textile. Cotton was first introduced to the Chinese mainland from India during the Song dynasty and was grown in both northern and southern China. Cotton became the most popular fabric for Chinese peasants and workers; as a result, despite widespread production in China, imports from India and later the United States and England were necessary to meet demand.

Silk was highly valued, but only the wealthy could afford it. Silk production in China, which dates back to around 3000 B.C., is accompanied by numerous legends about silk's invention. Tradition links the invention of sericulture to the Lady Xi Ling, wife of the legendary Yellow Emperor. As early as the second century B.C. Chinese silks were exported to the West along the Silk Route from Changan to Afghanistan to Iran to Syria. By the nineteenth century, silk had become China's leading export because of the beautiful silks produced by famous silk-making centers like Hangzhou, Suzhou, and Wuxi.

Most Taiwanese were far from wealthy. The majority needed clothing for working in the fishing industry or in the fields and thus wore simple outfits of blue or black clothing made of cotton or home-grown hemp topped with jackets buttoned down the center or the right side. Very little was spent on clothing, and often a single set of clothes sufficed. Cloth was usually imported from Zhejiang or eastern Guangdong Provinces and then dyed and assembled in Taiwan. Children and women sometimes wore more colorful clothing with patterned hems.

Subethnic groups in Taiwan had distinct clothing traditions. Each group followed slightly different traditions concerning women's headwear and the aprons worn over their clothing. The Fujianese, for example, wore conical bamboo hats to protect them from sun and rain. The Hakka hat, in contrast, was made of a flat circle of straw with black cotton fringe around the edge. Rectangular cotton scarves were worn on the head by Hakka women, as well, especially when indoors.[9]

Textile and clothing traditions of Taiwan's indigenous peoples differ dramatically from those of the Chinese subethnic groups in Taiwan. Each group has its own preferred colors and its own weaving and appliqué styles. The clothing style, colors, and weaving techniques all emphasize the separate origin of these groups. Indigenous peoples wear the same modern clothes as the urban Taiwanese, but for important rituals and ceremonial dances they adorn themselves with their traditional attire. They also wear these bright distinctive costumes as part of tourist entertainment for foreigners or even the Taiwanese.

During the Qing dynasty, wealthier Taiwanese imported silk fabric and clothes from the Chinese mainland. The clothes of the wealthy were much more elaborate and symbolic than the garments of the working classes. Traditional clothing consisted of mainly loose, straight lines that could be worn either hanging from the shoulders or sashed at the waist. The *changpao* was a long one-piece robe worn by both men and women. The *shenyi* and *bianfu* were generously cut tunic and skirt combinations. Rather simple in design, traditional garments themselves required relatively little stitching. Of course, the wealthier the person, the more fabric would be used in constructing the clothing. The distinctive, elaborate design of the clothing was found in the embellished sashes, hems, bands, and drapes.

Embroidery was the primary means of decoration. The art of embroidery was a valued skill for women as early as the Shang dynasty (sixteenth through eleventh centuries B.C.). As early as the Han dynasty eight different stitches were employed to create beautiful, intricate designs on silk clothing: Included were the chain stitch, the couched stitch, the seed knot stitch, the satin stitch, the stem stitch, the buttonhole stitch, the quilting stitch, and appliqué.[10] In combination stitches could create images as detailed as fine painting with a rich three-dimensional surface. Embroidery designs were often handed down

7.1 Rich embroidery used in temple banner.

from mother to daughter, although patterns were also available to expand the design repertoire.

Whatever our culture, we can easily appreciate embroidered designs of flowers or birds; but to understand the symbolism of these and other designs, we must know which plants and animals are traditionally used to symbolize particular ideals or wishes. Some objects used to embellish clothing or other textile items are chosen because they are homophones of Chinese terms for good fortune (*fu*), official position (*lu*), long life (*shou*) and happiness (*xi*). The bat is a popular animal, especially on boys' clothing, because the word for bat (*fu*) sounds like the word for good fortune. Five bats represent the five blessings of long life, good health, official position, love of virtue, and natural death. Fruits containing many seeds, like the pomegranate, are symbols for the many sons that Taiwanese traditionally hoped for. Continued fertility is expressed by a lotus blossom because its name sounds like "continually giving birth" (*lian sheng*). In addition to the depiction of the birds, fish, and animals that were part of everyday life, in their embroidery embroiderers often used mythological beasts, especially the dragon (*long*), the *qilin* (a one-horned creature quite unlike the Europeans' unicorn), and the phoenix (*fenghuang*). Young women would embroider to prove their worth as future daughters-in-law, to prepare their wedding clothing, and later to prepare special clothing for their children, especially their precious sons. In their wedding items, women embroidered the symbol for marital happiness: the Chinese characters *shuangxi,* "double happiness." This auspicious double-character is one traditional symbol that has, if anything, increased in popularity as more and more money is spent on wedding banquet decorations, foods, invitations, and the like.

Historically, both wealthy Taiwanese and peasant Taiwanese shared the same understanding of color symbolism, even if the peasants were less often able to express the symbolism fully. Blue, the most often worn color, is considered a dignified, ritually neutral color. The two colors with the most powerful symbolism are red and white. Red represents all things auspicious and especially those things related to fertility and life, namely, weddings, births, New Year's, and all joyful celebrations of life. Unlike in the West, white symbolizes death and sorrow. The Taiwanese are the inheritors of a developed elaborate etiquette for proper mourning attire based primarily on the use of white fabrics and undyed, coarse hemp cloth.

Children's clothing in old Taiwan was modeled on adult clothing styles, consisting of a jacket, robes, and trousers. Most children's clothing was made of cotton, but silk would be used for special occasions and by the wealthy. Bright colors made children's clothing distinctive; particularly popular were the auspicious colors of red and pink or the royal colors of gold and orange. Children's clothing often included symbols of long life and protection from evil spirits. The gods of good fortune, auspicious fruits and flowers, and protective animals could be depicted on clothing or accessories for children. Popularly depicted on boys' hats or clothing was the tiger, known not to be aggressive toward humans but fierce in attacking evil spirits that might harm a child. Since survival of the first month of life was an important celebratory occasion for Taiwanese babies, specially decorated clothing would be offered along with other gifts. Infant boys' clothing was elaborate and decorative, symbolizing the greater value placed on the birth and survival of sons in the family.

The Taiwanese who follow traditional practices give their children numerous accessories to protect them. Bells tied on clothing or string frightens the evil spirits. Necklaces with jade or gold charms are worn by anyone but are particularly important for the protection of children. Coins worn around the neck with a red thread are thought to bring good fortune. Different subethnic groups have specific hat designs for the protection and celebration of their children on special occasions such as the first-month celebration, New Year's, and temple festivals.

Religious, Ceremonial, and Ritual Attire

Although seen only occasionally on the elderly for everyday wear, traditional clothing is important for ceremonial occasions, religious rituals, and theatrical performances. For formal wear, men and women may still wear the simple traditional *changshan* for men and *qipao* for women. The *qipao* is an elegant Manchu dress that became popular for women during the Qing dynasty. A slender dress with a high, closed collar, slits up the sides, and buttons down the right side, the *qipao* developed into numerous forms appropriate to season and occasion. The dress could have long, short, or no sleeves; the length could be short or long. Taiwanese women today sometimes wear variations on the *qipao*, especially for formal or ceremonial occasions. Men in Taiwan also may wear traditional dress for these occasions by putting on a dark *changshan* or long gown.

In Taiwan, as in many cultures, religious attire is the most traditional attire of ordinary life. Buddhist monks and nuns, Taoist priests, and even members of some sects wear traditional religious attire that dates back centuries. For everyday wear Buddhist monks and nuns put on simple gray or saffron yellow robes made of pieced cotton, but on ceremonial occasions their attire consists of elaborate embroidered robes of silk and ritual headdresses.

Taoist priests also wear elaborate embellished robes when they perform public temple rituals. Depending on the Taoist sect, the priest's robes may be white, black, or bright red.[11] The ritual attire of a Taoist great master is given at his ordination. In the ceremony he goes from the simple Taoist black robe to the ornately embroidered robes decorated with designs of gods riding animals, elaborate palaces, constellations, and mountains and water. On his feet are richly embroidered thick-soled boots; on his head is a crownlike headpiece.[12] Lay devotees of Taoist and Buddhist temples may wear long blue robes while chanting scriptures or helping out at the temple.

Not surprisingly the Taiwanese have special symbolic clothing for weddings and funerals. Taiwanese wedding attire is elaborate and varied. Young Taiwanese patronize wedding studios to have beautiful, romantic photographs taken in a variety of costumes, including white Western wedding dress and tuxedo, colored evening gown and formal Western suit, *qipao* and long robe, or the traditional Chinese wedding attire of elaborate red costume for the bride and formal robe for the groom. One of the most popular prewedding photographs is with the bride in white wedding gown with her Western-attired groom in a beautiful landscaped park. The popularity of the white wedding gown shows the power of Western culture in Taiwan, especially since white has traditionally been a color of mourning. The auspicious color for weddings and other happy events, red continues to be the dominant color of wedding banquets, invitations, and decorations.

Mourning attire has been less influenced by Western traditions than has wedding attire. Funerals are still taken very seriously as a matter of honoring ancestors, ensuring the well-being of the living, and publicly establishing family roles and status. No single correct attire exists for funerals because clothing is dictated by a person's familial and economic relationship to the deceased. In a study of mourning clothes in Sanhsia in northern Taiwan in the 1960s, Arthur Wolf found perhaps 100 different forms of attire expressing specific relationships to the deceased.[13] Sons wore coarse, undyed hemp, grandsons wore yellowish-gray flax, and great-grandsons wore dark blue muslin. Fourth- and fifth-generation mourners would wear gowns and hats of red or yellow respectively. At funerals red had two meanings. Red worn by great-great-grandsons was meant to celebrate the long life and many descendants of the deceased. The wearing of small patches of red cloth by friends of the deceased or by hired workers, though, was not at all for joy; rather, it was for protecting the wearer from the negative influence of death. Brothers of the deceased wore white, but if they had established economically independent households, they would wear some red on their headbands to prevent negative influences coming into their own families. Shops in Sanhsia rented the clothing to family members for the funerals. In much of Taiwan in the 1990s, the funerals have become perhaps even more elaborate and expensive than in the past, but the mourning attire has been simplified. Siblings, children, and grandchildren might simply wear a cape and hood of undyed coarse hemp over ordinary clothes. Mourning is often expressed outside the funeral ritual itself simply by a piece of black cloth safety-pinned to one's dress or business suit.

Theatrical Costumes

Elaborate symbolic costumes brighten the stages of both Taiwanese opera and Beijing opera. Costumes convey information about the character of the wearers. Thus at a glance one can see the gender, status, and moral attributes of the role. Color may indicate status, such as the red worn by emperors and nobles. It may distinguish age by dressing the young in pink and the old in white, or it may express personal character through the blue robes of a loyal, brave official. Facial makeup adds to the symbolism of opera characters through the color and shape of the bright masklike makeup. Other accessories convey meaning as well. Officials wear black hats with wings, for example, and the warriors may wear pheasant plumes.

Opera and puppet theater costumes vividly express the nature of the characters. The attire does not, however, convey information about context. The costumes are the same regardless of the historical period of the drama or the season of the scene. In opera, performers express seasonal changes with their movements. In a winter scene, for instance, the actor expresses cold by crossing his arms over his shoulders.

Traditional costumes remain visible in Taiwan, but mainly in a ritual or performance context. Numerous historical dramas on television and in movies present the rich history of Chinese costume, and the gods and goddesses depicted in paintings, woodblock images, and statuary are often portrayed wearing the official or imperial costumes of the Ming or Qing dynasty. Indeed, the modernization of Taiwanese costume has had little effect on the ritual costume of religion and theater.

Modern Fashion

In recent decades the Taiwanese have eagerly modernized and Westernized their clothing for daily wear. Until the late 1980s much of Taiwanese fashion was Taiwan-made clothing of relatively poor style from a Westerner's perspective. Although not exactly world-class fashion, the clothes could be purchased inexpensively at the thriving night markets. Women's clothing tended to have more frills and flounces than the Western dresses on which they were based. Many men in business and government wore the light-weight Asian suit rather than the heavier Western suit and tie. Although many Taiwanese factories were making shoes and clothing for export to the West, these Western-designed items were not widely available until the cutting of the high tariffs on textile imports in the late 1980s.

The Taiwanese quickly embraced Western designer clothes, however, as soon as they become available and affordable after the 1980s tariff reductions. Although imports from Hong Kong and Italy increased in the mid-1990s, imports from Japan began the trend. In Taipei the large Sogo department store, a Taiwanese-Japanese joint venture, concentrates on moderately priced imports for a younger crowd. European, Japanese, and American designer labels are found not only in Taipei but also in department stores in Kaohsiung, Taichung, and Tainan.[14] As air conditioning spreads throughout the island, the wearing of Western business suits is seen not only as more stylish by businesspeople but also as relatively comfortable.

Taiwanese designers have become more international in style as well. Many were educated abroad and chose foreign names for their labels. Some designers draw on Chinese tradition for design inspiration. Imagery from Chinese paintings or patterns from ancient bronzes appear in modern dresses. The continuing presence of traditional Chinese clothing in ritual and performance influences and inspires designers wishing to incorporate traditional Chinese esthetics into their modern styles.

Furthermore, young people in Taiwan have become increasingly experimental with their fashion. In school, Taiwanese children and teenagers still wear uniforms of blue, khaki, or green with their shirts bearing the name of the schools. Recently a strict and unpopular requirement of short hair for boys and girls has been dropped, and there is somewhat less uniformity in the schoolday look of children. Out of school, children are dressed in bright colors and teens wear the latest of styles. Yet the importance the Taiwanese attach to dressing their infants, and the joy they feel in doing so, continues. Even in children's clothing, traditionally full of symbols of protection and good fortune, many Taiwanese have started to embrace Western styles and brand names.

In funerary ceremonies, local opera and stage performances, some contemporary adaptations, and the Lukang Folk Arts Museum, a visitor to today's Taiwan can view a splendid tradition of fashion. Much more dominant in current culture, Chinese and Taiwanese cuisine occupy every alley, street, back road, and aspect of contemporary life on Taiwan. Food and dress are interesting in their contrasting manifestations in the everyday life of today's Taiwan. These contrasts and the particular attractions of Taiwanese cuisine and fashion are among those many facets of the customs and culture of Taiwan that make the island such a fascinating place to visit, live, and study.

NOTES

1. E. N. Anderson, *The Food of China* (New Haven, CT: Yale University Press, 1988), pp. 194–95, uses this classification. Anderson himself is following Emily Hahn, *The Cooking of China* (New York: Time-Life Books, 1968), and Fu Pei-Mei, *Pei-Mei's Chinese Cookbook*, vol. 1 (Taipei: by the author, 1969).

2. Anderson, pp. 197–202, has a good review of Fujianese and Taiwanese cooking, very helpful to us in writing this section.

3. See, for example, Wei Chuan Cultural-Educational Foundation, *Taiwanese Style Chinese Cuisine* (Monterey Park, CA [U.S. distributor]: Wei Chuan Publishing, 1991).

4. The cuisine writer is Francine Halvorsen, whose enthusiasm for this form of *tofu* is recorded in her book *The Food and Cooking of China: An Exploration of Chinese Cuisine in the Provinces and Cities of China, Hong Kong, and Taiwan* (New York: John Wiley & Sons, 1996), p. 127.

5. Halvorsen discusses these notable figures in her Chapter 8, "Taipei, Taiwan," pp. 117–31.

6. Robert Storey, *Taiwan: A Travel Survival Kit* (Hawthorn, Victoria, Australia: Lonely Planet Publications, 1994), has a good review of current facts and rules governing drink and drinking rituals in Taiwan.

7. Storey, pp. 98–99, provides a good review of tea drinking in Taiwan, as does Halvorsen for Chinese society generally in her Chapter 11, "Tea and Yum Cha," pp. 171–88. Halvorsen includes recipes for goodies considered particularly worthy accompaniments of tea.

8. Anderson has a fine summary of Chinese traditional medicine in his Chapter 11, "Traditional Medical Values of Food," pp. 229–43, to which we often refer in writing this section. Halvorsen covers some of the same topics in her Chapter 9, "Herbal Specialties," pp. 141–56. Her chapter is particularly valuable for its listing of recipes for many of the herbal remedies.

9. A good introduction to traditional clothing is Valery M. Garrett, *Traditional Chinese Clothing in Hong Kong and South China, 1840–1980* (Oxford: Oxford University Press, 1987). Although Garrett's study focused on Hong Kong, the description of Fujianese and Hakka clothing during the late Qing period is relevant to the Taiwanese situation.

10. Nancy Zeng Berliner, *Chinese Folk Art* (Boston: Little, Brown, 1986), p. 156.

11. Michael Saso, *The Teachings of Taoist Master Chuang* (New Haven, CT: Yale University Press, 1978), p. 132.

12. Kristofer Schipper, *The Taoist Body* (Berkeley: University of California Press, 1993), pp. 69–70.

13. The information on funerals in Sanhsia is from Arthur Wolf, "Chinese Kinship and Mourning Dress," in *Family and Kinship in Chinese Society*, edited by Maurice Freedman (Stanford, CA: Stanford University Press, 1970), pp. 189–208.

14. For a recent discussion of Taiwanese fashion, see Eugenia Yun, "That Certain Look," *Free China Review*, vol. 46, no. 11 (November 1996), 46ff.

SUGGESTED READINGS

Anderson, E. N. *The Food of China*. New Haven, CT: Yale University Press, 1988.

Garrett, Valery M. *Traditional Chinese Clothing in Hong Kong and South China, 1840–1980*. Oxford: Oxford University Press, 1987.

Halvorsen, Francine. *The Food and Cooking of China: An Exploration of Chinese Cuisine in the Provinces and Cities of China, Hong Kong, and Taiwan*. New York: John Wiley & Sons, 1996.

Wei Chuan Cultural-Educational Foundation. *Taiwanese Style Chinese Cuisine.* Monterey Park, CA: Wei Chuan Publishing, 1991.

Wolf, Arthur. "Chinese Kinship and Mourning Dress," in Maurice Freedman, ed., *Family and Kinship in Chinese Society.* Stanford, CA: Stanford University Press, 1970, pp. 189–208.

Yun, Eugenia. "That Certain Look," *Free China Review,* November 1996.

8

Marriage, Family, and Gender

UNMARRIED CHILDREN represent potential unfulfilled and burden unrelieved, according to the traditions of Taiwanese society. An unmarried man well into his twenties is regarded as a boy; the twenty-year-old married male, by contrast, is considered a man. Until he has married, a son is perceived as having received mainly what is his due: food, shelter, parental instruction on matters of personal conduct and social behavior, and education. He has not yet entered into that matrimonial union whereby he can give back to those who have given him life, namely, to his parents and, through and beyond them, to his ancestors. The son represents to his parents unfulfilled economic, social, and religious potential. They expect him to pay them back for their efforts expended during his childhood. Until he marries, he is handicapped in realizing his economic potential and paralyzed in achieving his sociorelig- ious potential.[1]

His sister remains a burden unrelieved. In her youth she was quite possibly a delight, especially to her mother, and conceivably to her father as well. Unless a few brothers had already been produced by her parents by the time she was born, however, her birth was a disappointment to both her mother and her father. And whatever delights her existence eventually may have afforded them, she was held to be a burden if she had not married by the time she was eighteen, nineteen, or, certainly, twenty. Before the advent of abundant opportunities for factory and urban jobs as the contemporary economy burgeoned, any economic contribution a woman could make by the age of twenty was minimal; hence, materially she was held to be a burden. In the traditional conception, living independently is not something a decent woman does, but living with her parents into adulthood is socially unsatisfying for a daughter. Her family and the villagers of her community believe that to do so is to leave unfulfilled her destiny as a wife and mother in someone else's household, in some other village, worshipping someone else's ancestors, providing someone else's descendants. Until she fulfills this destiny, a daughter is not only an economic burden but an unrelieved socioreligious burden as well.

Marriage unfolding according to traditional Taiwanese culture is rarely an event of great personal joy for the two individuals involved in the union, but it is an instance of great joy for the families of the male and female thus joined. Only in experiencing some measure of the joy of their families in proceeding toward potential fulfilled and arriving at that moment when burden is relieved do the betrothed themselves take satisfaction in the event and its rituals. In the course of the last thirty years, the economy of Taiwan has changed and grown dramatically. Economic developments have brought with them changes and challenges to the island's social and cultural institutions. Women's economic value to their families has increased manyfold with these developments. More urban opportunities have resulted in a larger number of young people separating themselves from their parents residentially and generally assuming a more independent pose.[2] Nonetheless, the continuity in many aspects of the traditional system of family and kinship in Taiwan remains striking. Even in cases in which traditional norms have been altered considerably, older forms are alive in the contemporary memory; they have greatly informed and continue to inform the development of today's Taiwan. At the end of this chapter we will return to the matter of contemporary change. But given the prominent presence of traditional familial values even in contemporary society and the extent to which these values have contributed to economic development on Taiwan, the first several sections of this chapter are presented with the intention of presenting forcefully the key features of the traditional kinship system, suggesting along the way its abiding presence and importance in contemporary society.

MARRIAGE RITUALS

Taiwanese marriage customs dictate that bride and groom not only have different surnames but also be from different villages. The two young people to be joined ideally have little familiarity with each other; important parts of the marriage ritual imply that bride and groom are seeing each other for the first time.[3] Typically the marriage pool is found among those twenty or so villages economically and socially linked to a township government seat or other important urban center, and within those twenty villages a handful come to be regarded as particularly good sources of mates.[4] Traditional marriages are arranged by the families of the young man and woman, a duty assumed mainly by their mothers, who frequently employ a go-between. According to custom, the ideal age of marriage for females is about eighteen, and for males, twenty; but the deal might well have been struck years before, say, when the girl was twelve and the boy fourteen. The ideal prospective wife is physically strong enough for successful childbearing and skilled in the domestic arts. The ideal prospective husband is from a family in good economic condition and has personal habits appropriate to his role of provider.

When the families come to a tentative agreement regarding the match, the boy's family sends a letter to the young woman's family requesting engagement. Shortly after this letter is delivered, the young man, his father, other male relatives, friends of his family, and the go-between pay a visit to the young woman's family in observance of the "lesser engagement" (*xiaoding*)[5]; the young woman's father plays the role of the host. The young man's family gives such gifts as clothing, jewelry, an engagement ring, engagement cakes, substantial food items, and a small portion of the brideprice. The brideprice looms large in the economic exchanges between the two families. It is a substantial amount of money given by the groom's family in expression of their sincerity and goodwill in making the match; the brideprice ritually strengthens the tie between the two families. The young woman's family reciprocates with gifts that could well include a suit, shirts, neckties, a pair of new shoes, an engagement ring, accessories such as a gold pin to go with the groom's necktie, sweets, fruit, and substantial food items to be distributed to the young man's relatives and friends as an engagement announcement. If nothing happens to spoil the prospective union, the next important step in the direction of marriage takes place. This "greater engagement" (*dading*) finds the young man's family paying a formal visit to the young woman's family to set the date of the wedding. At the "greater engagement" the boy's father presents the final, larger amount of the brideprice, additional gifts for the family as a whole, and frequently a few small items for the young woman herself.

In the month or two after the "greater engagement," the family of the groom busies itself preparing food, purchasing utensils and other items the young couple will need, and decorating the room (*xifang*) where the young couple will live. Neighbors and relatives close at hand give presents and words of congratulation. Invitations are sent to relatives who live at distances, pre-

8.1 Modern bride and groom in search of the perfect garden location for photographs.

cluding word-of-mouth announcement of the wedding. In the bride's home, mother tenderly offers final words of advice to daughter and assists her with preparations of wedding attire and dowry.

On the wedding day, if full observance of traditional Taiwanese marriage rituals holds, the groom's family sends a decorated bridal chair into which the young woman, wearing a bridal gown of red or deep pink, her face covered with a piece of red satin, enters promptly. The scene typically finds the bride's mother weeping while the father, whatever his emotions, stands stoically. The bridal chair is closed so that no one on the road can see her as four able-bodied men of the groom's family carry her to her new home. The bride's family has proudly displayed the young woman's dowry in their house and courtyard before members of the groom's party load the items on an accompanying vehicle, where the typically enormous haul can be clearly viewed by onlookers. This dowry has multiple categories. It includes a sum of money under the bride's exclusive control, items for personal use, other items for the express use of her and her new husband, and still other items that the broader family may utilize. Typically the dowry is twice again as much as the young woman's family received in the brideprice.[6]

Upon arrival at the home of the groom, the bride is taken to the front court, where the wedding is performed. In the center of the court she finds a table on which are placed offerings to the gods of Heaven and Earth, a pair of red candles, and three sticks of incense. Standing beside each other, the couple face forward giving honor to the gods; the bride then turns with a bow to the groom, who returns the gesture. Family members then lead the couple into the house to the *xifang*; according to tradition, the girl is assisted by women as, head still covered, she steps over some object intended to symbolize ritually her ability to surmount all obstacles to a successful marriage. Inside, the couple pay homage to the ancestors at the altar just inside the front door and then proceed to the *xifang*. In their room, bride and groom face each other. The groom, following instructions from attending females, removes the red cloth from his bride's head; according to tradition, husband and wife now cast eyes on each other for the first time. After a while the bride leaves to pay respects to her new parents-in-law; she then returns to take her seat on the bed beside her husband. As feasting and words calling for many progeny and great prosperity reign in the household, young members and friends of the family come into the *xifang* at will, deepening the embarrassment of the young man and woman, so recently turned husband and wife. Young people shoot barbs at the groom, request silly performances of the couple, talk, and take up time so that the moment when bride and groom can be alone is delayed. At last the young people leave. Someone brings wine and food to the couple; they toast each other and consume some of the food together, ritually completing the transition to husband and wife. An interesting period begins in which the young couple seek to balance their own interests against the interests of the other *fang*, all of which ideally work together in the greater interest of the *jia*.

FANG WITHIN THE JIA

Thus far, we have referred to the young man or the young woman's "family," a term useful enough in its general meaning to convey the necessary information regarding the marriage ceremony. But in the United States when we discuss family, we most typically have in mind either the nuclear family specifically or kinfolk very broadly and nebulously defined. In addition to the nuclear family, two other main forms are identified by anthropologists: the stem family, which includes a married son and his family unit in addition to his mother, father, and unmarried siblings; and the "extended" family consisting of at least two married sons and their familial units living with their mother, father, unmarried siblings, and any other kinfolk oriented to-

ward the same home. Both of these family forms have great relevance to
Taiwanese society. In Taiwan, as in other Chinese societies, the cultural ideal
is the extended family, with the ultimate goal being "five generations under
one roof."[7] The extended family is difficult enough to achieve; five generations (ranging from young children to their great-great-grandparents) under
one roof was and is nearly impossible. But the ideal says much about the
value the Taiwanese place on familial unity, cohabitation, and cohesiveness.

Jia is the Mandarin term for an ideally cohesive and inclusive family unit.
Fang are any constituent families. Three important aspects of the *jia* are the
economy, the group, and the estate.[8] Which form the *jia* takes depends on
the members or claimants associated with those aspects. The *jia* estate is the
sum total of agricultural, industrial, commercial, and residential property to
which a member of the *jia* has a claim of inheritance. The *jia* economy refers
to the precise ways in which the resources of the *jia* estate are put to use to
generate still more resources for the enlargement of the estate. The *jia* group
includes those members with either active or potential claims on the *jia* estate
or participation in the *jia* economy. If the *jia* is of the extended form, multiple
fang must be participating in the *jia* group, involved in the *jia* economy, and
most importantly, retaining claims to their share of inheritance of the *jia*
estate.

Because it was the basis of traditional society, agriculture served as the
foundation for most *jia* estates. Yet Taiwanese folk readily gave their labor
to nonagricultural pursuits if these were economically advantageous to the
expansion of the estate. Investment might also be made in human potential,
for example, funding of higher education for *jia* members who showed the
kind of talent that could yield position, influence, income, and status to the
glory of all in the *jia* group. The familiar image of the *jia* is its concentrated
form: an extended family whose group members are geographically situated
in a single residence or residential compound; there they participate in an
economy concentrated on the cultivation of surrounding fields, exercising
claims on an estate the economic origins and expansion of which are based
in agriculture and the management of which is concentrated in the hands of
the extended family patriarch. In fact the *jia* may maintain a common budget
while dispersing its *fang* economically and residentially. Although many
scholars of the family predict that modernization will lead to the decline of
the extended family in favor of smaller units, in Taiwan larger family structures have proved highly adaptable and valuable to the modernizing economy. The Taiwanese *jia* have always responded flexibly to economic
opportunity, a propensity that has increased under conditions of rapid development.

An extended *jia* can very well turn into a corporation featuring diverse agricultural, commercial, or industrial enterprises. As long as several *fang* continue their interest in participating in the *jia* group, fulfilling their particular roles in the *jia* economy and participating in the expansion of, as well as deriving benefits from, the *jia* estate, the *jia* maintains its cohesiveness. As pressures for division of the *jia* estate intensify, usually an extended *jia* ultimately breaks into its constituent *fang*, which then establish their own separate *jia*, probably nuclear at first but possessed of the potential for extension.

JIA UNITY, JIA DIVISION

When a Taiwanese woman enters the *jia* of her husband, her position is extremely insecure. The greatest asset she brings to her new family is her childbearing potential. Divorce was rare in traditional Taiwanese society and remains rare in Taiwan today; however, failure to produce sons specifically can lead either directly to divorce or to those familial and marital tensions the relief from which might come only through divorce.[9] Concubinage, formerly a means of providing progeny outside the primary marital arrangement, is today illegal. In some cases a male, in reversal of the usual pattern, goes to live in his wife's village and agrees to give his first son the surname of his wife's heirless parents so that their line of descent might be maintained. (This is a matrilocal marriage.) Remaining in the familiar surroundings of her natal village may give some comfort to a wife; however, the norm looms large in Taiwanese society, and this option is not truly satisfying for any of the parties to the marriage. If anything, pressure to produce not just one but additional male progeny, with the male offspring subsequent to the first taking their father's family's surname, was greater for the wife than ever.[10] Giving birth to sons in particular and children in general was critical for the woman for at least two reasons. First, only by giving birth to children who can expand the family and ensure the maintenance of the descent line is it possible for a woman to fulfill her destiny, make secure her position in her new family, and ensure descendants to sustain her soul in the afterlife. Second, with the arrival of children, her *fang* increases in size and the unit more clearly representing her own interests grows in power. The young woman increasingly finds herself impelled to advance the interests of her own children against the interests of other members of the *jia*, and in the meantime to cultivate the affections of her own children within her own *fang*.[11]

Even for the Taiwanese, who clearly envision the extended family ideal and who at some point in their lives are likely to pass through this familial developmental stage,[12] this large family group contains a collection of individuals with a cornucopia of particular interests and personalities, frequently at odds with each other. The young wife's relationship with male members of her husband's *jia* is subject to strict taboos ensuring physical and emotional distance.[13] The mother-in-law interacts with the young woman much more closely, both physically and emotionally, but is typically not affectionate. Arguments between mother-in-law and daughter-in-law classically arise over proper ways to wash clothes, prepare meals, discipline and train children, and a host of other matters pertaining to domestic management. Initially the daughter-in-law defers to the mother-in-law and by convention should continue to do so. Inevitably, though, a daughter-in-law with some spirit will assert herself, particularly with the birth of a son and perhaps the addition of another child or two. If the daughter-in-law does manifest an independent streak, the stage is set for a test of wills that undermine *jia* unity.[14] The husband's sisters may offer sympathetic companionship, but they are, after all, destined to leave the patrilocal *jia*. The wives of the husband's brothers are less emotionally remote than the males, but they are competitors with the newest female arrival to the *jia*, and are already engaged in spirited competition among themselves. Rather than join forces to advance their own interests within the *jia*, each young wife tends to see that institution as hopelessly dominated by men and forever subject to the goals of a patriarchal system.

The young wife who has given birth to children has already set about creating a "uterine family" composed of mother and her offspring.[15] Usually the young mother is very aware of the need not to overpamper her son as he grows up; she is as likely as the father to administer physical punishment, particularly of the reactive rather than the calculated kind: The father's corporal blows are administered with greater cool, more dispassionately, in response to offenses that have crossed the borders delineating ideal child respect for elders and their authority. But mother is in a position to grant favors, make treats, soothe the pain of childhood stumbles, and in general draw her son emotionally close to her. This is at least as true of the daughter, who despite her expected departure at eighteen or twenty nevertheless remains close by her mother's side learning domestic arts and proper female behavior from her chief role model. Children are thus a young mother's chief sources of general emotional satisfaction and love, yet they are also her main constituency in the politics, the maneuvering for power, within the *jia*. Furthermore, though not a part of her personally cultivated "uterine family," the young husband frequently grows in his general affection for his wife, and in many cases he considers her a valued counselor and sounding board for his own frustrations within the *jia* group, the *jia* economy, and the *jia* estate.

Brothers participating in the extended *jia* evidence their own tensions. As children, their relationship normally featured many characteristics not conducive to smooth relations as adults. An elder brother in Taiwanese society is expected to be highly tolerant of the behavior of his younger brother. He is forbidden to strike his sibling, even to retaliate for a blow leveled by the younger one. The elder brother is expected to share his treasured possessions with his younger brother and in general give rein to his whims without expecting like return. The Confucian ideal holds that younger brothers should respect the authority of elder brothers, and eventually this ideal is invoked in everyday life—but in adulthood rather than childhood. Parents place higher demands on older children, who are expected to care for their siblings even while the younger ones are treated with leniency. Then, once the responsibilities of adulthood arrive and the brothers establish *fang* within the *jia*, fraternal hierarchy is formally moved to the fore of human relationships. Until division of the estate occurs, the father first but then brothers in descending order according to age hold authority in making joint decisions regarding the *jia* group and the *jia* economy. All brothers participate in those decisions, but ultimately opinions of the older males carry more weight. This can be irritating to younger brothers, who resent their subservient position, even as their elder brothers quite possibly maintain lingering resentment over the trouble the younger ones caused them as they were growing up.[16]

Such tensions mean that the extended family ideal eventually gives way to pressure for division of the estate. In dividing the estate (*fen jia*), younger brothers are given neither wider latitude as in childhood nor less priority as in the administration of an undivided estate in adulthood: The Taiwanese, as do all Chinese societies, follow the system of equal inheritance. According to social precedent, any adult brother can demand his share of the estate at any time. In some places in Taiwan, division typically occurs soon after brothers marry and the birth of children enlarges the various *fang*. In other places brothers usually defer to their elderly father as at least formal head of the *jia*, delaying division until after his death. In a few instances brothers find it economically advantageous to remain jointly invested in the *jia* group, economy, and estate throughout their adult lives, but this is in practice the exception rather than the rule. At some point during their young to middle-age adulthood, brothers usually dissolve their joint social and economic arrangements.[17]

Whether or not the *jia* remains extended, the extended family ideal makes itself felt even in cases in which the *jia* estate has been divided. An examination of rights and obligations in the Taiwanese family shows clearly the long shadow cast by the extended *jia* ideal.

RIGHTS AND OBLIGATIONS IN THE FAMILY

Social custom in Taiwan dictates that a person has certain highly defined rights and just as highly specified obligations by virtue of her or his membership in the family. Inheritance is a prized right that accrues to children in the Taiwanese family. In the United States a bumper sticker reading, "I'm spending my children's inheritance," reflects a cavalier attitude toward the family estate that is unthinkable in Taiwan. People in the United States ideally rear their children with moral care; they instill a success ethic based on individual initiative; they send their children to college if the family can afford to do so; and then they cut them loose, to prosper but also perhaps to fail if their individual preparation and effort prove insufficient. The dissatisfaction with the phenomenon of adult children adrift on the vagaries of the contemporary U.S. job market returning home to live with mom and dad shows how much Americans expect adult children returning home to live as dependents with their parents. Children in the United States, for their part, dread the thought of elderly parents becoming a burden, knowing that even old folks believe that living in their children's home is a hold-the-nose option delayed as long as possible.

Things are different, indeed, in Taiwan. Parents and all adult members who can be held together in the *jia* group work hard, diversifying their labors as much as possible, sparing no reserves of energy toward the building of a large *jia* estate. Great personal sacrifice is made and much denial of creature comforts is endured for the sake of saving, investing, and expanding *jia* resources. This is the meaning of life. Building a bountiful *jia* estate honors the ancestors, makes lavish ritual offerings to them possible, and ensures their happiness in the afterlife. Constructing a secure and growing economic foundation provides for the generations to come: children, grandchildren, and ideally all descendants to follow. Adult children returning home is an unimaginable problem: Ideally they never left, and that they will be welcomed if they return is a given. Conversely, children accept their eternal obligation to care for their parents. As Confucian dictum goes, "When we are young, our parents nurture us; when our parents are old, we sustain them."

Even after division of the *jia* estate, Taiwanese children and parents maintain close contact. Although they may no longer be contributing to a joint economy and expanding a jointly held estate, parents watch carefully to see if their children are living frugally, working hard, and investing wisely; for the children's behavior reflects the upbringing given by the parents and also affects their ability to be responsible to all those along the descent continuum. The children have received a great deal if their *jia* estate was sizable, and they are in any case expected to accept their inheritance with the accompanying understanding that they will be responsible for the living conditions of their parents. This responsibility can take several forms and evidences considerable variability from place to place and family to family in Taiwan.[18] When the *jia* estate is divided, some sons set aside enough land for a physically able father to work to sustain himself and their mother. If the father has grown elderly or if, as happens frequently, he has died and their mother is their lone remaining responsibility, they may set aside land to work either jointly or in rotation for the benefit of their parents or parent. Still another, highly interesting alternative is known as meal rotation, whereby the parent or parents live and eat by turns with two, three, or more sons.

Elderly Taiwanese men frequently face an unpleasant, if secure, fate.[19] Having cultivated a paramount position in the *jia* group as long as possible, they eventually find themselves having to give way to the leadership of sons, who afford them a degree of formal respect but likely hold little natural affection for them. Elderly mothers, by contrast, often have a more agreeable fate. The young mother planted the seeds of affection when she drew her uterine family unto her. As an elderly woman, she can sew and mend clothing and cuddle small children, thereby relieving the workload of the son's wife. The wife, now the ruler of her own domestic realm, finds herself more favorably disposed to her mother-in-law. The children also welcome their grandmother and the treats and favors she dispenses. Thus, in many cases the obligation to care for a mother after *jia* division and in her old age is undertaken in good cheer. Her visits are anticipated with delight by her son and his family.

Ancestor worship falls in the category of familial obligation that one returns in exchange for rights received. In the absence of a significant inheritance, a Taiwanese child may be lax in making good on this obligation; one study found that only in the cases of substantial inheritance did children conscientiously complete the ritual observances due to deceased parents.[20] A sizable inheritance of the *jia* estate obviously enlivens the memory and makes more secure ritual attention to parents as they dwell in another realm: A strongly felt right received is likely to make a son feel a more eternal sense of obligation.

To her own parents the female is obligated to learn the domestic arts, help with chores, assist with young children, and maintain a healthy, energetic physical demeanor that will make her an attractive partner in marriage. From her parents she receives proper training in the required domestic skills, cultivation of her moral character, and proper treatment as she is offered for marriage. The generous dowry a woman receives upon marriage—part of which goes to the husband's *jia*, part of which is shared by members of her *fang*, and a sizable portion of which is for her own use to dispose of as she wishes—represents a form of inheritance; it is smaller than that received by her brothers, but so are her eternal obligations to her parents.[21] After marriage, a woman's prime responsibility to her own parents lies in her proper conduct as a wife, which reflects her parents' skill in raising children and makes her natal *jia* and village good sources of marital partners. Her parents will monitor how she is treated in her husband's *jia* and oversee intervention should treatment be truly cruel.

Thus, familial rights and obligations operate within the rubric of patriarchy but offer both men and women some form of inheritance, promise of care in old age, and eternal sustenance of the soul in exchange for rendering of obligations according to social role. Social role and familial role have been so closely related in Taiwanese society that the student of Taiwan comes to observe numerous social extensions of the familial ideal.

SOCIAL EXTENSIONS OF THE FAMILIAL IDEAL

Southeastern China, from which most of Taiwan's Chinese population emigrated, is famous for the number and extent of those social formations known as lineages.[22] Lineages form when a number of related *jia* agree to endow an ancestral hall or otherwise provide for the common care of ancestral tablets. The lineage primarily honors an ancestor to whom all members of the constituent *jia* can trace blood relationship. Usually this ancestor in some way brought his kinfolk great honor, whether by success in business, service in the community, or attainment of a coveted government position. Implied in any measure of success would be the wherewithal to leave behind a large estate, a substantial portion of which relatives would set aside to endow the lineage and its hall in the great ancestor's honor. From income generated by the estate, lineage leaders could invest in land and enterprises from which all male lineage members would derive benefit. Profits generated by the estate could be used to establish schools, fund relief efforts in behalf of lineage and community in times of natural disaster, establish local militia to provide for the physical security of lineage members, provide welfare services for poor lineage members or to meet special needs, and conduct lavish rituals and provide bountiful feasts in honor of ancestors. Having the greater capability to endow the lineage estate, families of substantial means were more likely to form lineages than were families of poor or moderate means. Relatively humble folk, though, might form lineage organizations. Through these strong ritual connections they would secure networks conducive to common advancement and, especially, joint security in areas short on the rule of law and government policing efforts.

Provision of common security was of utmost concern to people on the Taiwanese fringe of traditional empire. Families related by traceable ancestry came together to enhance their power to control land, water, and other resources to which others sought to stake claims. On the mainland, lineage territory tended to expand as contiguous units whereby a particular lineage became the chief power in a given region. This pattern was in evidence to some extent on Taiwan, but the island is also notable for having produced dispersed lineages, linking kinfolk in different and noncontiguous villages, frequently with the ancestral hall located in one village to which nonresident lineage members traveled on particularly important ritual occasions. Because individuals with common needs of security and mutual aid, regardless of blood relations, immigrated at different times, multiple-surnamed villages are numerous. With the arrival of more or fewer kinfolk, particular kinship groups tended to grow more dominant within the village. In time two or three lineages would typically dominate, their power enhanced by links to lineage members in other villages.

Given frontier conditions, considerable leniency was frequently exercised in the matter of proving descent. Similarly, people of the same surname might come together to form a clan, an organization anthropologists distinguish from lineage. Members of a clan claim ancestry of questionable veracity: Descent lines are spurious, and the link to the putative common ancestor is for many, if not all, clan members fictitious. Lineage members generally offer compelling proof of ancestry. Taiwanese people, including anthropologists within Taiwan, are more flexible and less exact when referring to lineage and clan than are Western anthropologists; trained anthropologists in Taiwan recognize the formal distinction but argue that the Taiwanese frontier tended to blur the distinction and that trying to establish it involves terminological difficulty in the Chinese language.[23] Lineages, clans and hybrid forms live on to provide support networks for many in Taiwan today.

What is striking about the clan and the more flexible lineage is the attractiveness of the familial ideal beyond the *jia* form. The value that the Taiwanese place on this attachment to kinship is seen also in relationships that they have outside the family. In single-surnamed villages dominated by people with lineage ties, kinship terms are naturally used. Even in multisurnamed communities, villagers are given to referring to one another in kinship terms. They use subtle cues to distinguish real kin from close friends, but they call one another uncle, aunt, elder brother, younger sister, cousin, and so on. A wife marrying into her husband's family and establishing herself in her new village acquires a whole set of new relatives genetically unrelated to her. She refers to these people as father, mother, younger brother, and older sister. Her husband likewise employs limited kinship terms when addressing his wife's family upon their visit to her natal home; her children do not live close to their maternal grandparents, but they employ similar terms with certain differences to distinguish paternal uncle from maternal uncle and the like. A common differentiating character is *nei* (internal) for paternal kin and *wai* (external) for maternal kin.[24]

One study shows how relatives by marriage are more important than suggested by much of the scholarly literature, which emphasizes the patriarchal nature of Taiwanese society.[25] This study emphasizes how ties to a daughter-in-law's family have the potential to link people of two villages in matters that speak to their common good. These associations with maternal relatives, and through them to people in other villages, have become more important as economic and political opportunities have become diverse and abundant. Often it is the well-connected person, someone with close maternal kin in communities other than his own, who succeeds in a real estate or construction venture or who prevails over an opponent in a closely contested political event.

Long a tradition in Taiwan, sworn brotherhoods are fascinating extensions of the familial ideal.[26] These associations are classically sworn by two or more close friends who seek to strengthen an already established bond. In a temple ritual, the friends swear an oath of mutual assistance and loyalty. They offer incense, and then burn the written text containing their names as parties to the agreement and the terms upon which they swear their loyalty, thus enabling the document to rise to the celestial archives. The new brothers by oath share food and wine; in the midst of their meal, they cut their fingers to let their blood flow together into a common cup of wine. The newly sworn brothers then drink this wine, blended with the blood of their now eternal bond. Their families become, on some level, families of each other; thus they use kinship terms for members of each other's families, entailing dowry contributions, funeral expenses, and even mourning obligations.

Sworn brotherhood is a social extension of the kinship ideal, which originated on the Chinese mainland. The height of its literary expression comes in Luo Guanzhung's classic fourteenth-century novel *Romance of the Three Kingdoms* (*Sanguo yanyi*), which focuses on the union of Liu Bei, Guan Yu, and Zhang Fei and their daring deeds in the period just after the fall of the great Han dynasty. On Taiwan, Xu Yu's *Traditional Folktales of Taiwan* (*Taiwan minjian liuchuan gushi*) heavily features the adventures of two sworn brothers. The popular guards depicted on the entrance doors to many temples in Taiwan, General Fan and General Xie, are sworn brothers famous for their rock solid mutual fidelity; and some groupings of local gods are considered sworn brothers by their adherents. In contemporary Taiwan sworn brotherhoods frequently bring together from different parts of the island migrants who agree to loan each other money, encourage each other's business enterprise, and support each other in disputes with nongroup members. A unique case in the city of Tainan found two groups of sworn brothers with a linking member coming together to solve a sticky situation brought on by the misdeeds of a sworn brother in one of the groups; successful resolution of this incident proved so rewarding that thenceforth members regarded each other as half-brothers, further expanding networks of human support and economic cooperation. A sworn brotherhood founded by eight male migrants to Taipei in 1954 eventually expanded to twenty members, with alternate expulsions for "outrageous behavior" and additions of members holding some advantage for the group. Two of the new members transformed the organization into a "sworn siblinghood": These two were females admitted because their membership held advantages for the "fraternity's" economic network.[27] This leads us to consider the position of women as they take on new roles and acquire new status in a society into which patriarchy has traditionally been woven as surely as Taiwanese factory workers today stitch Nike cross-trainers.

FEMALE INDIGNITY AND DIGNITY

Clearly, women are subordinate in the traditional Taiwanese kinship system. As in many other premodern systems, efforts to subordinate and control women were undertaken by men who both admired and scorned them. Men's awe of women's ability to bear and give birth to children resulted in belief systems that attached great importance to procreation even as the physical processes involved in procreation were scorned. Emily Martin Ahern has carefully studied the power and pollution of women in Taiwanese society and provided fascinating detail on associated beliefs.[28] The sex act itself is held to be polluting. One who has recently had intercourse is forbidden to participate in religious rituals, for example, or even to come into the presence of a god's image. Anyone, male or female, who has come into contact with menstrual fluids is likewise unworthy of worshipping the gods. As a practical matter, women rather casually dispose of menstrual napkins or pads in ways that return them to the earth; this results in a sullying of the earth and certain ritual taboos: A god's image may not be carried under a clothes-drying pole, for instance, because feet soiled with dirt, and thus potentially the pollution of women, have passed through clothes hung out to dry. Both mother and newborn child are soiled with birth fluids and are therefore confined to the house for a month to spare the highest god in the traditional pantheon, Tian Gong, the sight of them. Elaborate rituals are carried out to protect a child from permanent harm due to birth pollution and also due to contact with other polluting occurrences, most notably death. The Kitchen God dwells dangerously close to where women work and is easily angered if washcloths, baskets, or clothes, all of which in some way have potentially come into contact with the bodily fluids of women, should brush against the stove. Female pollution displeases the greater gods: But women frequently lead ritual observances to relatively minor gods such as the Bed Mother or those designed to appease the souls of dead ancestors and hungry ghosts—in their association with sex, birth, and death, all subject to the kind of pollution tied to women.

Life and eternity, though, are also associated with sex, birth, and death. Here, of course, lies the power of women and the origin of the awe and fear men have of them. A child's very soul is held to reside for four months in the placenta. Indeed, menstrual blood is perceived as the physical essence from which springs life. Marjorie Topley powerfully illustrates the consequences that accrue should women choose to withhold their sexuality, their birth-giving potential, and their service to families in the raising of children.[29] She describes young women in the sericulture economy of Guangdong Province who swore oaths to one another to refrain from marriage and to live together in sisterhood. Given the women's unusual ability to make money in the sericulture industry, many families tolerated their unorthodox life plans. In the families that held to the traditional marriage ideal, women intent on following through with their oaths bound their bodies to make intercourse impossible and ran away as soon as possible, never to return. In Taiwan, becoming a nun in a Buddhist convent has afforded and continues to offer a similar respite from unwanted marriage. More tragically, the old society featured enough cases to be notable of women who looked at their life options as so abhorrent that they ended their lives by their own hand.

More typically, women strive mightily to carve positions for themselves upon the stone of patriarchy. Even as water, according to the Taoist image, shapes with its patient power the apparently tougher stone, so women leave enduring marks on the patriarchy. They form uterine families. They work to maximize the advantages of their *fang*. They shape community opinion through their verbal communication. They actively manage the household and handle its day-to-day finances. They take an active role in the social life of the community and handle rituals that, though polluting, are the very stuff of life in this world and in eternity. In the last decade or two of their lives they experience the love and gratitude of children and grandchildren. Frequently a woman will rise to the position of matriarch, wielding influence over her sons after the death of their father, making decisions for the *jia*, having patiently arrived at her position like some queen who outlives the male heirs to the throne.

Even in the traditional kinship system, women hold great power and achieve high dignity, finding ways to avert their putative pollution and to overcome the indignities thrust upon them. Taiwan at century's end highlights the powerful potential of women more than ever before.

THE TAIWANESE FAMILY AT THE CLOSE OF THE TWENTIETH CENTURY

At the end of the twentieth century there are two seemingly irreconcilable phenomena in the area of family and gender. The first is the durability of the extended family ideal. In his sociological study of the changing family pattern in Taiwan in the course of modernization, Chun-kit Joseph Wong showed that Taiwan is experiencing a definite trend toward fewer children, the result of a combination of an aggressive government birth control effort, the realities of crowded urban life, the increase in two-wage-earning couples, and modern attitudes as revealed in a cross-island survey.[30] Wong also found movement toward the nuclear family, but even among those revealing "transitional" or "modern" (as opposed to "traditional") attitudes and behavior, he found that either stem or extended family forms prevailed in half of all cases. When people were asked to cite their ideal family form, the stem and extended arrangements made similar, even slightly better, showings.

Wong's data support our own observations and anecdotal findings made during our latest period of residence on Taiwan during 1988–1990. The farm family Huang, with which Gary spent much time, came from humble origins but had prospered through hard work. The family was very fortunate in the traditional view; it had produced three sons, one of whom had attended National Taiwan Normal University in Taipei and secured a teaching position in the county seat of Chiayi, some twenty-five miles to the north of the Huang's home village. This family was well in touch with modern life through this son's residence in the major city of the island and a smaller city of considerable population and local importance, as well as their access to mass media and convenient transportation to the reasonably close cities of Tainan and Kaohsiung. Even though the elder son had married, the family had not yet divided its family estate, and Gary's discussions with the middle son indicated that even after the other sons married, immediate division of

8.2 An urban family of the 1980s using the most available personal transportation system.

the estate was not a foregone conclusion. The unmarried sons lived with their father and contributed their labor when they were not working in the industrial district established in their county during the early 1980s. Other cases that came to our attention during our residence and a follow-up visit during the summer of 1995 suggested to us that the familial ideal is very much alive in contemporary Taiwan.

Phenomenon number two, though, seems to threaten that ideal: the rising position and increased status of women. Factory labor has provided a personal source of income for many women. They can live on their own if they wish, and those working too far away may take up residence in company dormitories; but most young women remain at home before they marry, making powerful contributions to the *jia* economy. Their financial contributions to family well-being have made them ever more insistent that their parents allot a generous dowry to them when they marry. Although they contribute to the joint estate if it is as yet undivided, they are conscious of the amount of their contributions and strive to take a substantial sum with them when they marry.[31]

Marriage rituals as described in the early pages of the chapter have increasingly been simplified and modernized. Wedding dress, transportation, and ritual have changed with contemporary society. The traditional forms provide the points of reference from which contemporary styles have evolved, and in most cases the symbolism is still decidedly patriarchal. But romantic love plays a greater role in marital unions now, and women have a higher sense of their rights in what they see as a partnership. Western styles of marital dress are very influential; the Taiwanese are inordinately fond of parading for photographers in beautiful natural surroundings, the woman clad in flowing white wedding gown, the man in tux or suit of Western origin.

Women who remain in rural villages can still fit rather neatly into the patriarchal system with its patrilocal residence. Taiwan's population is well dispersed by the standards of developing and recently developed countries, so many people do remain in rural villages, even if the bulk of their income is not derived from agricultural sources. Some young *fang* go with *jia* blessing to larger or smaller cities to establish businesses or take up other employment. Taiwan's rapid economic development has featured small business prosperity as a key feature. Small family-owned businesses also accommodate the traditional patriarchal ideal well; an energetic young wife, perhaps bringing a substantial dowry largely of her own making into her marriage and the *fang's* business, can work close to her children while at the same time helping to run the business. In many cases she effectively runs the business while her husband seeks other employment in the same town or city, very much in accordance with the tradition of maximally efficient use of family labor.

Opportunity to attend colleges and universities, both in Taiwan and abroad, is also available to women, and they have seized the chance to train themselves for corporate business and the professions. Still greatly outnumbered by men, they face an old boy's network that makes that in the United States look insignificant by comparison, yet they persevere and they endure. The professional woman is now a fact of the urban landscape in Taiwan. As women become highly educated, and as they contribute more powerfully to the economies of the family and the society in general, they become more insistent on their rights. These rights were officially secured under the Marriage Law of 1931, passed under Guomindang administration on the mainland as part of a push for modern change in economics and society. By this law, women were given formal equality with men in such matters as divorce and inheritance. Until recently women were in general hesitant to invoke the law in the face of family pressure and the patriarchal tradition. At the close of the twentieth century, women are increasingly demanding political and economic equality with men. Women have the formal right to equal inheritance, for example. This flies in the face of Taiwanese tradition, and until recent years women did not challenge that tradition in significant numbers. Beginning in the 1970s, however, women began to maneuver for the best share they could secure from their natal family's estate, pushing for their rights as far as family harmony would allow, then backing off with something less than equal inheritance but much more than they would have inherited under the fully traditional system.[32] In the course of the 1980s and 1990s, a vanguard of urban women has pushed for full equality in all matters of economy, politics, and family. In the case of divorce, the woman's position has been greatly bolstered when pushed into the courts; there now occur cases in which the wife gains custody of the children. Unthinkable just a few years ago, this offers a great challenge to the notion of patriliny, which has anchored the Taiwanese sociopolitical system for centuries.

Traditional Taiwanese notions of family and kinship continue to influence the development of contemporary Taiwan. The notion of the extended family as an efficient economic unit with the potential to become a corporation, probably small but with unlimited possibilities for expansion, has contributed powerfully to the island's astounding growth. The Taiwanese ideal of family and kinship creates great pressure for success and puts a premium on material prosperity. Women are now fed by the same ethic of success that has driven men, and they strive for material prosperity through increasingly independent routes. It is likely that essential elements of the Taiwanese system of family and kinship will endure into the twenty-first century; it also seems that an ever-increasing number of women will demand parity with their brethren. How this contradiction gains synthesis will be a development that all who hold an interest in this fascinating society will watch closely.

NOTES

1. Martin C. Yang, *A Chinese Village: Taitou, Shantung Province* (New York: Columbia University Press, 1945), pp. 103–22; Hugh D. R. Baker, *Chinese Family and Kinship* (New York: Columbia University Press, 1979), pp. 26–28; Margery Wolf, "Child Training and the Chinese Family," in Arthur P. Wolf, ed., *Studies in Chinese Society* (Stanford, CA: Stanford University Press, 1978), pp. 224–27.

2. Chun-kit Joseph Wong, *The Changing Chinese Family Pattern in Taiwan* (Taipei: Southern Materials Center, 1981), pp. 84–87.

3. Yang, p. 111.

4. G. William Skinner, "Marketing and Social Structure in Rural China," *Journal of Asian Studies*, vol. 24, no. 1 (November 1964), pp. 3–43; Lawrence W. Crissman, "The Structure of Local and Regional Systems," in Emily Martin Ahern and

Hill Gates, eds., *The Anthropology of Taiwanese Society* (Stanford, CA: Stanford University Press, 1981), pp. 116–24, especially pp. 120–21.

5. Chen Chung-min, "Dowry and Inheritance," in Hsieh Jih-chang and Chuang Ying-chang, eds., *The Chinese Family and Its Ritual Behavior* (Taipei: Institute of Ethnology, Academia Sinica, 1985), pp. 16–127, especially p. 118.

6. Ibid., pp. 121–22.

7. Baker, p. 1.

8. Myron L. Cohen, *House United, House Divided: A Chinese Family in Taiwan* (New York: Columbia University Press, 1976); see also Cohen's articles, "Lineage Development and the Family in China," in Hsieh Jih-chang and Chuang Ying-chang, eds., *The Chinese Family and Its Ritual Behavior* (Taipei: Institute of Ethnology, Academia Sinica, 1985), pp. 210–18; and "Developmental Process in the Chinese Domestic Group," in Arthur P. Wolf, ed., *Studies in Chinese Society* (Stanford, CA: Stanford University Press, 1978), pp. 183–98.

9. Wong, pp. 65–67, and 87–89; Baker, pp. 45–47.

10. Baker, p. 22.

11. Margery Wolf, "Child Training," p. 227; and her classic work, *The House of Lim* (Englewood Cliffs, NJ: Prentice Hall, 1968), pp. 75–98. See also Yang, pp. 60–61.

12. Arthur P. Wolf, "Chinese Family Size: A Myth Revitalized," pp. 30–49, in Hsieh Jih-chang and Chuang Ying-chang, eds., *The Chinese Family and Its Ritual Behavior* (Taipei: Institute of Ethnology, Academia Sinica, 1985); Cohen, "Developmental Process," pp. 183–98.

13. Yang, pp. 65–66.

14. Margery Wolf, "Child Training," p. 232; Baker, pp. 19–21.

15. Margery Wolf, *Women and the Family in Rural Taiwan* (Stanford, CA: Stanford University Press, 1972), pp. 32–37 and 164–67.

16. Margery Wolf, "Child Training," pp. 237–38.

17. Division of the *jia* estate occurs at different times in the development of the *jia* group according to the precise geographical, economic, and social factors prevailing. Myron Cohen found great incentives operating to keep the extended *jia* together in a tobacco growing village of Taiwan's Pingtung County (see note 8). Burton Pasternak found similar cohesiveness for different reasons in a rice and sugarcane economy of central Taiwan: See Burton Pasternak, *Kinship and Community in Two Chinese Villages* (Stanford, CA: Stanford University Press, 1972); see also his articles, "The Sociology of Irrigation: Two Taiwanese Villages," in Arthur P. Wolf, ed., *Studies in Chinese Society* (Stanford, CA: Stanford University Press, 1978), pp. 199–219; and "Economics and Ecology," in Emily Martin Ahern and Hill Gates, eds., *The Anthropology of Taiwanese Society* (Stanford, CA: Stanford University Press, 1981), pp. 151–83. Sung Lung-sheng has found size of a long-established *jia* estate to be a persuasive factor in extending *jia* longevity: See Sung Lung-sheng, "Property and Family Division," in Ahern and Gates, pp. 361–78. Cohen found labor demands and the need of coordination of economic activities inherent in the

tobacco economy to be powerful incentives for keeping the *jia* estate undivided, the *jia* group in an extended arrangement, and the *jia* economy in corporate form. Where local irrigation needs require careful attention and cooperation, Pasternak found, *jia* groups were more likely to maintain unity, prolonging the life of an extended *jia*. Sung found that if a *jia* estate was largely an inheritance passed down through the generations rather than a current creation of individual *fang* economic activities, extended *jia* arrangements were common; if, however, the current contributions of the *fang* were the larger share or a high proportion of the *jia* estate, individual *fang* were likely to withdraw from the *jia* group, demand their share of the relatively small estate, and thenceforth rely strictly on their own economic endeavors. Whereas Confucian ideological pressures motivate Taiwanese folk to strive for the extended family form, fragile human relationships generally threaten to undermine that ideal; the economic advantages or disadvantages of the extended *jia* as an arrangement usually tip the scales one way or another.

18. Hsieh Jih-chang, "Meal Rotation," in Hsieh Jih-chang and Chuang Ying-chang, eds., *The Chinese Family and Its Ritual Behavior* (Taipei: Institute of Ethnology, Academia Sinica, 1985), pp. 70–83.

19. Margery Wolf, "Child Training," pp. 224–31; Yang, pp. 57–58.

20. Emily M. Ahern, *The Cult of the Dead in a Chinese Village* (Stanford, CA: Stanford University Press, 1973), pp. 149–62.

21. Chen Chung-min, in Hsieh and Chuang, pp. 124–26.

22. Maurice Freedman, *Lineage Organization in Southeast China* (London: Athlone Press, 1958), and his *Chinese Lineage and Society* (London: Athlone Press, 1966). See also Baker, pp. 49–67, and the following articles in Hsieh Jih-chang and Chuang Ying-chang, eds., *The Chinese Family and Its Ritual Behavior* (Taipei: Institute of Ethnology, Academia Sinica, 1985): Burton Pasternak, "The Disquieting Chinese Lineage and Its Anthropological Relevance," pp. 165–91; David Y. H. Wu, "The Conditions of Development and Decline of Chinese Lineages and the Formation of Ethnic Groups," pp. 192–209; and Myron L. Cohen, "Lineage Development and the Family in China," pp. 210–18.

23. David Wu, pp. 195–96 and 204–7.

24. Yang, pp. 69–72.

25. Bernard Gallin and Rita S. Gallin, "Matrilateral and Affinal Relationships in Chinese Society," in Jih-chang Hsieh and Chuang Ying-chang, eds., *The Chinese Family and Its Ritual Behavior* (Taipei: Institute of Ethnology, Academia Sinica, 1985), pp. 101–16.

26. David K. Jordan, "Sworn Brotherhoods: A Study in Chinese Ritual Kinship," in Jih-chang Hsieh and Chuang Ying-chang, eds., *The Chinese Family and Its Ritual Behavior* (Taipei: Institute of Ethnology, Academia Sinica, 1985), pp. 232–62.

27. Ibid., p. 244.

28. Emily Martin Ahern, "The Power and Pollution of Chinese Women," in Arthur Wolf, ed., *Studies in Chinese Culture* (Stanford, CA: Stanford University Press, 1978), pp. 269–90.

29. Marjorie Topley, "Marriage Resistance in Rural Kwangtung," in Arthur Wolf, ed., *Studies in Chinese Culture* (Stanford, CA: Stanford University Press, 1978), pp. 247–68.

30. Wong, pp. 1–26.

31. Chen Chung-min, in Hsieh and Chuang, pp. 122–23.

32. Tang Mei-chun, "Equal Right and Domestic Structure," in Hsieh Jih-chang and Chuang Ying-chang, eds., *The Chinese Family and Its Ritual Behavior* (Taipei: Institute of Ethnology, Academia Sinica, 1985), pp. 61–69.

SUGGESTED READINGS

Baker, Hugh. *Chinese Family and Kinship.* New York: Columbia University Press, 1979.

Cohen, Myron L. *House United, House Divided: A Chinese Family in Taiwan.* New York: Columbia University Press, 1976.

Hsieh Jih-chang and Chuang Ying-chang, eds. *The Chinese Family and Its Ritual Behavior.* Taipei: Institute of Ethnology, Academia Sinica, 1985.

Wolf, Margery. *The House of Lim.* Englewood Cliffs, NJ: Prentice Hall, 1968.

Wolf, Margery. *Women and the Family in Rural Taiwan.* Stanford, CA: Stanford University Press, 1972.

9

Social Customs and Lifestyle

TAIWANESE PEOPLE are very frugal and industrious. They say so. A popular expression can be translated with those very words. The Taiwanese back up those words with action, and lots of it. One's dominant impression of Taiwan is that of a place of movement, ambition, energy, not wasted but purposeful. Taipei, Kaohsiung, and Keelung taxi drivers whiz by each other seemingly helter skelter but in fact with a kind of inspired order in disorder, all with the goal of getting where they are going as quickly as possible so as to have the most to show for their efforts at long (sixteen-hour) day's end.

Pedestrians seem to follow the same cult of motion as the cab drivers, and woe to the unwary (or overly wary) walker who gives a false signal of intended direction, causing an ungraceful bump on the path to greater fortune. Along those same sidewalks, street vendors peddle their noodles or fried cakes or quick and sumptuous stir-fry with great efficiency and much more profit than their humble presentation would suggest. Inside the tall buildings of the major cities important deals are being struck in international business, sophisticated financial arrangements are being made in banking and trust companies, and intricate strategizing is taking place in corporate boardrooms. Smaller towns in Taiwan are abuzz with much of this same energy, not quite so frenetic but no less diligent and purposeful in its application. Even in the much more placid countryside, one does not wait long for a motorcycle or truck to speed by, hauling fertilizer, insecticide, household consumer items, harvested crops, or people. And out in the fields one finds the hardworking farmers on whose bent backs Taiwan's economy came to stand tall.

Taiwanese children develop this diligence and display this energy from a young age.

CHILDREN IN FAMILY AND SOCIETY

Even before they enter school, children find themselves in the midst of the economic exertions that are woven into the Taiwanese family as surely as respect for ancestors. When still very young, children experience their family's economic endeavors as an integral part of their universe. In the countryside they would be privy to the comings and goings of the chickens, pigs, water buffalo, or field oxen that have played such a big part in the traditional Taiwanese farm economy. These animals might well include the family dwelling in their pathways, for in most rural Taiwanese homes the animals that contributed mightily to the family's sustenance were welcome inside, particularly during inclement weather and during the winter, when their body heat added economical extra warmth. In the families that celebrated such religious occasions as the Thai Ti Kong festival, the pig to be specially fattened over the course of a year or more would actually have an honored place inside the homestead, receiving meals at least as tasty and nutritious as those served to the human family and its guests.[1] In the old days a boy, especially, might well be asked to tend to the family's water buffalo, feeding it and making sure that it got to and from the fields safely and stayed within the family's unfenced property. In the course of the last twenty years, water buffalo have become much less conspicuous in the countryside, and small tractors have mostly replaced them in their formerly crucial roles. Older farmers nonetheless keep them around for spot work here and there, and so these sturdy bovine creatures remain a part of the universe in which rural children take delight. Undoubtedly some sentimentality is involved in maintaining a field ox or water buffalo these days, and the emotional attachment children have to animals seems universal, but such fondness for animals is not encouraged in Taiwanese children. Animals are respected for their economic, utilitarian functions, not for their attractiveness as pets.

Until the age of six, Taiwanese children have few responsibilities. They crawl and then walk around the home, beginning to make some sense of the domestic and social symbolism inherent in the altar to their ancestors and patron deities. They begin to sense the roles and importance of aunts, uncles, and grandparents, distinguished carefully as maternal or paternal. As soon as

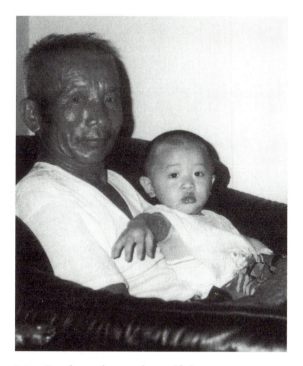

9.1 Rural grandson and grandfather.

rural youngsters can make significant sense out of the words spoken by parents, other kin, and friends, they learn that life holds a different vision for females and males. Within the family, in neighboring families, and throughout the village at large, rural children learn that save for unusual circumstances, it is father's kin who are close at hand. The children see that it is the paternal grandfather or grandmother for whom the family has responsibility and that it is paternal uncles who live close, frequently or always taking meals at the same table, sharing responsibility for the ceremonies honoring paternal ancestors, worshipping the family's patron deities, and keeping the hungry ghosts at bay.

In the rural Taiwanese family, the boy absorbs in the vocal tones and physical affection displayed by his kinfolk the message that his birth was special, particularly if he was the first male child, who could, assuming the requisite longevity, assure the continuance of the male line and the comfort of his parents in old age. He learns in time that he is not only welcome but expected to stay close, either proximally or economically, to the relatives of his father's line. He comes to know that regardless of birth order, he will have a share of his father's property, pooled with the shares of his brothers as long as the fraternal ideal can be maintained but then split as the conjugal units give way to pressures for independence. The boy learns that in the future he will have an essentially religious obligation to find a productive economic skill that will expand the family fortune, make the generations to come more prosperous, and with greater wealth make more sumptuous sacrifices to the ancestors possible, doing greater justice to their material well-being in the realm beyond this one.

Different messages, meanwhile, are conveyed to girls. The girl learns that the home in which she learns to crawl and walk does not in the long run house her most important family, not the family of her destiny, not if she does her duty and marries early and appropriately, however emotionally attached she may remain to the family of her nativity. She learns that her family will take care of her and lay claim to her productive labors as long as she remains in the household, but that her possibilities in the manifest world and in eternity depend on her agreeing to or securing for herself a good marital match. If she remains at home too long, she will only be a burden to her family; and if she should reach eighteen, nineteen, or twenty without good prospects for marriage, she should consider the nature of that burden and cooperate in more persistent efforts toward alleviating it by finding a husband. With her she will take a dowry that is generally granted by her parents, expected by the family of her mate, and of significant monetary value, within the economic capabilities of her natal family. She will retain control over that dowry in her marriage, she will cultivate the emotional loyalty of her children in the same way that she sees her mother build her own "uterine family" as a bastion within the patriarchal realm,[2] and she will endeavor to enhance the rights and interests of her conjugal unit within the extended family. But she will strive to make a place for herself within a patriarchal universe, and she knows that only through her sons will she have security and comfort in her old age. As a very young child, the little girl may play at will with her female and male siblings and cousins of comparable age, but during the elementary school years, at ages six through twelve, the girl increasingly finds herself physically oriented in the home, helping her mother cook, clean, and wash clothes, and receiving instruction in other domestic arts. The rural Taiwanese girl will usually tend a vegetable garden, scatter feed for chickens, or help maintain a pig in the yard adjoining the residential dwelling. During these same years, a brother falling in the same age range goes out to help with larger-scale agricultural endeavors in the rice paddies, vegetable fields, chicken coops, pigsties, or fruit groves.

Children in towns and cities are introduced to most of these same fundamental familial values and they, too, are incorporated into the rhythms of family economic endeavors at a young age. Boys and girls perch as soon as they can sit on tables where cash registers receive clinking coins and the quieter but more desirable paper currency along with which the family fortune grows. The youngsters absorb the smells, sights, and textures of the family enterprise and begin in small ways to contribute to its prosperity: carrying food to the tables of hungry customers in a restaurant, showing the way to umbrellas in a small store, just watching from a chair in an apothecary, and learning and lending the ambiance of the innocent, assuring customers of the continuation of this enterprise in the family's future and by extension the continuation of the prosperity of Taiwanese society in general. As do rural youngsters, children of an urban-based family of small-business proprietors receive numerous social, cultural, and religious signals embodied in the residential unit. The importance of the family economy is delivered powerfully in the very circumstances of the residence. Such dwellings and families make no clear distinction between business and residence. The business is ideally on the first floor, door opening to the sidewalk or street, maximally situated for convenient customer access. The family lives upstairs, where it displays a material culture that is in its luxury much less than the family can afford, and where people reside in much less space than an American of similar well-being would find comfortable. Typically a nuclear family of husband, wife, two or three children, and a grandparent or other relative live in a space not exceeding 500 square feet. The business establishment downstairs is nearly of comparable size, and family members utilize that space. A television may be in the business establishment, raised on a shelf so as to give a good view for those who want to watch. Small children explore the nooks and crannies of the store as they learn the ways of the world. Grandmother may sit by working on some household craft, watching the children, and greeting people from the neighborhood. Indeed, people from the neighborhood may drop by for chats and ensconce themselves more readily in a chair on the floor of the business downstairs than they would in the small *keting* (living room) upstairs in the domicile.

Sometimes the altar to the ancestors can be found downstairs; more typically the altar to Guandi, Milofo, or some other incarnation of the Buddha and other gods considered helpful to business enterprises is placed in the first-floor commercial area. In such a setting, the Taiwanese child learns that commercial prosperity is a higher-order goal interwoven with prime family activities. The youngster learns that the clinking of the cash register has priority over sumptuousness of living space and material conditions. The child learns that one spends generously on banquets securing social relationships, on weddings symbolizing the continuation of the patriarchal line, and on religious observances that tie one to one's ancestry and community; that otherwise one lives frugally and saves for the future. The Taiwanese child learns that personal space is not important, certainly way down on the list of life's priorities. One's bed is usually next to that of others, and it well may be set up in the living room. Perhaps a bit of the Japanese influence on the island's history and culture can be seen in a comfortable futon rolled out just for the purpose of sleeping, and then, with marvelous conservation of space, rolled back up in the morning to make way for other activities. As much as Taiwanese children are expected to read and study, they have no large, special place to do so in the family residence. A corner of the upstairs residential unit proper will suffice, or perhaps a relatively untraveled spot on the lower floor given to the family business may come to be favored. A chair placed outside the business on the sidewalk might in some cases offer the only remotely appropriate space. In all these circumstances people will be coming and going, talking, laughing, playing, so the student develops powers of concentration reminiscent of those pointedly cultivated by Mohandas Gandhi on the streets of London.

Taiwanese children born into families whose primary activities focus on factory labor will live in even more confined settings, situations much like that just indicated but minus the additional space afforded by the lower-floor commercial establishment. In contrast, the child born into a family whose economic endeavors unfold in a well-placed government position or in the executive ranks of a modern corporation has a quite different residential universe. Some of the messages conveyed to the children in the various circumstances described above are delivered more diffusely to upper-middle- and upper-class children. The living space may be a luxury modern high-rise apartment or condominium; or it may be a single-family dwelling of Japanese provenance in the city proper or a Western-style rambler in the suburbs. Such a child may well go to the American school in Taipei or some other private school, but more commonly would go to one of the many fine, highly reputed public schools accessible to those with the right combination of wealth and connections. The upper-middle- and upper-class child has personal space closer to Western expectations. Such a child is much more removed from family economic endeavors than are children born in farm-based or small proprietary families. The wealthier child is likely more pampered and less supervised by ever-present relatives than is the poorer and middle-class child in the more intimate settings of rural families and shopkeepers. Yet long-term expectations for upper-middle- and upper-class children are higher. To fail to take the family's inherited fortune and expand it is a failing of serious magnitude in Taiwanese society, and so the pressure on the upper-middle- and upper-class girl or boy to succeed is strong indeed. The boy of such a family today is expected to carry on the tradition of the family company, or to expand the family economy through success in some other business enterprise, or to establish family connections and reputation in another field, perhaps medicine or academics. The girl would be expected to marry well to help secure or expand family connections in business, government, higher education, or high culture. These days she may well succeed in one of these realms on her own terms, but she neither feels pressure nor receives encouragement, as her brother does.

Whatever their social class or community of origin, Taiwanese children are expected to maximize their chances for future success by doing well in school.

EDUCATION

Girls and boys begin an arduous climb through the educational system at the age of four or five, when their parents enroll them in one of the 1,725 private or 793 public kindergartens found on the island.[3] Public kindergartens are usually attached to one of the 2,472 elementary schools, administered by county or special municipality. Taiwanese children normally enter these elementary schools at age six and establish their educational foundations in the first through sixth grades. When students graduate from the sixth grade, they proceed to the American equivalent of junior high school. The three years of education at this level have been offered free of charge since 1968; however, between 1968 and 1982 students took exams to gain entrance to junior high school and to determine which one to enter if they passed the tests. These tests initiated Taiwanese children into the competitive system of Taiwanese higher education, with the quality of school into which one tests at a given level greatly influencing one's ability to gain entrance into a quality school at the next level. Since 1982, however, education through the ninth grade has been compulsory, and the examination to gain entrance to junior high has been eliminated. As a result, intense competition has since that time been deferred until the conclusion of junior high, at which time Taiwanese students are dispersed along several very different educational paths, determined greatly by performance on a standard examination administered at the end of ninth grade but in part decided by the students' families.

Three general paths are possible. Students performing at a high level on the examination can gain entrance into one of the academic high schools, each having a rank within the county or municipal systems and accepting students appropriate to that rank. Students manifesting less talent in the core academic subjects but giving evidence of solid fundamental skills and technical aptitude may choose one of two paths. The first is secondary vocational school that over the course of three years helps a student gain experience in a technical field such as machinery operation, carpentry, architectural drafting, plumbing, pharmacology, accounting, and various other technical subjects relevant to industry, agriculture, or commerce. Alternatively, a student testing well enough to embark on such training may choose to enter a program run by a five-year junior college; such a student therefore bypasses the technical high school in favor of this longer-term commitment. There are also two- and three-year junior colleges offering technical training, and beyond this there are three-year technical colleges offering still more advanced training. A student who rises through the various levels of technical training has completed four to five years beyond high school and emerges as a very highly trained technician. Whereas most students enter the job market at this point, the most apt or ambitious students may continue into master's and even doctoral programs in such fields as engineering, architecture, and computer technology. Such a student may emerge with as much prestige as a student who early on seemed through examination performance to indicate the most academic potential.

Gaining entrance into an academic high school, though, is the surest way to the highest level of social prestige and makes possible early entrance into the best academic colleges and universities. At the end of the three years of academic high school training, students take an exam encompassing a wide range of liberal arts and sciences; this exam determines the rank of college or university that the student may enter. There are good colleges offering undergraduate and very limited graduate courses of study, but the most prestigious schools in Taiwan are the universities offering a full range of undergraduate and graduate curricula. The most prestigious school in all Taiwan is National Taiwan University, excellent performance and well-established connections at which almost certainly assure a person high success in such fields as medicine, law, economics, or academics or improve one's chances of landing a position as research fellow at Academia Sinica or an important job in the government bureaucracy.

Education as a key value in Taiwanese society is reflected in the highly literate nature of the populace. Attendance at and graduation from elementary school is nearly 100 percent of students in the appropriate age categories, and most of these students complete junior high school. Of junior high school graduates, 75 percent go on to additional academic or technical training. Of those students graduating from one of the academic high schools, about 85 percent test into one of the academic colleges or universities. In all, there are 107 institutions of higher learning in Taiwan, including 68 junior colleges, 23 colleges (academic and technical), and 16 universities.

Education in Taiwan is high quality, teacher focused, and exam driven. It is delivered in a style now considered ill-suited to the needs and demands of students in the United States. In Taiwan, students rise when the teacher enters and greet their instructor with a reverent verbal salutation. The teacher talks. Students listen and take notes. The system is very efficient and produces students who have an enormous mental store of facts and figures. The system is not designed to produce highly creative, original, free-thinking students, but it produces students who have a large body of knowledge in history, geography, math, and science. Until recent years students received indoctrination in the "Three Principles of the People," and they still learn to cultivate filial piety, respect for authority, personal honesty, and a range of other virtues. As if the regular school day were not demanding enough, many students enroll in after-hours and night schools called *buxiban*, which are best understood in English to be cram schools offering an even more rapid flow of information for acquisition and review, geared toward high performance on the entrance exams that so greatly affect the future of the Taiwanese child and adolescent.

Whatever the level of education attained by the Taiwanese young person, she or he enters a very different world of work than would have been true even ten or twenty years ago; the comparison of the job opportunities and work situation available today with those available forty or fifty years ago is astounding.

A CHANGING ECONOMY'S IMPACT ON THE FAMILY

In 1950 Taiwan's economy was firmly embedded in the soil, which gave forth mainly rice, sugarcane, sweet potatoes, pineapples, and a variety of fruits or vegetables, the latter of which were mainly for family consumption.[4] The majority of Taiwan's workforce remained in agriculture into the middle 1960s, at which time a decade of great change began. The percentage of Taiwan's labor force associated with agriculture fell below that of industry by 1968, then continued to fall so that by the mid-1980s agriculture claimed no more than 16 percent of the total labor force. By this time, though, even the great majority of those households classified as farmers in fact sent forth multiple members into the factories, the concrete manifestations of the central government's decentralized industrial strategy. By the 1980s it was rare to find a fifty-year-old male who made his living solely or even primarily in agriculture. Most typically, he and his late-teen sons and daughters sought to augment the agriculturally derived portion of the family's income through work found in a nearby industrial park, where could be found factories producing textiles, machinery, chemical products, shoes, furniture, and even yachts. Increasingly farm labor was left to the women and older males, who stayed daily on the farm while other family members went off to work. Taiwan's small-scale farms, averaging no more than one hectare (two and one-half acres) precluded large-scale mechanization by individual farmers, but by the 1970s a good number of farming households had motorized power tillers that one walked behind as one had traditionally walked behind the field ox. Others hired one of the teams of workers from enterprising farm households that had invested in bigger, more powerful machinery and offered themselves to plow and prepare the soil for a fee.

Technological developments made possible the release of additional family labor to take advantage of expanding off-farm job opportunities. Through these shifting approaches to the tasks of farming, agriculture served as the solid base on which Taiwan's economic transformation took place. Exports of rice and sugar and pineapple generated foreign exchange for the Taiwanese economy and was used to start factories and establish new businesses. The government used various extractive devices to claim additional revenue from the agricultural economy, including most especially a rice-fertilizer barter system, a land tax paid in kind, and a compulsory purchase of about one-quarter of the rice crop at low prices. Until the mid-1960s, farmers did not feel the pinch from these government extractions too heavily. Many had prospered in the aftermath of a land reform implemented between 1949 and 1953; landholdings in excess of three *jia* (in all, about two and one-half acres) had been confiscated, so that the Taiwanese countryside rapidly turned into an owner-cultivator dominated sector. Demand for farm commodities was strong in urban areas, mushrooms and asparagus were added as high-value export items, and chemical fertilizer and pesticide were expensive but more readily available than ever. But by 1968 industry was, as evidenced by several indicators, overtaking agriculture as the leading sector; service-commerce was eclipsing even industry as the most important employment sector. It took five years, though, for the government to wean itself from the extractive policy and move instead toward subsidization. By that time Taiwan was experiencing industrial growth rates unparalleled across the globe. Industrial and commercial enterprise looked ever more appealing as lucrative employment opportunities and life invested in agricultural labor became less and less desirable. In the course of the 1980s, Taiwanese youth expressed next to zero interest in farming as a profession. Gary found during research in Tainan

County during 1989–1990 not a single youth reporting to him personally that she or he wanted to be a full-time professional farmer.

Hard work was not being lost as a value among Taiwanese youth. To the contrary, Taiwanese youth worked harder than ever during the 1970s and 1980s. The lifestyle of a farmer lost its appeal because farming, while technically successful, had become economically unrewarding, no longer sufficiently profitable to raise a family in a style consistent with Taiwan's growing standard of living. Many youth remained in the countryside, commuting to their jobs in the industrial parks while still helping out their families on the farm during evenings and weekends. When significantly higher pay beckoned, though, some youth moved farther away, to one of the Export Processing Zones, or to a factory job offered by big corporations located typically in areas ringing the major cities.

Young women were among those who sometimes made this move to distant factory jobs. This phenomenon was not entirely new to Taiwanese society. In the nineteenth century, women dominated among the tea leaf pickers on the hillsides of northern Taiwan, employed by companies running sizable operations and making handsome profits on the strength of international sales. In these fundamental characteristics the operation of Western Electronics studied by Lydia Kung was very similar.[5] Making electronic goods for international sale, the company during the 1970s made general use of female labor to assemble components. Across the island employment of women in the textile and electronics industries was widespread, and opportunities for female contribution to family economies were unprecedented and irresistible. Although there were roughly comparable situations in Taiwanese history of female labor being used to benefit international enterprises and family economies, never had this happened on such a large scale. Although many of the jobs were located close to home, sometimes the opportunity took the young woman a substantial distance from home; in some cases, a young woman from a family of humble means might make a cross-island move to take a job particularly well paying by the prevailing Taiwanese 1970s standard, perhaps at a factory on the outskirts of Kaohsiung, Keelung, Taichung, Tainan, or Taipei. Here she would most likely find cheap housing in a company dormitory, to which she would retreat after eight- to twelve-hour days.

Whether male or female, 1970s factory labor involved tedious, monotonous work in conditions better than the England of Charles Dickens but still ill-lit, minimally sanitary, and even mildly toxic. Some women combined their labor experience with study in night school. Sometimes the latter might actually be run by the company, but in many cases the young woman would be studying in one of the varieties of vocational schools or technical colleges, though rarely in an academic college or university. For some women this life was a liberating experience, an opportunity to see more of the universe outside the local community where she had been raised. It was a chance to meet new people, find a more independent space in the world, see movies, read more widely, expose herself to sights and sounds and ideas that ranged beyond the paternally controlled world from which she came.

Although freed from immediate parental control, the young woman still found herself in a patriarchal world. Her group leader at work most likely would be a woman, but her foreman was almost certainly a male; and if a woman appeared in the ranks of those above the level of floor foreman, it would have been shocking indeed. Most group leaders, proletarian and female, maintained cordial relationships with their fellow workers; they could not afford to put on airs if they were to be effective in securing the cooperation of the workers whom they led. Male supervisors, though, generally kept their distance and strove to maintain an aura instilling awe and even mild fear. A few foremen could be found who sought to shorten the distance between themselves and a worker by making unwanted sexual advances. There were proper channels of redress for such circumstances; and if pursued, a woman could reasonably expect justice to prevail. Nonetheless, such potential situations constituted an added consideration in the young woman's world, which factory women perceived as being much more complex and threatening than the universe encompassed by the rural community.

If all this complexity had been perceived as leading to a better life, with more and more challenging employment opportunities and greatly enriched social and cultural experiences, the sentiment on the part of the young women might have been uniformly and unreservedly positive. But most of these women sent checks home to fathers who pooled these with other family income, returning a portion to their daughters or trusting them to deduct an agreed-upon amount for personal needs. Most of these women perceived themselves as stuck in a wage range from which they were unlikely to climb in their later work lives. If such a woman could find no suitable mate, or if in line with Taiwanese tradition her family could not secure a mate for her, she would be doomed to a lonely life at the low end of the economic scale. If a young factory woman did find a mate, she was then likely to enter a family situation that although changing with modernization was still male dominated and certainly not descriptive of some fantasy novel plot wherein a young factory girl finds romance, adventure, fame, and fortune worlds away from her humble village. Her alternative employment opportunities at a female factory worker skill level were likely to be found as department store

clerk, restaurant waitress or hostess, railroad ticket-taker or onboard attendant, and the like. If she advanced in her education, she might find her way
into the ranks of bank teller, secretary, or hotel clerk, but these were prized
positions open only to those of polished personality, with the verbalisms of
the well educated and most likely having excellent social connections.

Males who began to leave the farms and move into the cities as the economy advanced in the 1970s and beyond had a much wider world of work
open to them. If they hailed from substantial farm family economies, they
might open any number of small businesses: restaurant, shoe store, hardware
store, vehicle repair, and specialty stores running the gamut: handbags, pad-
ded jackets, umbrellas, baby beds, household furniture, office supplies, electronic goods, and on and on. If their families could not stake them to the
relatively humble startup capital necessary to launch such businesses, they
might find work as railroad conductors, common laborers, janitors, auto or
motorcycle mechanics, security guards, or bus drivers. A very, very popular
job for males with no advanced education is that of taxi driver. Taiwanese
people are highly independent, so that a male finding his way to the city
might well endure the sixteen-hour days productive of a decent income in
exchange for the freedom from a boss looking over a shoulder. These taxis
constitute notable features of the urban landscape, carrying people intent on
getting quickly to where they are going; to people willing to buy, sell, wheel,
deal; by people working hard to build a better life for a family in place, back
home, passed on, yet to come.

Taiwanese family and community organization have always been flexible
in their responses to economic opportunities.[6] A seeming paradox in Chinese
societies generally and Taiwanese society specifically is how people so tied to
local family and community so readily pick up and move to other places.
The answer is that the paramount duty for a family unit and its individual
members is to maximize family income and wealth. Although agriculture was
always taken as the base, when other areas beckoned and economic expansion
was possible, family members had an obligation to seize the opportunities.
Market towns serving about twenty villages offered opportunities for entrepreneurial endeavors, and it was here that rural families most often sent excess
or expendable labor to establish businesses. Attempting to stay in the general
region, some males of the family might hire themselves out as laborers building roads or irrigation works. Women might do piece work at home for some
textile operation; others might take jobs picking tea leaves. In its economic
aspects, a family was a small corporation, extending its enterprises into as
many different areas as possible. If the family was successful enough in these
economic endeavors, the incentive was high to stay in the extended family

9.2   One of Taipei's many small-scale entrepreneurs: a shoe repair shop on a side-walk.

arrangement that was the Taiwanese ideal: Although various pressures tended in time to split most families into nuclear arrangements, if pooled resources were significant enough, the various brothers and their families might decide it wise to stay together. Staying together, though, did not necessarily mean co-residing. Cohabitation and sharing meals was the norm for the Taiwanese extended family, but if the incentives were powerful enough in an area at some distance from the village, one of the family units might be designated to move to the area where the opportunity prevailed. In such a situation, the family that moved would continue to send its income to the village-based family head according to a joint agreement for equitable distribution. Members of this distant economic extension of the family would return home for important ritual occasions and remain psychologically connected to their place of origin. They would certainly intend to be buried in the home village. Thus, when the Taiwanese family is seen in its corporate aspects, the traits described by love of village and willingness to migrate become less paradoxical.

Economic policy devised by the Guomindang brilliantly catered to this Taiwanese preference to stay close to the rural home if possible but move if powerful incentives existed elsewhere.[7] Seen from this perspective, decentralized industrialization gave farm families additional economic opportunities, similar to those that market towns had provided historically. The pull of farm and family was strong; if lucrative work could contribute to the family economy while allowing the person to remain in the ancestral home, this was ideal. Decentralized industry and a Taiwanese preference for staying near the home village combined to give the island relatively slow migration rates by the standards of other modernizing economies. At the same time, the rational way in which Taiwanese families used their capital and labor meant that some units proved ideal for entrepreneurial endeavors in the big city. Most of these family businesses were small in scale, and as other sectors eclipsed agriculture, these small businesses were at the forefront of Taiwan's economic transformation. But while these small concerns proved to be the backbone of the modernizing economy, some families inevitably realized their corporate potential: The extended family ideal contributed powerfully to both small-business growth and corporate growth in the Taiwanese economy.

Whether a person was motivated by survival or truly grand economic opportunity, the pull of the rural village remained strong. Much was left behind besides the immediate family. Taiwanese people have traditionally felt a keen identification with kinfolk beyond the immediate family, and they tended to reside close to other members of their lineage, that is, to people who traced their ancestry to the same historical personage.[8]

Taiwanese people identify first with their family and kinfolk, and by extension with others of the same surname; but they also value numerous nonkin relationships.

COMMUNITY VALUES

Traditionally, the Taiwanese placed great importance on the welfare of the people in their village. During periods of peak agricultural activity they would lend mutual assistance, thus providing needed hands in a labor-intensive, small-farm economy. They would lend this same sort of assistance when a neighbor needed a new roof, was establishing a fish pond, or was adding a new wing to meet the needs of an expanding family.

Villagers who needed to cooperate to complete some task of mutual benefit likely had an enhanced sense of loyalty and mutual responsibility: The need to build irrigation works, canals, or dams to enhance the value of and protect the property of all strengthened that bond among villagers.[9] Many festivals in Taiwan are celebrated on a very particular day, according to the lunar calendar. Such festivals include the New Year, the Dragon Boat Festival, *Qing Ming* (sweeping of ancestral grave sites), and the Mid-Autumn Festival. These occasions are observed throughout Taiwan. An islandwide spirit unites people across demarcations of village, township, and county, as well as across the boundaries of family, lineage, clan, and ethnic group. There are other occasions, though, that are particular to certain villages or that are celebrated at different times from village to village. Among these celebrations would be those honoring Tho Te Kong (*tudigong* in Mandarin, the earth deity of specific locality), Co Su Kong (*cushigong*, honored in the festival known as Thai Thi Kong [*taizhugong*], the "Slaughter of the Honorable Pig"),[10] and certain heroes identified with specific villages or village clusters. For these celebrations different levels of community organization may well be proudly activated. At one level, pride in village is operational, since the activity may involve the whole village. When surrounding villages are in fact celebrating the same festival at about the same time, this villagewide pride gains added strength during intervillage rivalry. Often prime responsibility for a celebration involving the whole village will be rotated from year to year, first falling upon certain lineage or surname groups within the village, which in turn designate particular families to take prime responsibility or to assume certain roles in the celebration. Loyalty to village has been an observable fact of community organization in Taiwan generally; prevailing circumstances can strengthen or weaken that loyalty. Villagewide loyalty and identification were traditionally strongest, similarly noted for lineage affiliation, when residents regularly faced physical danger from groups external to the village or when the demands of the agricultural economy placed a premium on cooperation across family, lineage, or surname.

People of a given region in Taiwan, then, have been potentially linked beyond the village on the basis of lineage; they also might be linked through subethnic identification. Given that Taiwan's Chinese population manifests characteristics commonly identifying an ethnic group, the Hakka, Quanzhou Fujianese, and Zhangzhou Fujianese may be understood as subethnicities.[11] The Hakka migrated to Taiwan from the Guangdong-Fujian border regions, whereas the Fujianese population came overwhelmingly from Zhangzhou and Quanzhou in southern Fujian Province. The Hakka speak a dialect mutually incomprehensible with Minnan, the language of the Fujianese, and they evidence certain cultural characteristics such as the relative independence of women (who did not bind their feet and did work in agricultural fields), a greater tendency to diversify family economies on an agrarian rather than a mercantile basis, the wearing of wide-brimmed hats and other distinctive attire, and the worshipping of certain deities and rituals particular to their own subethnicity. The two Fujianese groups speak a common dialect, but their accents are distinctive; and they, too, evidence some differences in the deities and rituals to which they are partial. In eighteenth- and nineteenth-century Taiwan, conflicts between a region's Hakka and Fujianese populations could be fierce. In the absence of such conflict, tensions between the Zhangzhou and Quanzhou subethnicities were often magnified, resulting in disputes every bit as violent as those evidenced in Hakka-Fujianese rivalry. On the more positive side of these rivalries, subethnic pride led to mutual aid, cooperative projects, and celebration of religious occasions incorporating subethnic members beyond the village.

Implicit in these nonkin relationships—cross-lineage, intravillage, and subethnic multivillage relationships—was a Taiwanese value brought from the mainland and expressed in the term *ganqing*.[12] *Ganqing* involves a feeling of cordiality most especially among friends but also among all those people with whom regular interaction transpires. Relationships are important in Taiwanese society; it is *ganqing* that infuses relationships with civility and good feeling. *Ganqing* permeates relationships of a horizontal nature, but it is also the value and characteristic that smoothes out vertical relationships in a society that gives great attention to hierarchy. Thus, although landlord-tenant relationships could be quite contentious, as could the relationships between rulers and ruled, lender and borrower, and any number of other groups in which the balance of power was tilted to one side, good *ganqing* could ameliorate the potential harshness and friction in such relationships.

Relationships, connections, and networks, so important in Taiwanese society, are so much more intricate than those articulated by most Americans that an introduction to the term *guanxi* becomes useful. In establishing the necessary contacts to contract marriages, buy land, expand commercial operations, get into preferred schools, gain access to jobs, and obtain appointment to government posts, for example, good connections are of paramount importance. People in Chinese societies elevate these connections, summarized in the term, *guanxi*, to a high art and a great social value. The Taiwanese cultivate and employ *guanxi* to great effect. As with the pursuit of economic gain, establishing and using *guanxi* to improve one's station in life is a practice unashamedly followed in Taiwanese society. Establishing good *guanxi*, increasing the number of people with whom *guanxi* prevails, and utilizing the resulting human relationships to maximize one's chances of economic success contribute to the greater glory of the eternal family and to the achievement of a more stable social order. These are high values, representing not just pragmatic and utilitarian strategies but also, ultimately more important, religious imperatives.

Politically ambitious Taiwanese have a greater chance than ever to explore the potential of *ganqing* and *guanxi* to achieve government power and to influence social policy. The Taiwanese political scene has been transformed since the lifting of martial law in 1987. Although the bureaucratic structure of government has varied over the years of Qing, Japanese, and Guomindang control, the current hierarchy of village, township, county, and province incorporates many traditional characteristics of the formal bureaucracy and reflects continuity in political structure. The Taiwanese traditionally focused most especially on family, surname or lineage group, village, market town, and township, with the latter two frequently one and the same, uniting in one locale the commercial and political functions most relevant to the area's population. The county could also be important and was fairly manifest in the lives of most people. Because islandwide identification was traditionally much weaker, politically township and county have been on the outer rings of the concentric progression affecting the lives of most Taiwanese people. Today islandwide identification has increased greatly. In the last fifty years expanding transportation and communication systems and enhanced economic interconnectedness have served to increase islandwide identification, and the advent of genuine political democracy has increased the stake most people feel they can and do have in the life of the whole island.

Although migration rates in Taiwan have been smaller than rates in most other geopolities at comparable stages of industrialization, Taiwanese cities have nevertheless grown enormously in the course of the last fifty years. Relatively little migration has taken place in Taiwan because of the lure of the big city. Migrants continue to come seeking economic betterment. In some cases this has been just a matter of expanding the family economy; in others it has been a matter of economic survival.[13] A famous study done by Bernard Gallin and Rita Gallin indicates that long-distance migrants to Taipei from several villages in Changhua County, with particular focus on a village given the pseudonym Hsin-hsing, tend to be those relatively low in economic status, education, and skills.[14] Many were tenants or operated extremely small parcels of land. They arrived in a chain migration in which the father or an older son of the family made the move first, followed later by a wife, children, and other family members. Three-fourths of those who migrated from the village of focus by Gallin and Gallin retained small landholdings in the village of origin; even when they sold off their land, they tended to retain their old family residences. Long after they migrated to Taipei, they returned to their villages on important ceremonial occasions, especially New Year and occasions involving ritual expression of respect for ancestors. Eighty-five percent of those who had migrated remained in Taipei permanently, while maintaining ritual connections to the home village and continuing to draw upon the *ganqing* and *guanxi* established with their fellow migrants hailing from the same village and village cluster in Changhua County. These migrants overwhelmingly sought employment in the vegetable section of Taipei Central Market, where the first migrants from their village had early on found jobs and established *guanxi*. Furthermore, the great majority lived in the same district in Taipei. They formed a trade association to advance their interests against legitimate competitors in the marketplace and to protect their mutual interests against police who frequently sought bribes and against local toughs who demanded their own payoffs. These migrants found themselves disparaged as newcomers by long-term Taipei residents. To advance mutual interests beyond the marketplace, they lent each other money, helped each other out at weddings, sent each other the red envelopes (*hongbao*) containing gift money at appropriate ritual occasions, and in general maintained many ties they had developed in the village. Many of them sought out others who had migrated from their general area of Taiwan, eventually signing on as members of the Changhua County Regional Association. At the same time, they did eventually cultivate new *guanxi* and express *ganqing* in new friendships formed with work and neighborhood associates not from their region of Taiwan. Some sought to expand socially and politically by forming sworn brotherhoods of the sort frequently recorded in Chinese and Taiwanese history. Those who moved beyond labor service to the level of merchants had inevitably been able to cultivate and extend *guanxi* to powerful and influential people in the city broadly construed. In such cases, for economically practical as well as socially rewarding reasons they maintained ties with their less-well-off fellow migrants, even as they moved in circles far above those who had made the move to the city under similar initial circumstances.

Alexander Chien-chung Yin found many of these same features among migrants from a very different area of greater Taiwan, the Penghu Islands to the southwest of Taiwan proper.[15] These migrants typically moved not to Taipei but to Kaohsiung, the second largest city and one of the island's two most important ports. These migrants also came from tough economic circumstances, perhaps the most challenging economic environment of any in greater Taiwan: The ecology of the Penghu Islands sustains fishers much better than farmers, but only so many people can fish profitably. So the nineteenth and twentieth centuries have witnessed much seasonal and permanent emigration from Penghu to the main island. During the Japanese period many served as laborers when Kaohsiung harbor was being redesigned into the major shipping center that it has become. During Guomindang rule more and more female laborers from Penghu have made the move, for reasons evident in the industrialization policy discussed earlier in this and other chapters. As in the case of migrants from the Changhua County village studied by Gallin and Gallin, Penghu migrants have tended to locate residentially close to one another, in the familiar chain migration pattern: People back home were kept abreast of opportunities discussed in the generally favorable reports of those who had already arrived, so other kin and community members followed those who blazed the migratory trail. In the course of the twentieth century, Penghu migrants have founded thirty-three temples in Kaohsiung. Interestingly, these have focused worship not on deities from the home region but, rather, on deities perceived as helpful in present circumstances, serving the economic aspirations so evident in many aspects of Taiwanese life. A number of temples have been built by Penghu migrants in honor of Confucius, in deified form the god of learning and therefore of great help as one moves through school, faces crucial examinations, and in so doing improves one's lot in life and that of one's family. Penghu migrants have built numerous other temples to Guandi, historically the god of war but valued today more for his assistance in commercial endeavors. Penghu residents have also formed a major moneylending association to assist one another, and a great Penghu regional association has undergone several incarnations advancing Penghu migrant interests in education, social welfare, culture, and, especially, politics. Toward the latter end, Penghu migrants have formed a bloc with real clout in Kaohsiung political circles and are among the movers and shakers in Kaohsiung society. As in the case of the migrants studied by Gallin and Gallin, Penghu migrants have inevitably expanded their *guanxi* and expressed *ganqing* among people outside their own migrant group. They have also increasingly varied their residential pattern. As they have found new places to live and found new contacts and friendships in sports clubs, school societies, professional groups, and political organizations, they have also maintained intimate relationships with one another and continued contact with those back in Penghu.

Taiwanese people are very frugal and industrious. They say so, and they display their frugality and their industry in a wide range of human endeavors. They are trained from childhood to be attentive to their religious and cultural imperative to expand the family fortune. Their success ethic in the realm of education is high. When they work, they work not just for themselves but for the family broadly construed, for all those generations that have been, are, and are yet to come. In their community organization they cultivate a wide variety of kinship and nonkinship relationships with great emphasis on *ganqing* (good feeling) and *guanxi* (well-developed social connections). They delay their move away from home as long as possible, but they move with great flexibility to take advantage of urban opportunities when those become too compelling to ignore, and in the city they employ their frugality and industry with results that have attracted the admiration of the world. When the Taiwanese make such a move, there is both continuity and change in the way they go about conducting their cultural, economic, and residential lives. Taiwan's emergence as a genuine political democracy with a capitalistic economy that hums loudly on the strength of the frugality and industry of the populace presents new challenges internally as the society becomes more complex and potentially contentious; it also presents a challenge externally, with the island's very success posing major challenges to the Chinese colossus on the mainland. The turbulent history of Taiwan gives every evidence that its people will be equal to the new challenges they face, and that they will employ their time-cultivated and time-tested frugality and industry to address successfully the pressing issues of the twenty-first century.

NOTES

1. See Emily Martin Ahern, "The Thai Ti Kong Festival," in Emily Martin Ahern and Hill Gates, eds., *The Anthropology of Taiwanese Society* (Stanford, CA: Stanford University Press, 1981), pp. 397–425.

2. Margery Wolf develops this concept in her classic work, *The House of Lim* (Englewood Cliffs, NJ: Prentice Hall, 1968).

3. The statistics on the Taiwanese educational system cited in this section are from Han Lih-Wu, *Taiwan Today* (Taipei: Cheng Chung Book Company, 1968), pp. 241–61.

4. For an overview of changes in the Taiwanese agrarian economy over the last fifty years, see Gary M. Davison, *Agricultural Development and the Fate of Farmers in Taiwan, 1945–1990* (Ph.D. dissertation, University of Minnesota Department of History, 1993), pp. 48–175.

5. The account of the life of the female factory worker found herein follows Lydia Kung's account in her "Perceptions of Work among Factory Women," in Emily Martin Ahern and Hill Gates, eds., *The Anthropology of Taiwanese Society* (Stanford, CA: Stanford University Press, 1981) pp. 397–425.

6. The classic account of the economic flexibility of the Taiwanese family is Myron L. Cohen's *House United, House Divided: A Chinese Family in Taiwan* (New York: Columbia University Press, 1971).

7. See Davison, pp. 48–106.

8. See Burton Pasternak, "Economics and Ecology," in Emily Martin Ahern and Hill Gates, eds., *The Anthropology of Taiwanese Society* (Stanford, CA: Stanford

University Press, 1981), pp. 151–83, for a concise treatment of the community functions of Taiwanese lineages.

9. For his full treatment of the impact of economics and ecology on rural Taiwanese community structure, see Burton Pasternak, *Kinship and Community in Two Chinese Villages* (Stanford, CA: Stanford University Press, 1972).

10. See Ahern's chapter as given in Ahern and Gates, pp. 397–425.

11. For an excellent discussion of Taiwanese subethnicity, see Harry J. Lamley, "Subethnic Rivalry in the Ch'ing Period," in Emily Martin Ahern and Hill Gates, eds. *The Anthropology of Taiwanese Society* (Stanford, CA: Stanford University Press, 1981), pp. 282–318.

12. Our application to Taiwan of a key concept in Chinese societies is indebted to Morton Fried's classic treatment of the importance of *ganqing* in *The Fabric of Chinese Society: A Study of the Social Life of a Chinese County Seat* (New York: Praeger Press, 1953).

13. See Alden Speare, Jr., "Migration and Family Change in Central Taiwan," in Mark Elvin and G. William Skinner, eds., *The Chinese City between Two Worlds* (Stanford, CA: Stanford University Press, 1974), pp. 303–30.

14. See Bernard Gallin and Rita S. Gallin, "The Integration of Village Migrants in Taipei," in Mark Elvin and G. William Skinner, eds., *The Chinese City between Two Worlds* (Stanford, CA: Stanford University Press, 1974), pp. 331–58.

15. See Alexander Chien-chung Yin, "Voluntary Associations and Rural Migration," in Ahern and Gates, eds., *The Anthropology of Taiwanese Society* (Stanford, CA: Stanford University Press, 1981), pp. 319–37.

SUGGESTED READINGS

Fried, Morton. *The Fabric of Chinese Society: A Study of Social Life in a Chinese County Seat.* New York: Praeger Press, 1953.

Gallin, Bernard and Rita S. Gallin. "The Integration of Village Migrants in Taipei," in Mark Elvin and G. William Skinner, eds. *The Chinese City between Two Worlds.* Stanford, CA: Stanford University Press, 1974.

Han Lih-Wu. *Taiwan Today.* Taipei: Cheng Chung Book Company, 1968.

Yin, Alexander Chien-chung. "Voluntary Associations and Rural Migration," in Emily Martin Ahern and Hill Gates, eds. *The Anthropology of Taiwanese Society.* Stanford, CA: Stanford University Press, 1981.

Glossary of Chinese Terms

bagua 八卦 eight trigrams

baibai 拜拜 devotional worship of a deity; temple festival honoring deity

baihua 白話 "plain speech" (vernacular Chinese)

bao en 報恩 repaying a deity with sacrificial offerings in return for its benevolent help

bayin 八音 "eight sounds" or materials out of which musical instruments are made (stone, earth, bamboo, metal, skin, silk, wood, gourd)

beiguan 北管 Northern Chinese opera and musical style

Ben cao gang mu 本草綱目 Ming dynasty medical text

bianfu 弁服 traditional long tunic and skirt combination

bianwen 遍文 popularizations of narratives

biqing 筆情 the feeling of the writing pen

bu 補 "supplementing" or "strengthening," as with certain foods

budai xi 布袋戲 traditional Taiwanese hand puppetry

buxiban 補習班 cram school

cao 草 "free-flowing" script of Chinese calligraphy

changmian 場面 "face of the show" (orchestra)

changpao 長袍 long one-piece robe worn by both men and women

changshan 長衫 traditional long gown for men

chi 恥 Confucian virtue of having a sense of shame

chou 丑 male clown in traditional Chinese drama

choudan 丑旦 female clown in traditional Chinese drama

chuandou 穿斗   pillar and transverse tie beam system of construction

chuanqi 傳奇   wonder tales

dabo 大鈸   large cymbals

dading 大定   greater engagement

Dajie 大戒   "Great Restraints," a musical composition

daluo 大鑼   big gong

danpigu 單皮鼓   one-headed drum

Dao 道   the Way

daoma dan 刀馬旦   "saber horse" warrior woman or a military sprite in
      traditional Chinese drama

di 笛   wooden horizontal flute

dongfang meiren 東方美人   "Eastern beauty" tea

dongxiao 洞簫   traditional Chinese flute-like instrument

du 毒   poisonous

erhu 二胡   two-stringed instrument played with a bow (lower pitched than
      huqin)

fagu 法鼓   "drum of the law" used in religious rituals

fang 房   households, families within the larger family

fanguan 反管   "turning the pipe," a musical improvisation technique

feng ru song 風入松   "Wind in the Pines" (a tune)

fenghuang 鳳凰   phoenix

fengshui 風水   "wind and water," Chinese geomancy

fenjia 分家   division of the family estate

fu 蝠   bat

fu 賦   a type of Han Dynasty poetry with prose introductions

fu 福   good fortune

gan bei 乾杯   call for "empty the glass" in Chinese drinking rituals

ganqing 感情   feeling of cordiality in human relationships

gaoliang 高粱   Chinese sorghum

gezaixi 歌仔戲   traditional Taiwanese opera

gongting 公廳   central room of a traditional Taiwanese home

guan 管   melodic tunes

Guandi 關帝   Lord Guandi, a popular god in Taiwan

guanxi 關係   human relationships involving strong ties and mutual
      obligations

Guanyin 觀音   Guanyin, the bodhisattva of compassion

Guanyin shi 觀音石   Guanyin stone

guilei xi 傀儡戲   traditional Chinese marionette puppetry

guobian 鍋邊   "wokside" soup

guogong 國功   Chinese martial arts

guoshu 國術   "national arts"

guting 鼓亭　drum pavilion

guwen 古文　"ancient style" of traditional Chinese prose

hongbao 紅包　red envelopes (filled with gift money)

hongwa 紅瓦　red tiles

huaben 話本　story-teller's "prompt books"

huadan 花旦　flirtatious younger woman in traditional Chinese drama

huaigu 懷鼓　breast drum

huqin 胡琴　two-stringed instrument played with a bow

jia 家　inclusive family

jiao 醮　elaborate Taoist ritual of cosmic renewal

jiaozi 餃子　dough-wrapped, boiled dumpling

jiedu 解毒　poison-freeing

jieti 結體　"composition," or structure of Chinese characters

jing 淨　painted face character in traditional Chinese drama

jinguang 金光　"golden light" puppet shows popular now on Taiwanese television

kai 楷　"standard" script of Chinese calligraphy

keting 客廳　living room or parlor

Lao yuefenpai guanggao hua 老月份牌廣告畫　old-style calendar advertising

laodan 老旦　older, dignified woman in traditional Chinese drama

laosheng 老生　older male in traditional Chinese drama

li 里　a unit of distance roughly equal to one-third of a mile

li 禮　Confucian virtue of ritual propriety

li 隸　"clerical" script of Chinese calligraphy

Li ji 禮記　*The Book of Rites*, a Confucian classic

lian 廉　Confucian virtue of integrity

lian sheng 連生　continually giving birth

long 龍　dragon

longgu 龍鼓　"dragon drums" used to accompany the dragon dance

longjing 龍井　"dragon well" tea

lu 祿　official position and salary

Lu ban jing 魯班經　fifteenth century manual for building Chinese homes attributed to Lu Ban, the man deified as the god of carpenters

luo 鑼　gong

luoban 羅盤　compass (a special compass is used for *fengshui*)

luohan 羅漢　an early disciple of the Buddha (Sanskrit arhat)

mabei xing 馬背形　saddle (or "horse-back") shape of roof

maobi 毛筆　Chinese calligrapher's brush

Mazu 媽租　the goddess Mazu

Mei shemma cai 沒甚麼柔   polite phrase of pretended modesty: "This food isn't anything (worth complimenting)."

muyu 木鼓   "wooden fish" drum used in religious rituals

nanguan 南管   southern Chinese opera and musical style

nei 內   internal

Nei jing 內經   third century B.C. medical text

pian wen 駢文   parallel prose

pipa 琵琶   four-stringed traditional Chinese instrument

piying xi 皮影戲   traditional Chinese shadow puppetry

qi 氣   life force

qigong 氣功   form of physical exercise directing movement of *qi* for healing and energy increase

qilin 騏驎   Chinese unicorn

qing 磬   stone chimes or bells

qing 清   cleaning

qing bu liang 清補涼   herbal tea or soup mix, named for its ability to "clean," "strengthen," and "cool"

qingshi 青石   green stone

qingyi 青衣   virtuous woman in traditional Chinese drama

qipao 旗袍   traditional slender dress for women with high, closed collar, slits up the sides and buttons down the right side

Quanzhou baishi 泉州白石   Quanzhou white stone

ren 仁   benevolence, a fundamental Confucian virtue

Sanguo yanyi 三國演義   *Romance of the Three Kingdoms*

sanxian 三絃   traditional Chinese three-stringed instrument

se 瑟   stringed zither

sheng 生   general name for a variety of male characters in traditional Chinese drama

sheng 笙   mouth organ

shenyi 深衣   traditional tunic and skirt combination

shi 詩   poetry; the fundamental Chinese poetic form

Shi jing 詩經   *The Classic of Odes*

shigu 獅鼓   "lion drums" used to accompany lion dancers

shou 壽   long life

shuangxi 雙喜   double happiness (for married couples)

shuhua 書畫   calligraphy and painting

shuijiao 水餃   dough-wrapped, boiled dumpling

suona 嗩吶   traditional Chinese double-reeded instrument

taijiquan 太極拳   gentle martial art requiring considerable physical discipline

tailiang 台梁   pillar-and-beam system of construction

Taiwan minjian liuchuan gushi 臺灣民間流傳故事   *Traditional Folktales of Taiwan*

Taiwan ren zhen xihuan chi dongzi 臺灣人眞熹歡吃東西
   "Taiwanese people really like to eat stuff."

tanggu 堂鼓   large drum

taotie 饕餮   zoomorphic (animal-like) design found on many Chinese bronze wares

Tian 天   Heaven

tie guanyin 鐵觀音   "iron Goddess of Mercy" tea

tofu (doufu) 豆腐   bean curd

tong 桐   type of pine tree

tongwa 筒瓦   tiles made to look like rows of bamboo

Tudi Gong 土地公   earth deity of specific locality

wai 外   external

Wangye 王爺   a category of gods known to protect against pestilence

wawa sheng 呱呱生   male child in traditional Chinese drama

weiqi 圍棋   style of elegantly simple Chinese chess

wenyanwen 文言文   classical Chinese language

wu xing 五行   the five agents: wood, fire, earth, metal, and water

wulong 烏龍   "black dragon" tea

xi 喜   happiness

xiangqi 象棋   "elephant chess," a Chinese strategy game

xiangsheng 相聲   Qing dynasty dialogues of comic social criticism

xiao 消   dispelling

xiao 簫   flute

xiao 孝   filial piety; the Confucian virtue of respect for one's parents and ancestors

xiaobo 小鈸   small cymbals

xiaoding 小定   lesser engagement

xiaoluo 小鑼   small gong

xiaosheng 小生   younger male in traditional Chinese drama

xifang 熹房   bridal chamber

xing 行   "running" script of Chinese calligraphy

xun 薰   an egg-shaped musical instrument that is blown; ocarina

yang 陽   bright, active "masculine" side of yin-yang polarity

yanwei xing 燕尾形   "swallowtail" shape describing the profile of a type of tiled roof

yi 義   Confucian virtue of righteousness

yimin 義民   righteous citizens

yin 陰   dark, passive "feminine" side of yin-yang polarity

yu 餘   abundance

yu 魚   fish

yuefu 樂賦   type of Han dynasty poetry with imagery of daily life

yueqin 月琴   "full moon" guitar with four strings

yunluo 雲鑼   group of multiple gongs set in a musical framework

Zaojun 灶君   stove god or kitchen god

Zhonghua minguo 中華民國   Republic of China

zhuan 篆   "official seal" script of Chinese calligraphy

zongzi 粽子   boiled dumplings of rice wrapped inside bamboo leaves

zuo chan 坐禪   sitting meditation; to sit in deep meditation

Selected Bibliography

Ah Sheng. "The White Jade Ox," trans. by May Li-ming Tang, *Free China Review*, March 1995, pp. 58–61, reprinted from *The Chinese PEN*, autumn 1994.

Ahern, Emily M. *The Cult of the Dead in a Chinese Village.* Stanford, CA: Stanford University Press, 1973.

Ahern, Emily Martin. "The Power and Pollution of Chinese Women," in Arthur P. Wolf, ed., *Studies in Chinese Society*, pp. 269–90.

Ahern, Emily Martin. "The Thai Ti Kong Festival," in Emily Martin Ahern and Hill Gates, eds., *The Anthropology of Taiwanese Society*, pp. 397–425.

Ahern, Emily Martin and Hill Gates, eds. *The Anthropology of Taiwanese Society.* Stanford, CA: Stanford University Press, 1981.

Anderson, E. N. *The Food of China.* New Haven, CT: Yale University Press, 1988.

Baker, Hugh D. R. *Chinese Family and Kinship.* New York: Columbia University Press, 1979.

Balcom, John. "Modern Master, Native Son," *Free China Review*, December 1995.

Berliner, Nancy Zeng. *Chinese Folk Art.* Boston: Little, Brown, 1986.

Bosco, Joseph. "Yiguan Dao: 'Heterodoxy' and Popular Religion in Taiwan," in Murray A. Rubinstein, ed. *The Other Taiwan: 1945 to the Present.*

Brooks, Sarah. "Songs of the Universe," photos by Liu Chen-hsiang, *Free China Review*, March 1994, pp. 65–73.

Campbell, William. *Formosa under the Dutch.* Taipei: Ch'eng-wen Publishing Company, 1967.

Chang, Winnie. "The Colors of Taiwan," *Free China Review*, October 1995, pp. 64–73.

Chang, Winnie. "Paring down to Essentials," *Free China Review*, October 1996, pp. 54–65.

Chang Chin-ju. "If Taipei Had Been Designed in the Tang Dynasty," *Sinorama*, vol. 20, no. 4 (April 1995), pp. 6–17.

Chang Chin-ju. "Modern Problems, Ancient Strategies," *Sinorama*, vol. 20, no. 4 (April 1995), pp. 18–25.

Chang Chiun-fang. "A Brush with Immortality: The Long and Twisted Tale of Chinese Calligraphy," *Sinorama*, August 1996.

Chang Han-yu and Ramon H. Myers. "Japanese Colonial Development Policy in Taiwan, 1895–1906: A Case of Bureaucratic Entrepreneurship," *Journal of Asian Studies*, vol. 22, no. 4 (August 1963).

Chen, Jackie. "Ami Sounds Scale Olympic Heights," *Sinorama*, vol. 21, no. 9 (September 1996).

Chen, Jackie. "Architecture down on the Farm," *Sinorama*, vol. 20, no. 12 (December 1995), pp. 40–57.

Chen, Jackie. "Images of a Century of Taiwanese Music," trans. by Phil Newell, *Sinorama*, June 1995, pp. 124–29.

Chen Chung-min. "Dowry and Inheritance," in Hsieh Jih-chang and Chuang Ying-chang, eds., *The Chinese Family and Its Ritual Behavior*, pp. 16–127.

Chen Fang-ming. "Unexpected Encounter at Yuraku-cho," *Free China Review*, July 1995, pp. 36–40.

Chen Kang Chai. *Taiwan Aborigines: A Genetic Study of Tribal Variations*. Cambridge, MA: Harvard University Press, 1967.

Cheng, Jessie. "The Sound of Thunder," *Free China Review*, April 1995, pp. 66–73.

Ching, Yu-ing. *Master of Love and Mercy: Cheng Yen*. Nevada City, CA: Blue Dolphin Publishing, 1995.

Cohen, Myron L. "Developmental Process in the Chinese Domestic Group," in Arthur P. Wolf, ed., *Studies in Chinese Society*, pp. 183–98.

Cohen, Myron L. *House United, House Divided: A Chinese Family in Taiwan*. New York: Columbia University Press, 1976.

Cohen, Myron L. "Lineage Development and the Family in China," in Hsieh Jih-chang and Chuang Ying-chang, eds., *The Chinese Family and Its Ritual Behavior*, pp. 210–18.

Copper, John F. *Taiwan: Nation-State or Province?* Boulder, CO: Westview Press, 1990.

Crissman, Lawrence W. "The Structure of Local and Regional Systems," in Emily Martin Ahern and Hill Gates, eds., *The Anthropology of Taiwanese Society*, pp. 116–24.

Davison, Gary M. *Agricultural Development and the Fate of Farmers in Taiwan, 1945–*

1990. Ph.D. dissertation, University of Minnesota Department of History, 1993.

Dawson, Raymond, ed. *The Legacy of China.* London: Oxford University Press, 1964.

Dean, Kenneth. *Taoist Ritual and Popular Cults of Southeast China.* Princeton, NJ: Princeton University, Press, 1993.

Elvin, Mark and G. William Skinner, eds. *The Chinese City between Two Worlds.* Stanford, CA: Stanford University Press, 1974.

Fairbank, John King. *The United States and China.* 4th ed. Cambridge, MA: Harvard University Press, 1983.

Far Eastern Economic Review.

Fei, John C. H., Gustav Ranis, and Shirley Kuo. *Growth with Equity: The Taiwan Case.* Oxford: Oxford University Press, 1979.

Feuchtwang, Stephan. "City Temples in Taipei under Three Regimes," in Mark Elvin and G. William Skinner, eds., *The Chinese City between Two Worlds,* pp. 263–301.

Freedman, Maurice. *Chinese Lineage and Society.* London: Athlone Press, 1966.

Freedman, Maurice. *Family and Kinship in Chinese Society.* Stanford, CA: Stanford University Press, 1970.

Freedman, Maurice. *Lineage Organization in Southeast China.* London: Athlone Press, 1958.

Fried, Morton. *The Fabric of Chinese Society: A Study of the Social Life of a Chinese County Seat.* New York: Praeger, 1953.

Fu, Pei-Mei. *Pei Mei's Chinese Cookbook.* Vol. 1. Taipei: by the author, 1969.

Galenson, Walter, ed. *Economic Growth and Structural Change in Taiwan: The Postwar Experience of the Republic of China.* Ithaca, NY: Cornell University Press, 1979.

Gallin, Bernard and Rita S. Gallin. "The Integration of Village Migrants in Taipei," in Mark Elvin and G. William Skinner, eds., *The Chinese City between Two Worlds,* pp. 331–58.

Gallin, Bernard and Rita Gallin. "Matrilateral and Affinal Relationships in Chinese Society," in Hsieh Jih-chang and Chuang Ying-chang, eds., *The Chinese Family and Its Ritual Behavior,* pp. 101–16.

Garrett, Valery M. *Traditional Chinese Clothing in Hong Kong and South China, 1840–1980.* Oxford: Oxford University Press, 1987.

Gold, Thomas B. *State and Society in the Taiwan Miracle.* Armonk, NY: M. E. Sharpe, 1986.

Hahn, Emily. *The Cooking of China.* New York: Time-Life Books, 1968.

Halvorsen, Francine. *The Food and Cooking of China: An Exploration of Chinese Cuisine in the Provinces and Cities of China, Hong Kong, and Taiwan.* New York: John Wiley & Sons, 1996.

Han Lih-Wu. *Taiwan Today.* Taipei: Cheng Chung Book Company, 1968.

Hanan, Patrick. "The Development of Fiction and Drama," in Raymond Dawson, ed., *The Legacy of China*, pp. 115–43.

Hawkes, David. "Chinese Poetry and the English Reader," in Raymond Dawson, ed., *The Legacy of China*, pp. 90–115.

Hayase, Yukio. *The Career of Goto Shimpei: Japan's Statesman of Research, 1857–1929.* Ph.D. dissertation, Florida State University Department of History, March 1974.

Hsieh Jih-chang, "Meal Rotation," in Hsieh Jih-chang and Chuang Ying-chang, eds., *The Chinese Family and Its Ritual Behavior*, pp. 70–83.

Hsieh Jih-chang and Chuang Ying-chang, eds., *The Chinese Family and Its Ritual Behavior*. Taipei: Institute of Ethnology, Academia Sinica, 1985.

Hsü Shih-hua. "God Statues, Past and Present," *Sinorama*, vol. 9, no. 8 (August 1984).

Hu, Jenny. "The Presidential Palace Opens Its Doors," *Sinorama*, January 1995.

Hu, Jenny. "Sacred Battle Ground—The Lungshan Temple," *Sinorama*, April 1995.

Huang, Anita. "All for Love," *Free China Review*, October 1996, pp. 48–53.

Huang, Anita. "Make Art, Not War," *Free China Review*, January 1997, pp. 56–65.

Huang Wen-ling. "Symphonies in Stone," *Free China Review*, July 1996, pp. 28–33.

Huang Wen-ling. "Yingko: Making Money from Muck," *Free China Review*, December 1996, pp. 54–65.

Hwang, Jim. "Brushing up the Brushwork," *Free China Review*, July 1996, pp. 61–65.

Hwang, Jim. "Paper Tigers," *Free China Review*, April 1996, pp. 64–73.

Hwang, Jim. "Taiwan's Crystal Maze," *Free China Review*, April 1997, pp. 58–65.

Insight Guides: Taiwan. Boston: Houghton Mifflin, 1997.

Jordan, David K. *Gods, Ghosts, and Ancestors: The Folk Religion of a Taiwanese Village.* Berkeley, CA: University of California Press, 1972.

Jordan, David K. "The Recent History of the Celestial Way: A Chinese Pietistic Association," *Modern China*, vol. 8, no. 4 (1982), pp. 45–62.

Jordan, David K. "Sworn Brotherhoods: A Study in Chinese Ritual Kinship," in Hsieh Jih-chang and Chuang Ying-chang, eds., *The Chinese Family and Its Ritual Behavior*, pp. 232–62.

Jordan, David K. "Taiwanese *Poe* Divination: Statistical Awareness and Religious Belief," in *Journal for the Scientific Study of Religion*, vol. 21, no. 2 (1982), pp. 114–18.

Jordan, David K. and Daniel L. Overmyer. *The Flying Phoenix: Aspects of Chinese Sectarianism in Taiwan.* Princeton, NJ: Princeton University Press, 1986.

Katz, Paul. "Demons or Deities?—The *Wangye* of Taiwan," in *Asian Folklore Studies*, vol. 46, no. 2 (1987), pp. 197–215.

Kaulbach, B. and B. Proksch. *Arts and Culture in Taiwan.* Taipei: Southern Materials Center, 1984.

Knapp, Ronald G. *China's Traditional Rural Architecture: A Cultural Geography of the Common House.* Honolulu: University of Hawaii Press, 1986.

Ku Lin-hsiu. "Teresa Teng Forever," trans. by Phil Newel, *Sinorama*, July 1995, pp. 6–19.

Kung, Lydia. "Perceptions of Work among Factory Women," in Emily Martin Ahern and Hill Gates, eds., *The Anthropology of Taiwanese Society*, pp. 397–425.

Lamley, Harry J. "Subethnic Rivalry in the Ch'ing Period," in Emily Martin Ahern and Hill Gates, eds., *The Anthropology of Taiwanese Society*, pp. 282–318.

Levy, John. *Chinese Buddhist Music.* New York: Lyrichord Discs. LLST 7222.

Levy, John. *Chinese Taoist Music.* New York: Lyrichord Discs. LLST 7223.

Li, Chu-tsing. "Chinese Art," in John Meskill, ed., *An Introduction to Chinese Civilization*, pp. 418–61.

Li, Ping-hui. "Processional Music in Taiwanese Funerals," in Bell Yung, Evelyn S. Rawski, and Rubie S. Watson, eds., *Harmony and Counterpoint: Ritual Music in Chinese Context.* Stanford, CA: Stanford University Press, 1996.

Li Ji, the Li Ki, trans. by James Legge, The Sacred Books of the East, vols. 27 and 28. Oxford: Clarendon Press, 1885.

Li P'eng. "The Rise of the Well-Versed Society: A Poetry Renaissance in Contemporary Taiwan," trans. by Vincent Chang, *Sinorama*, December 1995, p. 129.

Liu, Claire. "Mothballing the Military Gear—The Kuo-kuang Opera Company," trans. by Brent Heinrich, *Sinorama*, March 1996.

Liu Lan-fang. "Taiwan's Living Poets' Societies," trans. by Jonathon Barnard, *Sinorama*, April 1996, pp. 40–53.

Meskill, Johanna. *A Chinese Pioneer Family: The Lins of Wu-feng, Taiwan.* Princeton, NJ: Princeton University Press, 1979.

Meskill, John, ed. *An Introduction to Chinese Civilization.* Lexington, MA: D. C. Heath, 1973.

Meyer, Roger. "Celestial Sales Force," *Free China Review*, July 1996, pp. 40–45.

Meyer, Roger. "Revaluing the Popular Past," *Free China Review*, August 1995, pp. 62–73.

Nerbonne, Joseph. *Formosa at Your Fingertips: Guide to Taipei and All Taiwan, Republic of China.* 8th ed. Taipei: Caves Books, 1985.

Pasternak, Burton. "The Disquieting Chinese Lineage and Its Anthropological Relevance," in Hsieh Jih-chang and Chuang Ying-chang eds., *The Chinese Family and Its Ritual Behavior*, pp. 165–91.

Pasternak, Burton. "Economics and Ecology," in Emily Martin Ahern and Hill Gates, eds., *The Anthropology of Taiwanese Society*, pp. 151–83.

Pasternak, Burton. *Kinship and Community in Two Chinese Villages.* Stanford, CA: Stanford University Press, 1972.

Pasternak, Burton. "The Sociology of Irrigation: Two Taiwanese Villages," in Arthur P. Wolf, ed., *Studies in Chinese Society*, pp. 199–219.

Perng, Ching-hsi and Chin-kuei Wang, eds. *Death in a Cornfield*. Hong Kong: Oxford University Press, 1994.

Polyphonies Vocales des Aborigenes de Taiwan. Paris: Maison des Cultures du Monde et Chinese Folk Arts Foundation.

Pulley-Blank, E. G. "The Historiographic Tradition," in Raymond Dawson, ed., *The Legacy of China*, pp. 143–64.

Ranis, Gustav. "Industrial Development," in Walter Galenson, ed., *Economic Growth and Structural Change in Taiwan: The Postwar Experience of the Republic of China*, pp. 206–62.

Reed, Barbara E. "Women and Religion in Contemporary Taiwan," in Arvind Sharma, ed., *Today's Woman in World Religions*. Albany, NY: SUNY Press, 1994.

Republic of China Yearbook, 1997. Taipei: Kwang Hwa Publishing, 1997.

Rubinstein, Murray A. *The Protestant Community on Modern Taiwan: Mission, Seminary, and Church*. Armonk, NY: M. E. Sharpe, 1991.

Rubinstein, Murray A., ed. *The Other Taiwan: 1945 to the Present*. Armonk, NY: M. E. Sharpe, 1994.

Saso, Michael. *The Teachings of Taoist Master Chuang*. New Haven, CT: Yale University Press, 1978.

Schipper, Kristofer. *The Taoist Body*. Berkeley: University of California Press, 1993.

Sheng, Virginia. "Lighting the Way," *Free China Review*, March 1995, pp. 50–56

Sheng Yen. *Dharma Drum: The Life and Heart of Ch'an Practice*. Elmhurst, NY: Dharma Drum Publications, 1996.

Shepherd, John Robert. *Statecraft and Political Economy on the Taiwan Frontier*. Stanford, CA: Stanford University Press, 1993.

Skinner, G. William. "Marketing and Social Structure in Rural China," *Journal of Asian Studies*, vol. 24, no. 1 (November 1964), pp. 3–43.

Speare, Alden Jr. "Migration and Family Change in Central Taiwan," in Mark Elvin and G. William Skinner, eds., *The Chinese City between Two Worlds*, pp. 303–30.

Stafford, Charles. *The Roads of Chinese Childhood: Learning and Identification in Angang*. Cambridge: Cambridge University Press, 1995.

Storey, Robert. *Taiwan: A Travel Survival Kit*. Hawthorn, Victoria, Australia: Lonely Planet Publications, 1994.

Sullivan, Michael. "The Heritage in Chinese Art," in Raymond Dawson, ed., *The Legacy of China*, pp. 165–243.

Sung, Lung-sheng. "Property and Family Division," in Emily Martin Ahern and Hill Gates, eds., *The Anthropology of Taiwanese Society*, pp. 361–78.

Taiwan Agricultural Yearbook. Taichung, Taiwan: Department of Agriculture and Forestry, Taiwan Provincial Government, 1990.

Tang Mei-chun. "Equal Right and Domestic Structure," in Hsieh Jih-chang and Chuang Ying-chang, eds., *The Chinese Family and Its Ritual Behavior*, pp. 61–69.

Tong, Hollington K. *Christianity in Taiwan: A History*. Taipei: China Post, 1961.

Topley, Marjorie. "Marriage Resistance in Rural Kwangtung," in Arthur P. Wolf, ed., *Studies in Chinese Society*, pp. 247–68.

Tremble, John. "Fuzzy Logic," *Free China Review*, February 1996, pp. 58–63.

Tyson, James. "Christians and the Taiwanese Independence Movement: A Commentary," *Asian Affairs*, vol. 14, no. 3 (1987), pp. 163–70.

Wang, Jane. "A Legacy to Build On: Japanese Architecture in the Po Ai Special District," *Sinorama*, January 1995, p. 29.

Wang, Jane. "Space and Power in the District of Universal Love," *Sinorama*, January 1995.

Wang Fei-yun. "Nostalgia in Oils," *Free China Review*, March 1995, pp. 62–73.

Wang Fei-yun. "Tribal Treasures," *Free China Review*, May 1996, pp. 64–73.

Wang Fei-yun. "Utopia, Ltd.," *Free China Review*, July 1996, pp. 50–55.

Watson, Burton. "Chinese Literature," in John Meskill, ed., *An Introduction to Chinese Civilization*, pp. 618–42.

Wei Chuan Cultural-Educational Foundation. *Taiwanese Style Chinese Cuisine.* Monterey Park, CA [U.S. distributor]: Wei Chuan Publishing, 1991.

Weller, Robert P. *Unities and Diversities in Chinese Religion.* Seattle: University of Washington Press, 1987.

Wester, Michael. "Making Waves in Mandarin," *Free China Review*, June 1994.

Wester, Michael. "The Queen of Taiwanese Music," *Free China Review*, June 1994.

Wolf, Arthur P. "Chinese Family Size: A Myth Revitalized," in Hsieh Jih-chang and Chuang Ying-chang, eds., *The Chinese Family and Its Ritual Behavior*, pp. 30–49.

Wolf, Arthur. "Chinese Kinship and Mourning Dress," in Maurice Freedman, ed., *Family and Kinship in Chinese Society*, pp. 189–208.

Wolf, Arthur. "Domestic Organization," in Emily Martin Ahern and Hill Gates, eds., *The Anthropology of Taiwanese Society*, pp. 361–78.

Wolf, Arthur P. "Gods, Ghosts, and Ancestors," in Arthur P. Wolf, ed., *Religion and Ritual in Chinese Society.*

Wolf, Arthur P., ed. *Religion and Ritual in Chinese Society.* Stanford, CA: Stanford University Press, 1974.

Wolf, Arthur P., ed. *Studies in Chinese Society.* Stanford, CA: Stanford University Press, 1978.

Wolf, Margery. "Child Training and the Chinese Family," in Arthur P. Wolf, ed., *Studies in Chinese Society*, pp. 224–27.

Wolf, Margery. *The House of Lim.* Englewood Cliffs, NJ: Prentice Hall, 1968.

Wolf, Margery. *Women and the Family in Rural Taiwan.* Stanford, CA: Stanford University Press, 1972.

Wong, Chun-kit Joseph. *The Changing Chinese Family Pattern in Taiwan.* Taipei: Southern Materials Center, 1981.

Wu, David Y. H. "The Conditions of Development and Decline of Chinese Lineages and the Formation of Ethnic Groups," in Hsieh Jih-chang and Chuang Ying-chang, eds., *The Chinese Family and Its Ritual Behaviors*, pp. 192–209.

Wu, Emma. "Carving a Life," *Free China Review*, January 1994.

Yang, Martin. *Socio-Economic Results of Land Reform in Taiwan.* Honolulu: East-West Center Press, 1970.

Yang, Martin C. *A Chinese Village: Taitou, Shantung Province.* New York: Columbia University Press, 1945.

Yin, Alexander Chien-chung. "Voluntary Associations and Rural Migration," in Emily Martin Ahern and Hill Gates, eds., *The Anthropology of Taiwanese Society,* pp. 319–37.

Yun, Eugenia. "Alternative Clothing," *Free China Review,* May 1996, pp. 60–63.

Yun, Eugenia. "The Great Awakening," *Free China Review,* April 1997, pp. 4–29.

Yun, Eugenia. "The Hakka: The Invisible Group," *Free China Review,* vol. 43, no. 10 (October 1993), pp. 4–17.

Yun, Eugenia. "Hats in Hand," *Free China Review,* March 1997, pp. 58–65.

Yun, Eugenia. "The Painting Employee," *Free China Review,* June 1997, pp. 57–65.

Yun, Eugenia. "Painting, Not Starving," *Free China Review,* February 1997, pp. 56–65.

Yun, Eugenia. "A Place on the Pop Map," *Free China Review,* June 1994, pp. 5–19.

Yun, Eugenia. "That Certain Look," *Free China Review,* vol. 46, no. 11 (November 1996).

Zung, Celia S. L. *Secrets of the Chinese Drama.* New York: Benjamin Blom, 1964.

Index

About the Authors

GARY MARVIN DAVISON has very diverse teaching experiences—he has taught in prison, at four high schools and two universities, and at English-as-a-Second-Language institutions in Taiwan, where he has lived for two lengthy periods and where he visits frequently.

BARBARA E. REED teaches in the Religion Department and Asian Studies Program at St. Olaf College in Northfield, Minnesota.